INSTITUTIONAL DIMENSIONS
OF REGIONAL DEVELOPMENT

UNITED NATIONS CENTRE FOR REGIONAL
DEVELOPMENT
REGIONAL DEVELOPMENT SERIES
Edited by M. Honjo and R. P. Misra

Volume 8: Institutional Dimensions of Regional Development

Edited by G. Shabbir Cheema

The papers included in this volume were contributed to the Senior-Level
Seminar on Institutional Capability for Regional Development: Focus on
Coordination, held from 16 to 20 August 1980, in Nagoya, Japan.

INSTITUTIONAL DIMENSIONS
OF REGIONAL DEVELOPMENT

Edited by
G. Shabbir Cheema

MARUZEN ASIA
For and on behalf of the United Nations Centre for Regional Development
Nagoya, Japan

ISBN 962-220-208-X
Distributed by
Maruzen Asia Pte. Ltd.,
P O Box 67 Pasir Panjang,
Singapore 9111.

Printed in the Republic of Singapore
by Huntsmen Offset Printing Pte. Ltd.

FOREWORD

THIS IS the eighth volume of the UNCRD Regional Development Series. The earlier volumes dealt with changing perceptions of development problems, regional development alternatives, urbanization, rural development, rural-urban relations and human needs. This volume is concerned with development administration for local and regional development.

In the light of the experience of the past three decades, an examination of the institutional support structure for implementing development policies and programmes has acquired added importance. It is often stated that the major hindrance to development is not inadequacies in policies or planning, nor even the lack of resources; it is rather the unresponsive administrative system. It was precisely for this reason that the UNCRD launched a research project in 1979 to assess the institutional capability for regional development in a number of ESCAP countries. This volume is the product of that project.

The focus of the research project was on interagency and intraagency coordination in programme and project implementation. The UNCRD has consistently emphasized an integrated and coordinated approach to development. The focus of the project was in line with this thinking as also to fill an important gap in development research.

The volume contains papers contributed by well-known authorities on various aspects of coordinated development process. After the theoretical analysis of key issues, the structures and mechanism of coordination in the selected countries of the ESCAP region (Bangladesh, India, Malaysia, the Philippines, Sri Lanka and Thailand) are discussed. The impediments to effective performance of coordination functions are identified and strategies for institutional reforms to facilitate regional and local development from below are elaborated. The peculiarities of and similarities among the countries selected for case studies have been taken due note of while analysing the problems and issues involved.

We are grateful to Dr. G. Shabbir Cheema, Development Administration Planner at the UNCRD, for having edited this volume and thus contributed immensely to the success of the UNCRD series on Regional Development. We would also like to take this opportunity to thank our colleagues who have contributed the papers included in this volume.

We are confident that the volume will be a welcome addition to the growing literature on local and regional administration and development.

M. Honjo & R.P. Misra

PREFACE

THE UNITED Nations Centre for Regional Development (UNCRD) launched the first cycle of a comparative study on institutional dimensions of regional development in 1979. A draft research design, national survey format, and case study format were prepared by UNCRD and presented to the Consultative Workshop attended by the collaborating experts at Nagoya, Japan from 22 to 28 January 1980. The modifications suggested by the workshop were incorporated into the final draft which served as the basis for the country papers and case studies undertaken by the institutions in selected Asian countries. The findings of these studies were presented at the Senior Level Seminar on Institutional Capability for Regional Development: Focus on Coordination held at Nagoya from 16 to 20 August 1980. The first ten chapters of this book are revised versions of some of the papers presented at the seminar.

I am indebted to Haruo Nagamine, Physical Planner, UNCRD who served as project coordinator until 21 August 1980. Due to other commitments, he was unable to co-edit the book with me, but I have greatly benefited from several discussions with him. Thanks are also due to Josefa S. Edralin, Documentation and Publications Officer, UNCRD, and Aminta L. Peters for doing more than their share of work in editing to ensure uniformity of style and accuracy of references; to Mitsuhiko Hosaka, Research Associate, UNCRD, for proofreading the volume with devotion and giving me extremely useful substantive comments about each of the chapters; and to Hiroko Okada, Sumiko Torii, Kuniko Kondo and Frances Miwa for diligently typing several drafts of the papers.

Finally, I am grateful to the co-authors of this volume for their willingness to revise the original versions of their papers for publication in the present form.

Nagoya, Japan   G. Shabbir Cheema
15 December 1980

CONTENTS

PART I: THEORETICAL ANALYSIS

PART II: COUNTRY PERSPECTIVES

PART III: CONCLUDING OVERVIEW

INTRODUCTION

G. SHABBIR CHEEMA

PLANNING FOR DEVELOPMENT

SINCE THE 1950s, developing countries have been attempting to accomplish optimal utilization of resources and give a direction to societal change by introducing development planning. The initial zeal and enthusiasm for planned change in these countries could be attributed both to internal and external factors. Internally, the policymakers and practitioners were under tremendous pressure to improve the worsening economic situations of increasingly vocal groups for greater political legitimacy and nation-building. Externally, the perceived, rightly or wrongly, contribution of planning to the European recovery and prosperity, and to the transformation of the Soviet Union, as well as the interest of the international and donor agencies in economic development planning, further strengthened the enthusiasm of policymakers in this regard.[1] It should be mentioned, however, that in actual practice, the main thrust of planning which took place in most of these countries was economic. Noneconomic aspects, such as social and administrative ones, received scanty attention.

Within the context of national development planning, regional planning took several forms: planning for cities, metropolitan areas, governmental administrative and political units, depressed areas, resource frontier regions and economic regions. Similarly, national level planners reorganized the significance of industry and investment locations and sectoral allocation among various regions. The last two decades have witnessed an increasing emphasis by policymakers and practitioners on the spatial dimensions of development. This is evident from the rapid expansion of statutory bodies for frontier region resource management; delegation of some planning functions to lower governmental and administrative units; establishment of regional level planning offices; decentralization of budgets for small-scale projects; and the creation of coordinating committees within the

---

[1] Albert Waterston, *Development Planning: Lessons of Experience* (Baltimore: Johns Hopkins University Press, 1969), pp. 28-44.

administrative system to provide integrated services to specific areas. The focus on spatial aspects has been necessitated, among other things, by the desire to reduce growing economic disparities within various regions; to fully utilize resources from the largely untapped frontier regions in the acceleration of national development; and to involve the various segments of society in the development process through emphasis on regional and subregional or local level planning.

The impact of national and regional planning upon development has been well documented.[2] For example, experiences in the Asian developing countries show with few exceptions that no substantial growth rates have been achieved in the annual average gross domestic product. Even in relatively more successful cases, there seems to be little evidence to suggest that centralized planning has significantly contributed to the promotion of growth.[3] Income disparities among various groups within the society and between various regions have further widened. Similarly, previous planned efforts failed to provide sufficient employment for burgeoning populations, to promote meaningful grass roots participation, to improve investment decision and to enable the rural poor to equitably participate in the benefits resulting from government programmes.

There are many reasons for the failure of centralized planning in achieving the intended impact. These could be divided into two categories: institutional and noninstitutional. Among the noninstitutional reasons, the most prominent were the uncertainties of the world economic situation which negated some of the basic premises of national plans, and the lack of political will to formulate and operationalize realistic plans taking into consideration national resource constraints. Despite the diversity of country specific situations, other noninstitutional reasons which led to the inefficacy of national and regional development planning included an overemphasis on industrialization-urbanization at the operational level; non-egalitarian patterns of land ownership and social structural rigidities which inhibited access of the rural poor to government programmes and the creation of a cooperative rural community; alarmingly high population growth rates which necessitated an emphasis on productivity-oriented programmes, often overlooking equity considerations; and policy styles and frameworks which were in several cases characterized by political instability, resulting in the discontinuity of operational goals.[4]

[2] Among others, see Dennis A. Rondinelli, "National Investment Planning and Equity Policy in Developing Countries: The Challenge of Decentralized Administration," *Policy Sciences* 10 (1978): 45-74; Waterston, *Development Planning;* Naomi Caiden and Aaron Wildavsky, *Planning and Budgeting in Poor Countries* (New York: Wiley, 1974); and Martin Rudner, *Nationalism, Planning and Economic Modernization in Malaysia* (Beverly Hills: Sage Publications, 1975).

[3] Rondinelli, "National Investment Planning and Equity Policy in Developing Countries."

[4] Inayatullah and H.S. Wanasinghe, "Concluding Review" in Inayatullah, ed., *Approaches to Rural Development: Some Asian Experiences* (Kuala Lumpur: Asian and Pacific Development Administration Centre, 1979), pp. 413-29.

The second set of impediments to the success of development planning dealt with the government's administrative machinery and non-governmental organizations which were directly or indirectly involved in the process of plan formulation and implementation.[5] With reference to this, the Asian experience shows that technocratic plans were formulated without adequate attention to the appraisal of administrative capacities to implement these.[6] The administrative systems in most cases were characterized by political interventions in recruitment and promotion, "red tape", low morale and rigid personnel regulations. In addition, centralized controls existed without adequate decentralization of financial and administrative authority which thwarted local initiative in the implementation process. Despite these controls, the proliferation of government agencies led to a situation in which both horizontal and vertical coordinations were negatively affected. In effect, projects chosen for implementation did not always reflect planned priorities. Nor were the administrative systems well-equipped for monitoring and evaluating the chosen projects in terms of the stated national policy goals. Interdepartmental rivalries, absence of viable linkages between multilevels of government and administration, and the failure to operationally link planning decisions with budgeting ones and the lack of qualified personnel, particularly at the lowest government levels, further weakened the implementability of plans.

In most countries non-governmental organizations were even weaker than the administrative machinery.[7] The role of local government systems was restricted for the most part, to the provision of civic amenities. People's organizations in rural areas, such as cooperatives, village development committees, farmer's associations, women's organizations, youth clubs, and social welfare organizations were dominated by the bureaucracy and the landed elite. These organizations were financially dependent. There were several consequences of the weakness of non-governmental organizations: The meaningful participation of people in the identification of local needs and the implementation of local plans did not take place despite the desire of governments; local, human and material resources could not be fully mobilized; bureaucratic responsiveness at the grass roots could not be ensured; the interests of the poor segments of society could not be safeguarded; governmental facilities and services could not be delivered in such a way that these could be accessible to all groups within the rural community; and planning at the subregional or local level in effect remained top-down.

---

[5] In developing economies, as Rothwell notes, "gaps are seen in the capability and efficiency of established institutions to attain social goals, and gaps are seen in established structures, systems and functions appropriate for new human values and relationships." See K.J. Rothwell, "The Scope of Management and Administration Problems in Development" in *Administrative Issues in Developing Economies* (Lexington, Mass.: Lexington Books, 1972), p. 3.

[6] Gabriel U. Iglesias, "Introduction" in *Implementation: The Problem of Achieving Results* (Manila: Eastern Organization for Public Administration, 1976).

[7] G. Shabbir Cheema, "The Rural Poor, People's Organizations and Development: Analysis of Asian Experience" [Paper prepared for the World Conference on Agrarian Reform and Rural Development, Food and Agriculture Organization of the United Nations, January 1979, Rome, Italy].

In the past, most attempts to introduce radical administrative reforms met with limited success due to old legacies and to the predominance of bureaucratic interests. At the same time, most countries were reluctant to encourage mass mobilization through people's organizations, as they were faced with problems of unifying manifold diversities. Thus, what actually took place was the emergence of two distinct administrative cultures with insufficient communication between them, i.e., those of the Western educated technocrats and the elite bureaucratic cadres within the planning bodies, on the one hand, and the regional and subregional level implementors, on the other.

INSTITUTIONAL DIMENSIONS

It may be contended that a country's regional development performance is affected by four interrelated factors. These are: the technical skills, values, attitudes and beliefs of individuals within the society; the sociopolitical structure which serves as an environment within which individuals perform their role as agents of change; the availability of resources which generates innovative ideas and programmes; and the institutional machinery through which regional development planning and implementation takes place.[8] The institutional machinery provides the channel through which various regional development ends are accomplished; relevant societal issues and priorities are articulated; short-term and long-term plans are formulated; regional development projects are implemented; people are involved in specific activities undertaken by the government; and the planning and implementation processes are integrated.[9] Indeed, it serves as the most critical intervening factor through which economic resources and human skills are utilized for promoting development.

There are two components of the institutional machinery for regional development planning and implementation, i.e., governmental and non-governmental. In most developing countries, due to the weakness of non-governmental institutions, the main tasks of promoting planned change are the responsibility of the government's multilevel administrative machinery. In any case, both institutional machinery components play a role. While government agencies actually formulate and implement regional development projects, non-governmental

[8] Among the related works are: Daniel Lerner, *The Passing of Traditional Society* (New York: Free Press, 1958); David C. McClelland, *The Achieving Society* (Princeton: Van Nostrand, 1961); Philip E. Jocob et. al., *Values and the Active Community* (New York: Free Press, 1971); Manning Nash, "Some Social and Cultural Aspects of Economic Development," *Economic Development and Cultural Change* 7 (Jan. 1969); J.J. Spengler, "Economic Development: Political Preconditions and Political Consequences," *Journal of Politics* 22 (Aug. 1960); Myron Weiner, ed., *Modernization: The Dynamics of Growth* (New York: Basic Books, 1966); and Rothwell, *Administrative Issues in Developing Economies.*

[9] Manifold functions which can be performed by government and non-government institutions in the rural development process were empirically tested in selected countries of the region under the auspices of Asian and Pacific Development Administration Centre. Among the relevant publications in this regard is Inayatullah, ed., *Rural Organizations and-Rural Development: Some Asian Experiences* (Kuala Lumpur, 1979).

organizations perform several related functions, such as facilitating the delivery of public services to people; ensuring administrative responsiveness; making claims on behalf of various segments of the society; and facilitating resource mobilization.

Institutional capability for regional development thus, implies the capacity of national, regional and subregional or local level administrative structures as well as non-governmental and semi-governmental organizations to optimize economic resource and human skill utilization in the process of development acceleration within the society through consideration of spatial and distributive dimensions. This is reflected in the extent to which governmental and non-governmental organizations (the institutional machinery) are able to perform their assigned tasks at multilevels of government and administration for achieving the above objective.

Measurement of institutional capability for regional development is a complex task due to the numerous organizations involved, the varying administrative and institutional requirements for specific development policies and programmes, the difficulty of delineating workable linkages among organizations at multilevels, and the shifting concerns of regional development as a field of study. Therefore, the search for indicators of institutional capability at the national, regional, and subregional levels should inevitably follow, once the components of the phenomenon under consideration are identified. If the planning and implementation experiences of developing countries earlier described are any guide towards this purpose, it would seem that the main components of institutional capability include:

1. The existence, both in theory and practice, of mechanisms within the administrative machinery for horizontal and vertical coordination in harmonizing and integrating government actions according to people's aspirations.

2. The decentralization of governmental functions and financial resources towards regional and subregional levels in order to create effective partnership between multilevels of government and administration.

3. The provision of mechanisms through non-governmental constituency organizations and the creation of conducive environments for increasing people's meaningful participation in the development process.

4. The administrative system's capacity to rationally undertake the programme and project formulations and effectively monitor and evaluate the consequences of government intervention in collaboration with the programme beneficiaries and people's organizations.

5. The existence of procedures and their actual extent of practice, given environmental uncertainties, for operationally linking planning and budgeting decisions.

6. Personnel structures and practices which may facilitate administrative innovation.

THE COORDINATION ASPECT

Coordination may be simply defined as the "harmonization of activities for the purpose of ensuring optimum collective contribution to the achievement of a common goal."[10] It may also be considered as a process "engaged in by two or more individuals, units and organizations to increase the availability of scarce resources and/or improve the impact of activities to more effectively and/or efficiently reach organizational and/or programme goals."[11] Thus, the need for coordination in government machinery arises from several factors:

1. To make the most efficient use of limited resources and to avoid wastage.
2. To eliminate conflicts in the goals of rapidly proliferating government agencies.
3. To accomplish uniformity in government policies at the operational level.
4. To establish effective linkages among public agencies so that these may assist each other.
5. To reduce overlapping functions of different government agencies.

There are several methods, techniques and mechanisms which may be utilized to ensure coordination in regional development planning and implementation. These include:

1. The exchange of information.
2. Negotiation to resolve differences.
3. Coercion if negotiations fail.
4. Specification of each agency's functional areas.
5. Institutionalization of procedures to ensure that views of all relevant agencies are, if possible, incorporated in decision-making.
6. Establishment of intersectoral committees.
7. Delineation of guidelines by the supreme coordinating body.

Coordination within and between governmental organizations may take many forms depending upon the methods utilized. According to one approach, coordination may take one of three forms: "integration", "domination" and "compromise".[12] In the first device every functionary has a feeling of participation, since the goal is to integrate diverse ideas without too much concern over hierarchy. If coordination takes the form of domination, the manipulation of

[10] United Nations Centre for Regional Development, *Role of Government in Regional Development Process* (Nagoya, 1977), p. 17.

[11] V. Chammong, *Coordination in the Implementation of Family Planning Programmes* (Kuala Lumpur: Asian and Pacific Development Administration Centre, 1978), p. 3.

[12] M.A. Muttalib, "The Theory of Coordination Rediscovered and Reformulated," *Indian Journal of Public Administration* (April-June, 1978).

hiérarchy or "the authority of office" becomes the most critical factor. The third device creates a balance between integration and domination leading to coordination activity performance among coequal agencies.

According to another approach, three forms of coordination may be identified:[13] (1) coordination by "standardization"; (2) coordination by "plan"; and (3) coordination by "mutual adjustment". Standardization implies the establishment of procedures or rules which regulate the actions of each unit into an interdependent relationship. This, in turn, necessitates task specifications for the units or organizations involved. Coordination by plan for "sequential task interdependency" involves the delineation of schedules for the interdependent units which become the basis for governing their actions. This form of coordination does not require the same extent of routinization required for coordination by standardization. The third form is coordination by mutual adjustment for reciprocal task interdependency. The greater diversity within a situation, the greater the need for mutual adjustments which, for the most part, involve the transmission of new information. Thus, a key element in this form of coordination is that the units involved must be willing to modify their internal operations. This implies that persons holding key positions within the units should be knowledgeable and should have a clear understanding of cost and benefit of adjustments through negotiations.

It should be pointed out that many systems of coordination may lead to over-centralization, extremely complex and unnecessary agencies and intervention in operational management. In this regard, the concepts of coordination and control should be differentiated. While the former does not necessarily involve direct sanctioning power, the latter requires mechanisms for direct supervision. Traditionally, the concept of control has been used to imply hierarchical, bureaucratic and unidirectional communication flow. The concept of coordination, on the other hand, emphasizes harmonious relationships and mutual influence. The concepts should indeed be separated since not all issues and reasons for both are the same.

Our argument in favour of coordination as a means of accelerating regional development does not entail that overcentralization in decision-making should take place, that innovative redundancy within the administrative system should be eliminated or that local initiative and competition among agencies should be curbed. Rather, it is contended that there is a need to harmonize activities with regard to regional planning and implementation for the purpose of integrating government developmental actions as far as possible. This may and should take place through decentralization of coordinating authority, greater involvement of people's organizations and through negotiation, adjustment and bargaining among individuals, organizations and units.

---

[13] Chammong, *Coordination in the Implementation of Family Planning Programmes*, pp. 61-2.

EFFECTIVENESS OF COORDINATION

From a systemic perspective, one of the most critical indicators of coordination effectiveness as an end-product within the administrative system, is the extent to which sectoral programmes and projects are clearly identified and integrated to achieve optimal consistency in government intervention. Similarly, the degree to which the responsibilities and functions for horizontal and vertical coordination are effectively shared among agencies at multilevels would also show the efficacy of the government machinery in harmonizing its activities. Another indicator in this regard would be the extent to which national priorities incorporated within various policy packages are in practice actually reflected in annual budgetary allocations.

The effectiveness of coordination within the government machinery may also be analysed by focusing on key coordinative agencies at the national, regional, and subregional levels. For this purpose there are six dimensions which, when considered cumulatively, may be assumed to delineate the effective performance of coordination functions by these agencies. These dimensions or components of criteria for measuring effective coordination at the agency level are, of course, not mutually exclusive. Furthermore, it is difficult to weigh these components with regards to their relative significance vis-a-vis the effectiveness of coordination.

The first dimension is the authority and status of the coordinating agency as indicated by, among other things, the degree of control and influence exercised by the coordinating agency on allocation of resources and personnel and the extent of formal authority statutorily or through administrative procedures granted to the agency. This implies that the coordinator and his agency need the authority and status to influence, and in some cases even force, those units or organizations which are consistently uncooperative in situations characterized by task interdependency.

Second, the location of the coordinating agency within the administrative system is of critical importance. The agency which has more direct access to the political decision-maker, and which is hierarchically well placed, is more likely to persuade other organizations and units within the government machinery to cooperate with each other in achieving common goals. This might be particularly true in developing countries in which most administrators are reluctant to make decisions unless guided by someone above them.

Third, the internal bureaucratic and organizational structure of the coordinating agency reveals its capacity to harmonize government actions. Free flow of communication within the agency, specification of its tasks, and more flexible internal organizational structure are conducive to increase the capacity of the agency to bargain, negotiate and informally influence organizational decisions. When the coordinative agency itself has a rigid organizational structure, it is not in a position to encourage task performance innovation by interdependent organizations.

Fourth, the leadership quality of key actors in the coordinating agency and human relations are important dimensions. The above are indicated by harmony within the agency; the extent to which personnel show awareness of and interest in the goals of the agency; and the rapport between the agency's key actors and those involved in organizations trying to achieve common goals.

Fifth, technical and professional competence within the coordinating agency, as measured by the actors' educational background and experience, enables it to take a leadership role in conflicts and differences among units involved in task performance. Given the complexity of public management tasks, it is indeed essential that the actor or agency responsible for harmonizing and integrating government actions within a particular area should have the necessary technical knowledge and experience.

Lastly, communication flow and the availability of essential information requirements commensurate with procedures to be followed at various levels, facilitate understanding of each other's role in achieving collective goals. Lack of such information would inevitably lead to duplication of efforts, mutual suspicions, and inefficiency in public sector management.

FOCUS AND ORGANIZATION OF THE BOOK

In this book an attempt is made to examine how and with what effect the coordination functions are being performed in developing countries at the multi-levels of planning, budgeting and implementation management processes. The first ten chapters are revised versions of papers presented at the Senior Level Seminar on Institutional Capability for Regional Development: Focus on Coordination which was held under the auspices of the United Nations Centre for Regional Development (UNCRD) from 16 to 20 August 1980 in Nagoya, Japan. The purpose of the seminar was to:

1. Examine the structures and mechanisms of coordination.
2. Discuss the effectiveness of coordination, including any impediments, to the effective performance of coordination functions.
3. Review other institutional dimensions which affect regional development performance.
4. Suggest strategies for institutional reform.

The papers in the first part of the book deal with theoretical issues. Milton J. Esman identifies two "parallel processes" for institution building in accelerating regional development, i.e., the establishment of structures and delineation of procedures within the administrative system to facilitate policy, programme and operational coordination, and the creation of viable people's organizations to ensure popular involvement in development activities and more effective interaction of "public" with government agencies. He argues that these necessitate deconcentrating administration, vesting of adequate authority within a single official in the field, encouraging the growth of constituency organizations and allocating financial resources to local units. After discussing the scope of coordination in the processes of regional development, A.P. Saxena identifies four categories of "blocks" to coordination which are "technical", "procedural", "structural" and "bahavioural". These blocks, he argues, lead to "dysfunctional administrative styles" which hinder the access of beneficiaries to regional development programmes. The author identifies two categories of coordination instruments, i.e., "tangible" and "intangible" and suggests that five factors should be taken into consideration while designing these, which are location of the instrument, its status within the administrative hierarchy, its internal structure, its linkages with other organizations and its leadership.

Dennis A. Rondinelli and Marcus D. Ingle identify major shortcomings in traditional approaches to development administration. The authors analyse the experiences of the selected developing countries in implementing decentralization programmes and policies, and suggest that impediments to programme implementation "extend beyond deficiencies in administrative procedures and organizational structures." Five factors which constitute the context of programme implementation are identified as political will, bureaucratic attitudes and behaviour, cultural tradition and practices, economic structure and spatial and physical systems. In his paper, Gabriel Iglesias suggests an approach for appraising administrative capability to perform coordination functions in plan formulation and implementation processes. Based on systems analysis, he argues that one could begin with examining the administrative capability of the "regional framework" to generate, allocate and utilize financial, human and physical resources. To undertake this, however, one would need to assess the management resources, i.e., "structure", "policy", "technology" and "support".

The papers in the second part of the book deal with structures, mechanisms, and effectiveness of coordination in selected countries of South and Southeast Asia. Though prepared on the basis of a common conceptual framework, the emphasis of the respective papers reflects country peculiarities. Shaikh Maqsood Ali, for example, discusses the Bangladesh experience in coordinating government activities at the grass roots and the mobilization of the rural poor. Johari Mat, on the other hand, describes in detail the mechanisms for coordination within each level in Malaysia. The studies by T.N. Chaturvedi and Chakrit Noranitipadungkarn emphasize the role of coordination agencies in India and Thailand, respectively. The study by Armand V. Fabella highlights the Philippine experience in regionalization of administration and development. K.P.G.M. Perera and Neil Fernando focus on the roles of the district minister and the Ministry of Finance and Planning. The last chapter presents an overview of the experiences of the particular countries discussed, and highlights key issues in institutional reform that might bring about the strengthening of regional development.

PART ONE

THEORETICAL ANALYSIS

1

FIELD LEVEL ORGANIZATION FOR REGIONAL DEVELOPMENT

MILTON J. ESMAN

MODERN GOVERNMENTS provide services principally through functionally specialized, hierarchically structured bureaucratic organizations. These organizations tend to be authoritarian in decision-making style and emphasize central control and uniformity of policy. Flows of information within them follow vertical channels and they maintain tight boundaries between themselves and other organizations. The more governments and administrative systems develop, the greater the proliferation of differentiated and specialized organizations, including not only government departments but also parastatal bodies of all sorts. The more governments succeed in spreading their presence and their services geographically beyond the main cities, the more the levels of hierarchy within their bureaucratic organizations. As they penetrate the periphery, central government agencies provide new and useful services; but they sometimes undermine established local capacities for collective action. The development of these networks of services confront all governments with administrative complexity, one consequence of which is difficulty in coordination.

DIMENSION OF COORDINATION

There are two major dimensions of coordination. The first is vertical — the achievement of coherence among related activities of the several levels of government and administration. As a practical matter, this has usually meant efforts to maintain central government control, national uniformity, and equity in policies and procedures, while at the same time recognizing the need to accommodate distinctive regional and local needs. Vertical coordination is especially important on matters of policy. Thus, the goal of increasing crop production and marketing at the local level requires national policies establishing sales prices that at least cover the costs of all the farmer's production inputs plus a reasonable margin of profit. The success of a regional programme to foster small-scale industry in rural areas may depend on national policies for infrastructural development (roads and electricity) and local action to make suitable land available.

Horizontal coordination involves the establishment of coherent priorities and the maintenance of operational consistency among the activities of specialized units serving the same publics in the same geographic space. Thus, the implementation of a local crop development programme may require the synchronization of credit, physical inputs (seeds and fertilizer) and the timely release of water for irrigation. This paper will emphasize horizontal coordination because it is operationally more feasible and can be a major institutional contribution to improving the productivity and the welfare of disadvantaged groups in rural areas.

Recent experience has demonstrated that public bureaucratic institutions are not sufficient vehicles for many kinds of public services, especially those which are oriented to mass publics and require positive responses and acceptance by members of those publics. In many countries, governments are unable to finance sufficient personnel to provide direct services to individuals and households, especially in rural areas. Even when this is possible, standardized rules and uniform procedures prevent bureaucratic agencies from responding to the distinctive and very unstandardized needs, preferences, capabilities and convenience of the diverse public they are expected to serve. Frequently the flows of information between publics, especially those which are more remotely located, socially marginal and economically weaker on the one hand and bureaucratic agencies on the other, are insufficient and unreliable. This is due to the physical, social and often psychological distance between educated and urbanized officials and low income, low status urban squatters, small rural farmers, tenants, landless labourers and especially the women among them.[1]

Because governments are frequently unable financially to provide a full range of services and because it is important that people participate more actively and assume greater responsibility for their own development, it is necessary to tap their information, skills, resources and latent managerial ability and combine them with the information and resources that governments can provide. Bureaucratic administration alone is not well suited to link with local publics and mobilize such local participation. The low productivity of the field personnel of many bureaucratic agencies is widely recognized and deplored; it is due in part to insufficient coverage, inadequate training and poor supervision and support; but in large measures, it is the consequence of their inability to establish appropriate linkages with their publics. This is a serious problem today for governments which are committed to rural development strategies aimed at enhancing productivity and meeting the basic needs of their poorer citizens. Since the administrative agencies of government cannot meet this challenge alone, other complementary kinds of organizations are needed.

---

[1] For an analysis of these phenomena, see Milton J. Esman and John D. Montgomery, "The Administration of Human Development" in International Bank for Reconstruction and Development, *Implementing Programs of Human Development* edited by Peter T. Knight (Washington, D.C., 1980) (World Bank Staff Working Paper; no. 403).

THE INSTITUTIONAL CHALLENGE

Regional development associated with basic needs strategies calls for two parallel processes of institution building:

1. Within the administrative networks which tend to function along strictly vertical lines, cross cutting structures and procedures must be established to foster policy, programmatic, and when necessary, operational coordination. This is needed at all echelons of administration and spatial jurisdiction, but it is especially important at the field level. Field level coordination will not simply happen; it must be structured. And the new structures must be endowed with sufficient political and administrative power and financial resources and control to induce and where necessary, compel coordinated programming and operations among related specialized staffs.

2. Organizations will have to be fostered at the local level to enable the various publics to interact more effectively with government agencies and to take greater collective responsibility for activities that affect their progress and well-being. These organizations should in large measure be accountable to their memberships.

These are mutually supportive processes. Improved coordination among government agencies cannot be counted on to activate the publics on whose cooperation their success as administrators must depend. Consequently administrative coordination, important as it is, cannot insure that services respond to public needs or that the people will contribute needed resources and support. Local constituency organization, without improved coordination among the agencies that provide services, will generate claims to which the latter are unable to respond. This will produce frustration and destroy incentives for local organization, because public needs are not fragmented along the lines of conventional, specialized, bureaucratic agencies.

Within the organizational complexity of contemporary states there are so many concrete variable factors to take into account when organizing public services that general prescriptions are impossible. The present state of knowledge does, however, suggest a number of propositions that seem to apply across a wide spectrum of countries and regions within countries and which ought to be taken into account in the design of improved local structures:

Horizontal Coordination

1. Centralized control of the details of programme operations is the enemy of local coordination. Thus coordination has major implications for the entire administrative system. Any serious effort at regional or local coordination requires the deconcentration or delegation of considerable decision-making authority within government agencies. If every departure from detailed, uniform bureaucratic rules and procedures or any variations from approved, standardized programme content must be referred to higher authority for prior approval,

then it is impossible to achieve operational consistency among the local units of departments providing complementary services to the same publics, or to respond in a timely way to distinctive or changing circumstances. Deconcentration cannot be sustained, however, unless field personnel are sufficiently trained that they can use discretion responsibly. This means that more attention must be focused on the hitherto neglected need for upgrading the performance of field personnel and on providing them with updated manuals and other forms of technical and policy guidance. Administrative practices must be simplified to permit timely adaptation of public services to distinctive and changing local needs.

2. If it is to be more than cosmetic, coordination requires the vesting of authority in a single official to guide the processes of field level planning and programme implementation. The more this authority depends on negotiations with and among local units of ministries, the weaker it will be; under those conditions regional administration becomes a political coalition in which every party has veto power. The more power the coordinating official is given over budgets and over the supervision of locally posted staff members and the more staff assistance he has for programme development and evaluation, the more effectively coordinated regional planning and programme management will be. There are many specific methods of patterning the coordinative role and for the authority of the coordinator over personnel and funds.[2] Whichever pattern is selected, the allocation of such authority is likely to produce continuous tensions between functionally specialized departments and units responsible for spatial coordination and integrated development. A useful antidote to the strength of the specialized departments pressing for vertical control are vigorous local government authorities demanding the right to integrate services within their areas of jurisdiction.

While the specialized departments may resist deconcentration and field coordination, national political leadership may favour that trend because it stands to increase their effective influence over field level decisions. This means, however, that national political leadership may find it necessary to control the selection of field level coordinators in whom so much power is vested and that the latter be responsible and responsive to them. This trend is evident in many countries and has contributed to the politicization of field administration. The latter has been further affected by the increased activity of elected politicians at local and regional levels. Thus, the inevitable consequence of administrative deconcentration, which is essential to responsive field operations and to effective horizontal coordination, is increased politicization of the field coordinating role. Under these circumstances, it is important that the selection of field coordinators incorporate administrative competence as well as political skills and political reliability.

[2] See James Heaphey, ed., *Spatial Dimensions of Development Administration* (Durham, N.C.: Duke University Press, 1971).

Field Levels of Services

3.   There are several layers of field level activity, each with distinctive potentialities for the organization, provision and coordination of services:[3]

(a) At the base level are hamlets, village communities or clusters of villages. Usually they have little or no taxing authority, employ no trained staff, and provide only routine services. They may, however, be organized into councils that can provide representation at higher levels where effective planning and operational coordination can take place. They may also contain informal groups which engage in mutual assistance and provide the base level structures for such associational groups as farmers' organizations, credit unions, cooperatives, or women's clubs.

(b) The district or subdistrict (the name varies from country to country) serving populations of 80 to 120 thousand is usually the lowest level at which funds, specialized expertise and competent coordinating authority can be brought together. This is the smallest region and the lowest administrative echelon at which integrated planning and programme management can be accomplished and in which representatives of organized local publics can conveniently participate on a continuing basis. In most countries, this is the level at which effective area development and programme coordination seem feasible.

(c) Between the village and the district levels there are opportunities to establish government service centres. These will usually be located in market towns where commercial facilities and services are also found. Here can be situated the offices of ground level representatives of specialized agencies. (Below them there will usually be only community based paraprofessionals whom they supervise). The service centres should be conveniently located no more than a day's return travel for people in the area. The primary interface between functional associational groups, e.g., water users' associations, farmers' organizations, mothers' clubs, and the bureaucratic agencies that serve them should occur at these service centres. The propinquity of the various government specialists, plus accessibility to their organized publics, should facilitate operational coordination of service delivery.

Organization of Publics

4.   An important dimension of organization for regional development is the participation of the publics whose lives are directly affected by development

---

[3] I am indebted for many useful insights to John Howell's (as yet unpublished) paper, "Administering Agricultural and Rural Development: Guidelines for Decentralization and Participation" (Rome: FAO, 1980).

programmes.[4] This participation affords them some influence over the content and style of government services. What organized publics can contribute to planning and implementation are:

(a) Information about their needs, capabilities, priorities, and preferences which might otherwise not be available to officialdom. This is especially important for disadvantaged and marginal groups whose members are unlikely to have ready access to officials or politicians and frequently have little confidence in them.

(b) Understanding and support for programmes as they are instituted, understanding and support that are needed if new programmes are to be taken up by the publics that are expected to use them and at times contribute to their implementation and maintenance. Most government services relating to rural development cannot be forced on rural people, but must be acceptable to them, viewed by them as useful and beneficial. This covers a wide range of activities from new forms of credit and innovations in cropping to family planning and environmental sanitation. Not only the substance but also the methods of service provision must be acceptable and convenient. The more that publics have a voice in these decisions, the more likely will the services respond to their priorities and preferences and the more likely will they be used. Both the relevance and the efficiency of service delivery depend on the participation of the publics who are likely to be affected. Effective participation of publics, especially those which are socially and economically disadvantaged, depends entirely on organization. Only through organization can they gain the power to participate.

There are two types of local participatory organizations: the general and the special. General organizations incorporate all members of the public within their area of jurisdiction. These are units of local government. While local governments have great potential for enhancing participation and for improving public services, in most developing countries they have been entrusted with few developmental responsibilities and have little access to funds or technical skills. As presently constituted, they can, however, be useful in articulating local needs and channeling them to the district level where their representatives can participate in planning activities and in the surveillance of programme implementation.

Special local organizations reflect the differentiation of rural life among groups with common economic, occupational, or ethnic interests. Rural areas are seldom homogeneous in the economic and social composition of their residents. These different interests must usually be reflected in separate organizations because conflicting interests (e.g., between landowners and landless

[4] See Milton J. Esman, "Development Administration and Constituency Organization," *Public Administration Review* (March/April, 1978).

workers) can seldom be promoted by a single organization. Common constituency relationship to an agency of government (e.g., water users' associations to the irrigation department, mothers' clubs to the family planning agency), is another basis for special local organization. These functional interest groups are likely to relate both to district level agencies and to the intermediate service centres, not only making claims but also providing information and facilitating service delivery.

The activation, especially of previously excluded or unmobilized groups, gives them the capability not only for greater mutual assistance, but also to make claims on their governments and on their more favoured neighbours. This initially introduces new political dimensions into area development. One reason that formal local organizations both of the general and special type are so underdeveloped is the fear of some governments that this political process may get out of hand, generate claims to which governments are not prepared to respond, and provide opportunities for oppositional or subversive activity. In addition, bureaucrats may not welcome activated publics because they complicate their routines and make "unreasonable demands". National leaders who in principle favour local organization, may hesitate, because of fear that local elites not supportive of the national regime will end up in control of the new organizations and convert them to their objectives rather than those preferred by the central government or by the poor who need assistance from government. Rural people often avoid the risks of collective organization, including the hostility of local elites, and prefer to depend on particularistic kinship or patron-client relationships for the satisfaction of their needs.

For such often inconsistent reasons combined with local factionalism which makes cooperation difficult and with the inexperience of rural people with formal organizations, local organizations in rural areas have been of limited use in dealing with governments. Yet if regional development is to serve the interests of the poor majority, they must be encouraged to act in concert in their collective interests; and governments must be willing to foster and protect general and special organizations, respect their autonomy (neither attempting to control them, nor to make them dependent on government largesse), and to tolerate the disagreements and the conflicts that active participatory local organizations are certain to generate.

If local organizations are to be effective they must have access to decision-making processes and their members must have the sense that this access is yielding tangible benefits. Isolated local organizations can do little for their members because the resources and the information they need to supplement their self-help measures are controlled by governments. Effective linkage to sources of information, funding, services, and resources are vital to their success. Without access to centres that allocate resources, the effort involved in participation will not justify the cost in time and strain, the interest of members will dwindle, the organization will wither or be taken over by unrepresentative minorities.

The strengthening of local organization depends in large measure on encouragement by governments. Governments of all ideological persuasions are recognizing the fact that local organizations which work within the system can make an important contribution to the effectiveness and legitimacy of their regime and expand the base of their political support. The fostering of general organizations — local authorities — depends on devolution to them of authority to act on matters of significant local interest. They should have access to funds, combined with staff training and other forms of technical assistance. The process of devolution should be gradual so that local publics, local leaders, and local staff can gain the necessary experience. Increased devolution can usefully be accompanied by financial auditing and other government measures, including conditional grants of funds, designed to foster probity on the part of local authorities. Accountability downward to their publics through elections and regular reporting and upward to government agencies are reinforcing methods of controlling abuses of authority.[5] Since many functions are likely to be shared by local authorities and government departments (water supply may be managed and maintained by local authorities, but inspected for sanitary standards by a bureaucratic agency), departmental administrators posted in rural areas must be trained and rewarded for working harmoniously with local authorities; conflicts between them will have to be mediated and settled by regional coordinating officials.

The most effective special organizations are usually built on a base of long standing trust and informal cooperation between kinfolk or neighbours. Thus, the specific form and structure of a local organization cannot be prescribed a priori, but should be derived from local experience. Where possible, attempts should be made to base organizations on established informal patterns. Their familar functions can be expanded in scope and where larger scale is required, second and third tiers of formal organization can be built on the base of informal groups, thus combining solidarity with scale.[6] Even more than with general organizations which are governmental, it is important that special organizations be permitted sufficient autonomy to represent the members' interests. Government assistance is usually required to provide needed resources and technical assistance, but too much patronage or too much control may destroy incentives for local initiative. It is not helpful for the government agency to "capture" the local organization, or vice versa. There must be continuing interaction, exchanges of information, and accommodation between special organizations and relevant government agencies, for despite the inevitable conflicts, each needs the other in order to accomplish its goals. The style of field administration must necessarily shift from command to negotiation; this can be facilitated by deconcentration to the field of discretion to adapt government programmes to distinctive local conditions and preferences.

[5] Norman T. Uphoff and Milton J. Esman, *Local Organization for Rural Development: Analysis of Asian Experience* (Ithaca, N.Y.: Cornell University, Rural Development Committee, 1974).

[6] Ibid.

Scope of Responsibility

5. What activities should be committed to district level planning and administration and what financial resources should they have? Clearly major investment projects which require large capital appropriations or sophisticated technology and management, and the impacts of which transcend the district, cannot be entrusted to district administration. They should, however, be coordinated with district level administration — which is all too seldom done — because they are likely to depend on and their consequences are likely to affect ongoing services under the authority of district or local governments. The latter may be inadequately informed and unable to act until crises develop. Thus, a major road building project with its heavy demand for labour could seriously disrupt agricultural production unless the project authority coordinates its schedule with the district administration.

Relatively small public works in all sectors seem ideally suited to district level planning and management because the necessary technical and management facilities can be built up at that level, and financial resources can be made available. Siting and specific services mix can respond to local priorities, capabilities, and convenience. Small or "minor" works are precisely those which are most demanded and appreciated by local people because they respond to their particular needs. Their management and maintenance are the special forte of district administration and local organizations. They are beyond the capacity of national level officials to plan or to manage. They are of little interest to them, and they compete only marginally, if at all, for financial, staff or physical resources. Usually small works activities are conceded, even by jealous or sceptical national ministries, to be suitable for district level planning and decision-making.

What is more frequently overlooked, however, is the capacity of district administration to manage ongoing services and to coordinate them in ways that the vertically organized ministries find impossible. Most government activity within a district does not involve new investments or new "projects", but the management of ongoing and recurring services. Yet the potential for district level management and coordination of such services tends strangely to be neglected, perhaps because they are incorrectly looked upon as routine and thus nondevelopmental and because central ministries resist what they regard as loss of control. Yet these recurring activities deal with agricultural and livestock production and marketing and involve the government-influenced inputs that affect the vital economic base of rural life. They also affect ongoing social services — health, welfare, and education — as well as the operation and maintenance of such important public facilities as roads and water supply systems. The planning and management (including the coordination) of these ongoing services are ideally suited for district administration and it is through district level processes that the contribution and participation of local publics can be most effectively and most responsively sustained.

6. Sufficient financial resources are required to make decentralized planning

and administration a reality. There are three sources of funds that district and local units can tap.

(a) Local and district levies of many kinds — on land, business transaction, consumption and fees for public services. Though many districts are poor and so are the majority of their residents, local levies are an underutilized source of funds in large measure because central governments have pre-empted them or do not encourage local authorities to act. The problem is aggravated by the weakness of regional and local governments and by well-meaning paternalism at the centre which discourages local financial initiatives and breeds an unhealthy dependency on the central government. In order to be seen as "benevolent" and in response both to local pressures and to the promptings of national level bureaucrats, governments often succumb to the temptation to "take over" local services or to provide them unilaterally. Such extension of government-financed services, without requiring some continuing counterpart local contribution, often stifles local initiative, undermines local action capabilities, and reduces incentives for participation at regional and local levels.

(b) The second source is block grants from the central government, usually for small and labour intensive public works. These grants should permit considerable discretion to district authorities so that they can respond to local initiatives. Central governments, however, for purposes of political patronage or technical control, often pre-programme such small works activities or subject them to time consuming review and approval procedures. To foster regional and local initiatives, governments should move toward financial block grants with limited central controls, but requiring some local contribution to projects, a challenge to local publics that can be met only if they are effectively organized.

(c) The third and most controversial source of locally available funds are those allocated by the national ministries for operations within the district. The main question is not the magnitude of these funds, but who controls them. Should these funds be allocated and their expenditure controlled by the specialized ministries and their field agents, or by the regional and district coordinating authorities, or by a process of negotiation in which both are involved? This is not the place to map out or evaluate detailed alternatives, except to say that if district level coordination is to be a meaningful process and if it is to incorporate the participation of local publics, it must include significant local influence on the programming and the use of funds and on the management and coordination of the activities they support. This means that control of substantial funds and programmatic and financial responsibility for their use should be delegated to regional coordinating officials or even devolved to local authorities. The major ongoing activities and expenditures of government within the region cannot be excluded from any strategy that attempts to foster regional development through administrative coordination and more active public participation.

PARTICIPATION, ADMINISTRATIVE REFORM AND REGIONAL DEVELOPMENT

There is so much concrete variation in the social structures, economic bases, government traditions, political processes and administrative institutions of Asian countries, that any concrete prescription for programme coordination, or for local organization in support of regional development would be presumptuous and useless. There are, however, a number of general considerations which might serve as points of departure for governments wishing to move in the direction of more participatory regional development:

1. Coordinating institutions must be as responsive as possible to the distinctive and varied needs of rural areas and their people. They should be established at the lowest level of administration that combines the presence of technically qualified staff members and sufficient resources to permit meaningful programme development and administrative supervision. This usually means the district level with populations of 80,000 to 120,000 persons.

2. Considerable discretion for the design and management of programme operations must be delegated by the specialized national ministries to their agents at the district level. Deconcentration must be a gradual process as field personnel are trained and equipped to accept greater responsibility. This has important implications for administrative operations. Departmental headquarters will have to shift their emphasis from supervising detailed programme operations to the establishment of policy, the training of staff, the provision of technical assistance, inspection and auditing, and the management of large projects and installations.

3. Sufficient funds must be available and sufficient operating discretion provided at the district level to make area planning and coordinated implementation worthwhile to the officials and the publics concerned. These funds will have to come from a combination of local sources and block grants from the central government.

4. Publics should be organized both in general units of local government and in functionally specialized interest groups to make inputs into the planning process, to mobilize locally available information, resources, and support, to make claims that reflect their priorities and capabilities, and to facilitate interaction between government agencies and the population they serve. Though governments must usually facilitate and protect these organizations, they must be allowed sufficient autonomy to reflect and express the interests of their members.

5. Officials and technicians posted in rural areas must be trained, equipped, guided and rewarded in order to accommodate two major administrative innovations: Working within the framework of area coordination, and working with organized publics which they can influence but cannot control.

6. Increased politicization is an inevitable consequence of administrative decentralization and public participation. Regional coordinators are likely to be selected and their performance evaluated in part according to political criteria. This may have detrimental effects on administrative impartiality, while increasing

the responsiveness of public services to organized publics.

7. Overambitious, "comprehensive", or integrated planning should not be attempted at the regional or district level. Simple and pragmatic methods should be adopted for programme planning and for coordination. Small working parties or ad hoc teams are preferable to large, formal structures. Elaborate formal machinery should be avoided in favour of flexible planning and operational coordination among service agencies and representatives of the concerned publics; the main objectives of planning and of operational coordination should be to establish programme priorities and achieve consistency among related activities, between investment projects and ongoing programmes, and among complementary ongoing activities in order to insure substantive compatibility, the timely availability of inputs, the maintenance of operating schedules, participation of the affected publics, and common learning from experience.

While it may seem heretical to academic planners, there is no technical or political reason for district level plans to be "consistent" with national plans; indeed the priorities of national planners tend to be quite different from those of the majority of rural people.[7] Nor has any method ever been found that makes such vertical coordination operationally feasible. For major investment projects such consistency between levels of government is indeed necessary and feasible; and national priorities such as malaria eradication or the upgrading of the livestock industry can and should be taken into account in district level plans and programmes. But the bulk of field level activities are likely to be small projects or the improvement of ongoing public services which are distinctive to local conditions. What is needed is not the dominance in rural areas of centrally determined priorities, but the ability to adapt and shape a meaningful share of government resources and services to locally determined priorities, reflecting the pluralistic character of developing economies. At the field level the achievement of consistency among related activities is a necessary and feasible objective. This requires substantial emphasis, as I have previously indicated, on building and restructuring institutions — the institutions of public administration and the institutions of popular participation.

Within these general guidelines, the concrete organizational factors that contribute to effective regional development can be put together and appropriate institutions built in a number of combinations that reflect political realities and the plurality of local conditions, country by country. Specific experience can be examined to determine what combinations work best under what sets of economic and institutional conditions. It is increasingly apparent that improved technical skills and better management performance in government, even when carefully planned and coordinated, will not suffice for regional development which is oriented to improving the productivity and the welfare of mass rural publics. If the intention is to share benefits widely, the publics must contribute

---

[7] For the development of this theme, see Michael Lipton, *Urban Bias: Why the Poor Remain Poor* (Cambridge: Harvard University Press, 1977).

and they must participate; to participate meaningfully they must work in and through organizations which are in some measure accountable to them and reflect their distinctive and often competing interests. The nurturing of such organizations may be the most challenging institution building problem that governments face in making vigorous area development a reality.

2

COORDINATION FACTOR IN REGIONAL DEVELOPMENT

A.P. SAXENA

IN RECENT years, the study of regional development has become an element of increasing concern in overall national development designs. Unlike today, twenty-five years ago, regional development problems were considered to be primarily technical.[1] In the intervening years, many factors made the situation more complex and unclear. In referring to the Third World, B. Higgins points to "an unprecedented lack of clarity as to the proper role, the day to day activities and the professional requirements of those engaged in this task."[2] R.P. Misra suggests that "the persistent questioning of the meaning of development has its repercussions on the meaning of regional development too," adding that "the disenchantment with the prevalent regional development policies is visible in all developing countries . . ."[3]

The subject of regional development, nevertheless, has been explored from an interdisciplinary perspective and pursued through a wide range of approaches. This has provided fresh insights into many of the issues facing regional development, especially those concerned with implementation. For example, it is increasingly appreciated that regional development, like the life span of the region within which it is directed, is made up of a number of indivisible elements. Its aim includes re-establishing economic and demographic equilibrium or establishing it at a higher or different level. It is inconceivable that such improvements should apply to only one aspect of a region's development to the exclusion of others. This might well result in a new disequilibrium being substituted for the one which was intended to be remedied. Regional development thus, presupposes an integrated view of all the constituent elements of human activity

---

[1] Lloyd Rodwin, "Regional Planning in Less Developed Countries: A Retrospective View of the Literature and Experience," *International Regional Science Review* 3 (1978): 113-31.

[2] Benjamin Higgins, "Planning Regional Development: Art, Science or Philosophy? The Challenge of the 1980s" [Paper presented at the Consultative Meeting of Experts on Training for Regional Development, Nagoya, United Nations Centre for Regional Development, 29 Jan.-4 Feb. 1980].

[3] R.P. Misra, "Training of Regional Planners in the 1980s — Challenges and Opportunities" [Paper presented at the Consultative Meeting of Experts on Training for Regional Development, Nagoya, United Nations Centre for Regional Development, 29 Jan.-4 Feb. 1980].

and requires coordination in all branches of such activity so that overall development is the result of simultaneous and harmonious uplifting of the elements. It is recognition of this disequilibrium and the inherent dangers in its delayed resolution that gives push to new regional development policies and institutional experiments. Since coordination could assist development activities by making goals clear, by observing the progress towards those goals and by taking initiative in ensuring further improvement, the underlying context and emphasis of these measures need analytical understanding of the coordination factor in regional development. It is often noted that our understanding of the coordination factor in regional development is unclear and represents an empty space in regional development thinking. This paper explores the nature and scope of the coordination factor, examines obstacles to coordination, and discusses the concept and design considerations for coordination instruments. It is expected this will provide some clarity regarding the coordination factor vis-à-vis the processes of regional development, especially with regards to the fulfilment of plans, programmes and projects within time and cost parameters.

NATURE AND SCOPE

At the outset, it may be reiterated that the coordination factor does not have an audit function, has no audit connotation, and therefore, may not be conceived as a coercive device. Coordination is between often widely dispersed activities, with the purpose of accomplishing events and tasks as part of a specified set of objectives. Coordination is defined here as a facilitating function and as an intervention instrument or device ensuring achievement of a plan, programme or project goals, and tasks within stipulated time and cost considerations. Coordination has a discreet function in space and time, oriented towards the achievement of specific objectives and goals within a targeted time frame. In essence, therefore, the purpose of the function is not to seek coercive coordination but to aspire cooperative coordination even though coordination objectives and contents would be oriented towards the solution of problems.

Decisions regarding coordination must be based on prior examination of how they can best be secured, e.g., by establishment of new objectives, policies, or procedures, by the delegation of new responsibilities or authority and centralization of command. Coordination must be distinguished from control here. Accountability or making individuals accountable for operation, plays an important part in the design of control devices and systems. Control focuses on policies, rules and standards to be enforced, while coordination stresses harmonious relationships and unity of activities among people organized for a common purpose. Thus, while both coordination and control pervade the process of regional development, the concept of coordination is more encompassing, positive and integrating than that of control.

As mentioned earlier, a whole new set of high priority, unprecedented tasks has emerged which is inherently part of the institutional proliferation of the current regional development pace. Regardless of our understanding of coordination, its problems will continue to increase as the scale of regional development intensifies. The need for coordination will be greater as more institutions are established in response to the multifaceted regional development framework. The importance of coordination in regional development, therefore, demands serious consideration in the assessment of institutional capability, as well as in the planning and implementation stages of regional development. In the overall scheme of regional development, coordination will be an ongoing integral part of such efforts and not a mechanical one-shot exercise.

Coordination is also necessary to initiate and establish linkages between different regional development institutions in order to ensure that the institutions so linked are mutually supportive. It is, therefore, necessary to comment on coordination vis-a-vis its response to the needs of regional development institutions. With the emergence of new regional development institutions designated as development devices, a stream of problems involving coordination are likely to surface. Along with these problems, the institutions will need to cope with a number of challenges and opportunities. It may be suggested, therefore, that the purpose of coordination is to effectively respond to institutional problems in the context of those challenges as well as the available opportunities. Although it is not always possible to establish institutional responses, including external ones, the responses must, nevertheless, take into account two major difficulties: (a) the problem of little control over the environment, and (b) the lack of means to anticipate the responses. A variety of environmental classifications of economic, political, social, demographic, and technological dimensions are available. Thus, the regional development process must be encompassed by the coordination factor and the institutions. In terms of planning and implementation, they help and organize the proper sequence for development with some objectives, for example:

1. To avoid the overlapping of major development elements, unless there be any compelling technical or functional reason for such overlap.
2. To help ensure a uniform basis for determining the sequence of regional development efforts in terms of potential and probability of success.
3. To minimize the cost of integrating related development efforts.
4. To reduce the number of personnel and of small, isolated functions wherever possible.
5. To provide adaptability to the regional development process and, thus, provide a foundation for consistent and comprehensive development.
6. To facilitate the continuation of both ongoing and *postfacto* regional development efforts.

Institutions here are visualized as intervening and implementing regional development vehicles, concerned with formulation as well as implementation aspects. In a way, the problems mentioned above are to some extent unavoidable, because in regional development, formulation usually take place at the macrolevel while implementation is carried out at the microlevel. It is the task of coordination to attempt to understand the situation and to eliminate or minimize these difficulties. Also, in the current reality of regional development planning and implementation, while tasks and responsibilities have been delegated to the lower levels, all effective power and authority necessary for discharging such tasks and responsibilities is retained at the centre. Coordination of different activities and services along the different levels is rendered extremely difficult because the lines of authority run vertically downwards from the central offices to the respective field offices. At the same time, any corresponding upward flow by means of feedback or otherwise, is extremely limited.[4] As a result, regional development activities remain uncoordinated and in some cases come to be mutually conflicting.

Brief mention may be made here about factors contributing to changes in the institutional environment. This is an important consideration because changes in the environmental profile of regional development institutions will influence the coordination design. Since it is recognized that institutions are part of the environment, any changes in regional and national development priorities, and in the regional and national economic and political situations, are considered to be of some significance. Similarly, the demands of beneficiaries, pressure groups, political, factional and ethnic groups and subregions, as well as changes in the procedures and policies of governmental operations, and in the structural relationship of institutions with other government agencies, may cause institutional environment disequilibrium. Frequently, conditions of resource scarcity and relative structural instability may also disturb the environment. Resource constraints would be one of the major reasons for coordination.

Environmental analysis is the identification of those existing and future conditions within the environment that have an influence on development institutions. The objective in performing this task is to identify new opportunities as well as future major difficulties. Regional development institutions should be able to identify opportunities within the environment that would fill a unique niche. These opportunities occur when there are specific needs which the institution is uniquely able to meet. The environmental continuum pertinent to regional development extends from the institutional to the national scene, reflecting a micro-macro distribution on a spectrum. In order to respond to institutional needs, the coordination factor in regional development must take due note of the above mentioned environmental features.

COORDINATION BLOCKS

Designing the coordination factor in regional development is a difficult task. There are several blocks to coordination in an aggregate sense, and more specifically in the context of regional development institutions, in the processes of

---

[4] See the background paper in A.P. Saxena, *Administrative Reforms for Decentralized Development* (Kuala Lumpur: Asian and Pacific Development Administration Centre, 1980), pp. 5-38.

regional development. Such obstacles may be found within institutions concerned with formulating regional development at the macrolevel as well as in those concerned with implementing regional development at the microlevel. In fact, blocks may exist within the coordinating instruments themselves which, as will be discussed later, include individuals as well as institutions. An attempt will be made here to examine the nature and content of internal and external blocks which are pertinent to an understanding of the coordination factor in regional development.

Generally speaking, these blocks may be divided into four categories — technical, procedural, structural and behavioural. Technical blocks relate primarily to the nature of the work, whereas the procedural blocks reflect the inhibiting rules and regulations. Structural blocks relate to the organizations, departments and inevitable hierarchies concerned over accountability and observational procedures, but not over performance. This is so because in its structural aspects, coordination within regional development institutions includes vertical, horizontal, intersectoral, interministerial (as part of the government set-up), interfunctional, intradepartmental and intrasectoral coordination. Behavioural blocks specifically relate to status-orientation and interpersonal relationships. To some extent, these blocks may partially overlap and the removal of one will affect the substance of another block. For example, structural rigidity produces distrust and insularity, and becomes the dominant characteristic of behavioural blocks.[5]

The purpose of alluding to these blocks is twofold. Individually and cumulatively these blocks lead to the evolution of administrative styles which, over a period of time, undergo formalization and thereby, generate internal institutional impediments to regional development. The emergence of dyfunctional administrative styles is marked by extreme concern for accountability and adherence to rules and regulations which are crucial. Relationships between people become increasingly impersonal. Written communications are preferred over face-to-face contact, because rules, regulations and procedures are ends in themselves, rather than means to ends. Interpersonal communications are also complicated by such factors as the psychological, social and cultural characteristics of the people, language and semantic problems, the social and formal structures of the institutions and the modes of communication.[6] The orientation is towards accountability instead of the results, which is the basis for decision-making and performance evaluation.

The higher levels of coordination within the administrative hierarchy are increasingly unavailable to the lower levels, resulting in independent entities within the organizational structure in pursuit of their own unidentified missions

[5] A.P. Saxena, "Administrative Improvement at Organizational Level — A System Design," *Economic and Political Weekly* 13 (1978): 51-2.

[6] Daniel Lerner and Schramn Wilbur, eds., *Communication and Change in the Developing Countries* (Honolulu: East-West Center Press, 1972).

that are oftentimes unrelated to the overall objectives of regional development. Styles are also characterized by a lack of cooperation which results in competing and confronting situations. Thus, lack of cooperation leads to intra- and inter-institutional conflicts, diminishing the efficiency and impact of the coordination factor in regional development. Cooperation may trigger other problems as well, including political ones. These formalized, uncooperative administrative styles inhibit efforts towards decentralization and bring about conflicting situations by reinforcing centralization. Regional development objectives are consequently blurred and common understanding is impaired. Emergence of such administrative styles creates a vicious circle which reinforces the blocks to coordination.

The blocks to coordination and the corresponding emergence of dysfunctional administrative styles seriously impair the access aspects of regional development. Perhaps, the consequences are far more serious to the beneficiaries of development. For instance, the beneficiaries may not be aware of the facilities, their locations or mechanisms for securing these benefits provided by the regional development schemes. Secondly, access mechanisms may be obstructed due to basic system inefficiency resulting from inappropriate coordination which is reinforced by formalistic and evasive styles at the institutional level. Thirdly, beneficiaries may not even be allowed to reach the services, and thus, are denied access. Continuing coordination gaps accentuate the complexities and result in eventual inefficiency of the disbursing system which, in turn, lead to mandatory requirements and compliance of procedures, regulations and formalities with which the beneficiary is in no position to comply.

The above difficulties have strong overtones, and primarily emerge because of coordination factor weaknesses. In spite of our long familiarity with regional development, the coordination factor as an important element in the equation has not been adequately analysed. In this context, and even more so because the factor has no outreach features, the problems of accessibility are more serious. It seems as if the blocks to coordination, the resulting administrative styles and the consequent obstacles to access mechanisms chase each other, preventing coordination and thus, inhibiting the processes of regional development. However, it is possible to meet these difficulties through appropriate coordination instruments which may be conceived and designed to strengthen the coordination factor in regional development.

The blocks to coordination mentioned here, and the resultant administrative styles must be further examined in order to isolate their causes before suggesting coordination instruments as prescriptions. Two causes seem relevant at this stage — lack of both administrative and information support. Administrative support is vital as a resource for the efficient performance of regional development plans, programmes and projects. Unfortunately, oftentimes administrative support is taken for granted and thus, is ignored in regional development planning. Administrative support, however, is a resource which must be sought and planned for like any other resource necessary in regional development and planning. Moreover, it must not be considered synonymous with manpower, which is only one contributing element to administrative support. Briefly, it includes components like an enabling legislation, effective organizational units, available decision-making systems and processes, skilled manpower, administrative leadership and, above all, institutional arrangements for coordination.[7] If these components are not available, the search for improved coordination may merely be an elusive one.

Today, as the scope and content of regional development has expanded, there are increasingly more unprogrammed decisions which underline the need for administrative support — both in terms of reliable availability and qualitative content. In this instance, administrative support has to be designed according to the strength of the coordination factor in order to overcome inhibiting factors in regional development. An incisive understanding of administrative support will facilitate the design of coordination instruments.

In addition to inadequate administrative support, lack of information support is also a major reason for blocking coordination or making it ineffective. Here again, information is seen as a resource to be generated and exploited for achieving regional development objectives. Inadequate information support may lead to serious difficulties.

> Top staff often lack reliable data needed to manage their own operations or to guide key policies. They are frequently embarrassed to learn about major new developments (private and public) of which they were not aware and which will create serious problems for services they should be providing. They are sometimes stunned by shocking errors — like zooming ahead with agriculture settlements in areas with fragile environments which will produce "green deserts" in just a few years.[8]

It is an immense problem to organize the information support required to sustain and service large regional development plans and programmes. This problem is not solved by providing more volume of data for all concerned, by faster accumulation and transmittal of conventional data or by wider distribution of previously existing data. Indeed to believe that such measures meet the requirments of information support is fallacious. What is required, instead, is a more systematic and comprehensive study of the regional development process in order to determine what, where and in which particular position information support is needed. Viewed in this context, qualitative and quantitative information support are a vital ingredient in the coordination factor. This factor should not be regarded as an information exchange counter or limited only to information exchange across the interface of departments. Information support is accomplished in accordance with several factors — flow, periodicity, timeliness and usage levels. The flow aspect, both vertical and horizontal, is crucial since periodicity, timeliness and usage levels without corresponding concern for

---

[7] Shelton Wanasinghe, *Administrative Support for Development Projects* (Kuala Lumpur: Asian and Pacific Development Administration Centre, 1978).

[8] Lloyd Rodwin, "Regional Planning Perspectives in Third World Countries" [Paper presented at the Consultative Meeting of Experts on Training for Regional Development, Nagoya, United Nations Centre for Regional Development, 29 Jan.-4 Feb. 1980], p. 29.

availability may not assist coordination. Timeliness and dimensions are particularly significant and need·to be seriously considered in the implementation phase of regional development.

COORDINATION INSTRUMENTS

It is suggested that there are two broad categories of coordination instruments — tangible and intangible ones. Tangible instruments include individuals as well as institutions. As far as individuals are concerned, the coordination of human beings is understood as ultimately necessary in any development effort. Individuals may be institutionally appointed, relocated or given new posts as part of the coordination strategy, although it is necessary to examine and take into account their location, span of authority, and status within the hierarchy. In real life situations, we are well aware of authority relationship problems connected with hierarchical structures. It makes little sense to designate or locate individuals as coordination instruments if their place within the hierarchy and corresponding activities are not commensurate with the expected tasks they are required to perform.

Institutions as tangible instruments are in a variety of forms. They may be new institutions, appendages to existing ones or existing institutions designated for a particular purpose. They may also have been created as modifications and changes within existing institutions. The question of structure, staffing, administrative capabilities and leadership within the institution, however, is of utmost importance before it is accepted as a tangible instrument.

The purpose of designing coordination instruments is to avoid *ad hoc* approaches and solutions via piecemeal informal arrangements which are at best part of a trial and error approach. An innovative planner concerned with regional development may develop procedures and relationships for handling a coordination problem of concern to him, but since this is an individual act, the principles involved in his successful efforts cannot be generalized and applied to other comparable problems.

A warning may be added that beyond a point, the proliferation of individuals and institutions as tangible instruments intended to provide coordination, may in effect create coordination problems. Thus, their proliferation becomes an obstruction to coordination in the overall scheme of regional development. Proliferation results in the overlapping of working relationships, aside from the ineffectiveness in dealing with social and political pressures at the field level. As a result, there is diffusion of responsibility as well as accountability.

Devising tangible coordination instruments does not necessarily imply that a dynamic modern structure concerned with new procedures will be added to or superimposed upon the traditional administrative structure. Rather it means that the existing structure will be altered and improved. Coordination is not simply a question of reorganization, of subdividing, merging or eliminating offices, improving methods, mechanizing, rationalizing or reducing staff. Although several of these steps are necessary, they are not sufficient and the results would not be lasting unless the other elements which give life and substance to regional development are also taken into account. Successful, pervasive coordination through tangible means require a complete change of attitude within all levels in the process and the institutions.

By intangible instruments, we mean information as a resource, as referred to earlier.[9] This is the least exploited instrument, but one with greatest potential for resolving regional development coordination problems. Information instruments may be entirely new procedures, systems or modifications of existing arrangements. Eventually, one can even conceive of a management information system specifically designed for a regional development programme or project or a cluster of such projects, to serve as a formal coordination instrument. The system would rely on speed rather than on fullest accuracy and would thus, avoid extraneous, unnecessary detail in the interest of timeliness. It would selectively emphasize continuous appraisal of progress and performance. It would be action oriented, dynamic and forward looking, and its operational design will include, (a) planned receipt of data, especially progress data; (b) quantitative and qualitative appreciation of development performance against predetermined targets; (c) variance analysis; and (d) critical review of lags and shortfalls in terms of performance schedules. In the context of regional development, the information system may thus, be conceived as a system for measuring performance changes that lead to decisions resulting in actions affecting performance.

Effective use of information as an intangible instrument ensures that the lines of communication are kept as short and as open as possible so that the content transmitted is as possibly similar to the content received. Generally speaking, as transmission is subjected to interpretation, problems of distortion and noise arise. In the regional development where language and cultural barriers are confronted, the messages are easily distorted. A suitable information instrument must ensure that partial communications be avoided and that only information be provided which the intended recipient understands, assimilates and acts upon. Too much information may be as harmful for coordination as too little information, because the recipient is only able to assimilate and utilize so much at one time.

Stating the design of coordination instruments — tangible as well as intangible — provides specificity to our understanding of the coordination factor. The exercise has iterative characteristics as indicated in Figure 2-1.

It is necessary to clarify that predesigned canned answers cannot be provided in the form of universal coordination instrument models, as design considerations depend on regional situations and development imperatives. In some instances, it may be even culture specific, e.g., where consensus values are dominant, specificity of instruments may be underscored. The choice of instruments and

---

[9] In an intangible sense, information is also behaviour — initiating stimuli between sender and receiver. It is important to remember this concept because the problem with most so-called information systems is that they are treated as data systems rather than information systems. For details, see: Adrian M. McDonough, *Information Economies and Management Systems* (New York: McGraw-Hill, 1963).

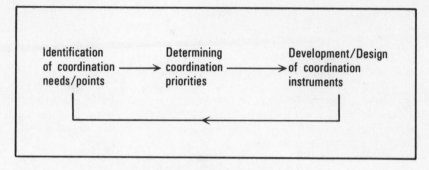

Figure 2-1. Performance-oriented Feedback

their design depend on the scope and size of regional development efforts in terms of the scale of programmes and projects which will eventually determine the instruments. A few guidelines for designing coordination instruments, however, may be briefly stated:

(a) Location of the Instruments: This is particularly relevant to tangible instruments — individuals and institutions. In the case of intangible instruments (information), the location implies the point where the information apparatus or system is located for its implementation and constructive exploitation of feedback on a continuing basis. Specifying the location, rather than leaving it loose and undefined, is useful in the interest of sustained coordination.

(b) Status within the System/Hierarchy: Status here is not considered in terms of rank or other nonfunctional attributes, but as placement within the overall scheme of regional development. This is equally applicable to individuals as well as institutions. Status within the design of the hierarchy influences the administrative linkages which may either facilitate or impede the efficacy of coordination instruments. Similar arguments hold well in the case of intangible information instruments.

(c) Internal Structure: This is particularly relevant to institutions considered as tangible instruments. The internal structure and corresponding staffing largely determines their facilitating capability. It may be suggested that ideally the structures should be flat and not multilayered with an extended vertical hierarchy. The obvious reason for this is that such structures will create problems of internal coordination within the instrument itself.

(d) Linkages with Other Organizations and Institutions: There is an obvious need for open and continuing linkages between tangible and intangible instruments wherever located, as part of the coordination scheme. In most regional development efforts, one may conceive of a multiplicity of instruments — individuals, institutions and information. All of these need a network relationship to mutually reinforce their expected output towards the common goal of improved coordination.

(e) Leadership: It is equally necessary to highlight the leadership vis-à-vis the coordination instruments functioning. If leaders controlling the instruments

do not *per se* believe in the development tasks, the result will be a routine maintenance approach designed at best to keep alive the administrative functioning of the instruments without concern for objectives. At its worse, it will be an internal, self-administering approach reflecting failure of the coordination instruments. The need to provide enlightened leadership with back-up technical and professional support thus, cannot be overemphasized.

The sophistication of any coordination instrument depends on the complexity of the regional development activities and the ability to implement these. A simple regional development project, for example, may require only limited coordination to ensure smooth functioning without unnecessary constraints. On the other hand, a major programme requires more extensive coordination in order to sustain continued progress. Regardless of the complexity of the development efforts, however, certain basic conditions must be met in order to provide workable coordination. Coordination instruments must be understood by those who use them and are responsible for their operation. They must relate to regional development and its institutions. Since institutions and coordination are interdependent, neither can function properly without the other. It must be sufficiently flexible so as to remain compatible with the changing institutional environment.

CONCLUSION

As a word of caution, it may be said that coordination will not *suo moto* improve the level of institutional capability for regional development. In fact, the reverse is also not true either. Coordination is only one of the intervening devices which may resolve impediments in the processes of regional development. It is not the only panacea for better regional development, since all the ills and failures of regional development cannot be traced to lack of or poor coordination, even though it may be justifiably called a crucial factor in accelerating regional development.

In the specific context of regional development, the coordination factor should be characterized by three specific features. It should be enduring, economical and acceptable. The first feature is a test of its validity. It will depend upon the extent to which it may perform the task in providing supportive integration of internal activities identified by function and/or level. It is one thing to design an instrument that contains the elements of coordination, but quite another to sustain its operation true to its objectives and design. This, in a way, indicates the content of the enduring feature.

The coordination factor should be economical for implementation and not be out of tune with the economic profile of the regional development programme or project concerned. It is conceivable that coordination instruments may be too elaborate, expensive, top-heavy or overstaffed, resulting in ineffective cost-benefit relationships. While it may not be denied that coordination instruments involve certain outlays over a period of time, the need for economy cannot be overlooked.

Finally, coordination instruments should be acceptable and their activities should be seen as legitimate. The acceptability should be endorsed by actors, doers, and implementors at various levels of implementation. It is necessary to remind ourselves that acceptance of coordination measures cannot be secured by administrative fiats, much less improved by a plethora of circulars and directives. Acceptance of coordination instruments should be equally forth-coming from the beneficiaries as well. It is imperative that the instrument be able to ensure credibility in terms of its ability in performing the tasks necessary for expeditious regional development. The instruments may not operate even at marginal efficiency and their output may be a mere illusion in the absence of acceptability by the beneficiaries.

During the process of implementation, coordination should be carried out along systematic lines. It should start with careful examination and analysis of the regional development institution in order to determine its structure and problems. These then should be listed in order of importance. How can coordina-tion be introduced without a clear knowledge of what has to be coordinated? There will be more favourable times than others when coordination will forge ahead. Even with outlines of systematic coordination, it should be possible to make full use of such occasions. These are often ignored because preparation begins too late. Worse still, introduction of coordination at the overall, sectoral or project levels of regional development is initiated without any prior preparation, clear-cut goals or adequate resources, thus, leading to discouraging results.

Coordination should remain flexible throughout the implementation process. It is, at the same time, equally important to appraise the progress of coordina-tion by making periodic comparisons with the original objectives. Adjustments may be made to the design of original instruments with the emergence of new factors which are easily foreseen at the outset. In other words, the original design must not be rigid. On the contrary, because coordination is a dynamic process, action to achieve it must always be based on the principle of innovation inherent in the changing scenarios of regional development.

Should total coordination be attempted or should it be progressive and partial? Should it begin with the modernization of the central institutions in order to improve their capacity to formulate and guide regional development, or should efforts be concentrated on the decentralized bodies, which are in a position to carry out programmes and projects more independently and flexibly? Or, should the emphasis be on institutions whose services have direct impact on the beneficiaries? Should coordination be backed by vertical action from the top downwards to break down resistance, or could it be carried out through the inculcation of new ideas for which support should be enlisted through cooperation, particularly at the field level? Would it be best to await a favourable political situation before implementing coordination measures all along or should this be a specialized process altogether removed from the political aspect? Rarely do favourable situations arise when political, social and other factors all permit the launching of coordination that is likely to be successful within a short or medium term. In most cases, because of the wide sphere of action, the obstacles to be overcome and the shortage of resources, it is advisable to undertake coordination wherever it is most urgently needed, especially in areas which, may become nuclei providing the driving force for broader, more far-reaching and more dynamic coordination.

These and many other questions are of basic importance for the coordination factor in regional development. Yet, available experience with coordination attempts in regional development shows that in many cases the nature and scope, the blocks and the design of the instruments had either not been properly analysed or were not sufficiently clear-cut.

3

AN APPROACH TO APPRAISING ADMINISTRATIVE CAPABILITY FOR REGIONAL DEVELOPMENT

GABRIEL U. IGLESIAS

INTRODUCTION

MOST EFFORTS at appraising administrative capability for regional development assume that the regional framework created for this purpose is an important factor in achieving regional development goals. Yet, it is fair to assume that in a number of cases the regional framework may not be an important factor at all (or may even be dysfunctional), since regional development has taken place even before such a framework was instituted. Regional development has also occurred despite weaknesses in the institutional machinery for coordinating regional growth and development. On the other hand, if the creation of a regional development coordinating framework is an important strategy for achieving regional development goals, then there is an urgent need for appraising its administrative capability in carrying out its assigned regional development tasks.

Initial interest in appraising the administrative capability of public organizations stemmed partially from the disappointing results of various national development plans implemented in developing countries during the 1950s and 1960s.[1] Because of the so-called "implementation gap", there has been heightened interest not only over plan implementation problems in the late sixties and seventies, but also an interest in appraising the administrative capability of organizations to implement national development plans.[2]

---

[1] See, in particular, Albert Waterston, *Development Planning: Lessons of Experience* (Baltimore: Johns Hopkins Press, 1965); and Bertram M. Gross, ed., *Action Under Planning: The Guidance of Economic Development* (New York: McGraw-Hill, 1967).

[2] See United Nations, *Appraising Administrative Capability for Development* (New York, 1969), United Nations, *Second United Nations Development Decade: A System of Overall Review and Appraisal of Objectives and Policies of the International Development Strategy* (New York, 1971); and United Nations Economic Commission for Asia and the Far East, *Problems of Plan Implementation in the Second Development Decade* (Bangkok, 1971). The 1969 monograph, *Appraising Administrative Capability for Development,* prepared by the International Group for Studies in National Planning (INTERPLAN) for the Public Administration Division of the UN Secretariat, served as a watershed in efforts towards developing a methodology for appraising administrative capability which INTERPLAN defined as "the capacity to obtain intended results from organizations," (p. 8). The appraisal of administrative capability was focused on three important dimensions: the organization's performance, structure, and environment.

Over the years, a number of approaches have been suggested for appraising the administrative capability of public organizations. One approach suggests the development of both quantitative and qualitative indicators to measure the performance capability of public bureaucratic organizations,[3] whereas another employs an analytical framework which incorporates input-output analysis[4] as well as the use of indicators to measure performance.[5] Another approach looks at aspects of administrative capability within a narrower framework of the plan implementation capability of administrative organizations, particularly at the capability of project level administrative organizations. These approaches generally use systems analysis.[6]

Shortfalls in national development plan implementation, and continuing inadequacies in the planning process, created pressures towards reforming the government machinery of some developing countries in order to improve their planning and implementation capability.[7] A reform strategy adopted by some governments was the creation of regional units as intervening levels between centre and local administrative or development units. Establishment of a regional framework was aimed not only at improving coordination in the preparation and implementation of sectoral and lower level plans, but also at serving as an important hub in efforts towards achieving regional and national development goals.

Focus on the region as the primary development unit interposed between the centre and the local level was seen as a strategy for improving the planning and implementation processes through decentralization of the coordinative and integrative tasks and responsibilities at a level closer to the area of operations. It also served as a primary vehicle for achieving a variety of development objectives — spatial, multisectoral integration, and coordinated planning and implementation of multisectoral programmes, projects and services.

In the case of the Philippines, regionalization by means of administrative deconcentration[8] of national functions through the creation of regional offices since the mid-fifties failed to achieve the main objective of decentralizing government functions and services. It also spawned other administrative problems,

---

[3] "Quantitative and Qualitative Indices for Appraising Administrative Capability for Development," *Public Administration Newsletter* No. 42 (October, 1971).

[4] Gabriel U. Iglesias, "Administrative Capability as a Neglected Dimension in the Implementation of Development Programmes and Projects," Eastern Regional Organization for Public Administration, *Pre-Conference Documentation* (Manila, 1973), v. 3.

[5] Norman Uphoff, "An Analytical Model of Process and Performance for Developing Indicators of Administrative Capability," *Philippine Journal of Public Administration,* 17 (July, 1973).

[6] In-Joung Whang, "Administrative Feasibility Analysis for Development Projects" (Kuala Lumpur: Asian and Pacific Development Administration Centre, 1978).

[7] Hahn-Been Lee and Abelardo G. Samonte, eds., *Administrative Reforms in Asia* (Manila: EROPA, 1970); Waterston, *Development Planning;* and Gross, *Action Under Planning.*

[8] Decentralization by deconcentration is the transfer of certain functions and responsibilities from the centre to lower level units without the corresponding transfer of authority; that is, final decisions relating to the performance of delegated functions are retained by the centre.

such as increased costs, more red tape and inter-unit squabbling. The shift in the early seventies to decentralization by devolution[9] of administrative and developmental functions through the creation of Regional Development Councils (RDCs) added an entirely new dimension to the concept of regionalization. Whereas the reforms of the mid-fifties focused on coordinating the planning and implementation functions of various bureaus and offices within the same department or ministry, the RDCs' functions included the coordination of regional planning and implementation of sectoral ministries (that is, through the ministries' regional offices, as well as those of other regional development authorities and local governments within the region). Although it would be difficult to export some of the lessons from the Philippine regionalization experience to other Asian countries, it is safe to assume that the trend in other countries is towards redefining and expanding the role and function of the regional framework in order to include planning and implementation coordination in the achievement of multilevel development objectives (e.g., multisectoral and intergovernmental development objectives). Therefore, the more multifarious and heterogeneous these activities — from irrigation projects in infrastructural development to family planning in the social development field — the greater the difficulties faced in the coordination process.

An additional strain in the regional framework's administrative capability for coordinating efforts towards the achievement of regional development emerged when some governments incorporated the integration of sectoral programmes, projects and services as a key feature in their overall regional development strategy (for example, integrated rural, agricultural, health, population and area development schemes). The evident failure of the traditional sectoral approach in solving coordination and integration problems spurred the incorporation of the integrative approach, particularly as a strategy in the acceleration of rural and regional development.[10]

Appraising Administrative Capability and the Problems of Focus

A fundamental problem in appraising the administrative capability for regional development is determining what is the most appropriate focus for analysis. This would help define the usefulness and limits of the appraisal

[9] Decentralization by devolution implies the transfer of authority from the centre to lower level units commensurate with the responsibility for performing delegated functions. For the Philippine experience on regionalization, see Gabriel U. Iglesias, "Political and Administrative Issues in Regional Planning and Development," presented at the 25th Anniversary of the College of Public Administration, University of the Philippines, National Conference on Public Administration: Promise and Performance, Manila, June 1977; and Raul P. de Guzman, "Administrative Reforms for Decentralized Development," in Saxena, A.P., ed., Administrative Reforms for Decentralized Development (Kuala Lumpur: APDAC, 1980).

[10] Generally, integrative approaches imply the coordination of both planning and implementation processes of programmes and projects within a specified geographic area defined as "region". For an approach which focuses on comprehensive regional development planning, see Haruo Nagamine, "Methods of Planning for Comprehensive Regional Development: A Paradigm," Asian Development Dialogue (No. 5 and 6, 1977).

technique or approach. Should focus be on appraising whether the broad regional development goals are attained, or should focus be on the role and functions of the regional framework in achieving more specific regional development goals? It would be useful to initially focus upon explicitly stated goals for which the regional framework is primarily responsible. This would limit the analysis to its administrative capability to perform the necessary functions for goal-attainment, and not to the more complex question of whether overall regional development goals have been achieved. Thus, the main objective of the analysis is on the appraisal of the regional framework's administrative capability for performing its assigned tasks or functions in attaining certain specified regional development goals.

Functional Focus

The next simplification stage is to determine with more precision the regional framework's set of functions and tasks (major and minor ones) and to rank these according to their importance. For example, for which of the regional framework's assigned tasks would it be held primarily responsible and accountable to some higher authority? One of the major functions for creating a particular regional framework is to coordinate regional development programme and project implementation. In practice, however, it has been predominantly preoccupied with simply gathering data to be used in regional development plan formulation. In this particular case, should an appraisal include its responsibility for coordinating the implementation of development programmes and projects? Its preoccupation with data collection for planning purposes may have been induced by its lack of power or authority to coordinate the implementation of regional development programmes and projects. In any event, an appraisal of administrative capability should initially focus on the major functions, and if time and resources permit, on the minor functions of the regional framework.

The focus delimited here is based on the assumption that activities and outputs emanating from the regional framework's function performance are not the only factors contributing to the overall development of a subnational space called the region. Not only are public and private organizations at various levels implicated in the entire process of regional development, but other factors like the existing land ownership patterns, peace and order situations, natural calamities, power distribution, resource endowment and others are often beyond the control of the regional office.

A related problem is the specificity and scope of the regional framework's functional responsibility. For example, it would be a far simpler task to appraise the regional framework's administrative capability if its main function were to promote regional growth. This could be accomplished by coordinating the planning and implementation of industrial development projects through industrial estates' development in various parts of the region rather than by appraising its administrative capability if its main task is to coordinate various activities needed to accelerate the region's socioeconomic development. Since the overall development of a major geographic subdivision like the region is the function of many institutions, factors, and influences which conceivably would implicate the total governmental and non-governmental system, to appraise its administrative capability to perform this herculean task will be not only expensive but also a fruitless exercise.[11]

Coordinating the Implementation Function as a Suggested Focus

It would be useful at this stage to further narrow the regional framework's major functions or tasks to a particular set of functions concerned with either coordinating the formulation of regional development plans or coordinating the implementation of plans, programmes and projects or both.

In view of the relative importance of the regional framework's implementation vis-a-vis its planning function, and the many difficulties and problems which have been identified in the implementation phase, it may be a useful strategy to initially limit the appraisal of the regional framework's administrative capability and responsibility over implementation;[12] and if time and resources permit, on its planning responsibility, if the latter has been specified as part of its functions.

Post-project or impact evaluation, an equally significant function, may not be explicitly stated as part of its major tasks although such is implied and inferred from its planning and implementation role. Because there are questions as to whether this task should be performed by "independent" institutions, it may be advisable to initially exclude this aspect from its administrative capability appraisal unless this is specified as part of its major functional responsibility.[13] However, ongoing evaluation and monitoring are included in implementation, so that this aspect is already included in the analysis. The focus on appraising administrative capability for coordinating the implementation aspects of regional development not only makes the appraisal manageable, but it also attends to

---

[11] It would be extremely useful if definitive studies could be done to determine the optimum limit on how many multisectoral programmes, projects and services could be effectively coordinated by a given type of regional framework. A typology could be assumed, based on resources which could be employed to achieve the task of coordinating the implementation process.

[12] As noted earlier, the initial interest in appraising administrative capability was spurred by the disappointing results in the implementation of national development plans. See UN, *Appraising Administrative Capability for Development;* Gabriel U. Iglesias, "Implementation and the Planning of Development: Notes on Trends and Issues, Focusing on the Concept of Administrative Capability," in *Implementation: The Problem of Achieving Results* (Manila: EROPA, 1976); UN, *Second United Nations Development Decade;* and UN ECAFE, *Problems of Plan Implementation.* However, focus on implementation does not obviate application of a modified version of the proposed framework on planning and evaluation processes appraisals.

[13] Evaluation of outcomes, including post-project impact analysis, is possibly an important area for examining the administrative capability of the regional framework as well as that of key sectoral and subnational level institutions. Because of the inherent bias towards subjective evaluations of one's own activities, there is less urgency in this particular field since this type of appraisal is best done in collaboration with academic or other institutions not directly concerned with performing the functions being evaluated. See U.S. Agency for International Development, *Evaluation Handbook* (Washington, D.C., 1974); United Nations, *Systematic Monitoring and Evaluation of Integrated Development Programmes: A Source-Book* (New York, 1978); and Kuldeep Mathur and Inayatullah, eds., *Monitoring and Evaluation of Rural Development: Some Asian Experiences* (Kuala Lumpur: APDAC, 1980), for materials dealing with problems of evaluation, particularly rural development programme and project integration.

an important problem area in the whole regional development strategy. This narrower focus seems logical, considering the fact that the regional framework's function goes beyond the coordination of multisectoral programmes and projects. In some cases, the major task of the regional framework incorporates a particularly integrated, multisectoral approach (e.g., comprehensive planning and integrated rural, agricultural, and industrial development), and integrated, spatial approaches as well, such as area-based development. Other approaches include the development of target clientele groups or beneficiaries (e.g., landless labour, the urban poor or ethnic minorities).

AN APPROACH FOR APPRAISING ADMINISTRATIVE CAPABILITY FOR COORDINATING PLAN IMPLEMENTATION

Focus on Critical Organizational Resources for Coordination Function

The regional framework, like any organization, would require certain resources to perform certain tasks. Therefore, the central problem in appraising the regional framework's administrative capability to perform its tasks is in the analysis of its capability to mobilize, allocate and utilize organizational resources, such as basic financial, human, physical and management resources pertinent to structure, policy, technology and support. Organizational resources *per se* are of critical importance to the organization if they can be mobilized and employed to achieve desired purposes and objectives. Funds, equipment and personnel may be idle and irrelevant resources unless they are (a) adequate in quantity and quality; (b) relevant to the needs of the organization; and (c) they can be mobilized and used when and where needed. Since in most developing countries there is generally a scarcity of these three basic resources, the regional framework should have financial, human and physical resources which are adequate, relevant and timely at the first level of analysis.

While it is not extremely difficult to construct quantitative and qualitative measures for the adequacy, relevance and timeliness[14] of these three basic resources, it may be useful to go to the next level of analysis which seeks essentially to answer the question: What is the regional framework's administrative capability for generating or mobilizing, allocating, and utilizing or employing these basic resources in performing its coordinating functions in the implementation of regional plans, programmes and projects? The mobilization, allocation

---

[14] These criteria may be operationally defined as follows: "adequacy" is a condition where a particular level of magnitude or characteristics of the resource (quantity and quality) may enable the performance of an activity based on a particular objective. "Timeliness" refers to the availability of a resource to achieve the purpose for which it is needed; and "relevance" is the appropriateness of a resource for the particular purpose or function being performed. Perception of these criteria vary and, therefore, are contentious, so that the appraiser will have to rely on the perceptions of the actors concerned, on the verification of data, and on arbitrary decisions based on objective and neutral grounds.

and utilization capability[15] of the regional framework to ensure adequate, relevant and timely financial, human and physical resources is influenced by another set of organizational resources which may be conveniently referred to as management resources: structure, policy, technology and support (see Figure 3-1).

Structure

The difficulty faced in designing the most appropriate institutional mechanism for performing the tasks of regional development coordination and management stemmed, in part, from the variety of existing organizational forms below the national or federal level which directly or indirectly perform the functions of regional development. Thus, the responsibility of coordinating and integrating regional development activities may be the sole or shared responsibility of the regional framework created for this purpose, as in the case of the Philippines; or of political subdivision, such as the states in the federal government as in India, and Malaysia, or provinces in Pakistan. The presence of national/federal entities operating within the region or the local government, such as the Muda Agricultural Development Authority (MADA) in Malaysia or the Southern Philippines Development Authority (SPDA) in the Philippines, tend to further complicate the tasks of coordinating regional development activities.

Special national/federal programmes or projects, such as the National Food and Agriculture Council (NFAC) food production programme in the Philippines, and the Federal Land Development Authority (FELDA) resettlement projects in West Malaysia, also operate at regional and local levels. Finally, national differences in terms of allocating and sharing functions and responsibilities between the national/federal and the local governments may affect both the structure and function of the regional framework, depending on whether governmental and developmental functions are centralized and/or decentralized to the lower level units.

On a continuum of organizational forms which has been devised, the coordinating committee/council and the public authority/public enterprise are at opposite ends. The committee structure is generally representational; that is, the various representatives of sectoral ministries, development authorities, and local

---

[15] Mobilization, allocation, and utilization capability vis-à-vis financial, human and physical resources is self-explanatory. It might be pointed out that to allocate budgetary expressions to the various projects in the plan represents an intended action (unless bound by law), and release of funds for the project is not assured. Utilization is the actual use of funds for projects in the plan whether they are allocated or not. Generally, resource allocation and utilization capabilities of the regional framework may be severely constrained by existing rules, procedures and conventions which preserve authority over resource allocation and utilization to central planning and implementation bodies and sectoral ministries. Mobilization capability is the more dynamic element since the regional framework could initiate efforts to tap governmental and non-governmental sources to enhance its human, financial, and physical resources. See M. Solaiman, "Mobilization and Use of Local Physical Resources," and Gabriel U. Iglesias, "Identification and Mobilization of Local Groups for Rural Development," in Raksasataya, Amara and L.J. Fredericks, eds., *Rural Development: Training to Meet New Challenges* (Kuala Lumpur: APDAC, 1978), v. 4.

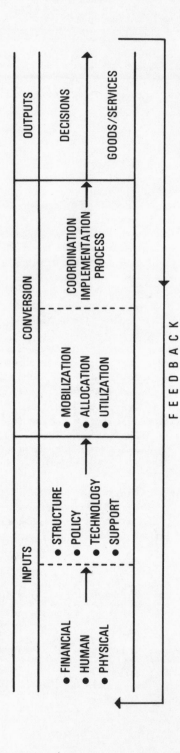

Figure 3-1. Administrative Capability System for Implementation

governments sit in the committee and the leadership is drawn from either among the members, as in the case of the Regional Development Council in the Philippines, or from the ministry which performs integrative functions within the existing governmental system, as in the case of the Ministry of Interior in Thailand. A secretariat composed of technical specialists is often created to assist the committee/council.

Since the committee/council depends to a large extent on who occupies the leadership position and on the cooperation of the sectoral ministries, its effectiveness as an institutional mechanism for coordinating planning and implementation of regional programmes and projects is often dissipated by internal wrangling, lack of cooperation, and inability of the coordinative body to impose collective decisions upon members, particularly when regional and departmental priorities and interests are in conflict.[16]

The public authority/public enterprise represents an attempt to overcome some of the problems of the committee structure through the creation of an organization with sufficient authority, resources and personnel to perform certain regional development tasks. The problem of interdepartmental coordination and integration appears to be less severe here since the development authority or public enterprise may perform the major brunt of the developmental tasks. This type of organizational structure has been found to be generally successful in dealing with narrower and more limited functional regional development responsibilities, but it is less effective for coordinating broader regional development functions, activities and areas.[17] As the Malaysian case shows, this type of structure tends to create linkage problems with other governmental units concerned with regional development.[18]

The importance of structure as a management resource is in its stable patterning of organizational roles and relationships. It achieves organizationally relevant goals by defining responsibility and authority relationships among individuals and units of the organization, particularly with regards to allocating, mobilizing and utilizing basic resources. The structural characteristics of the regional framework to a large extent determine its administrative capability to perform its major functions of coordinating the implementation of regional plans, programmes and projects in terms of its capability to make decisions or to influence organizational decisions, particularly those belonging to regional and subregional extensions of national ministries.

---

[16] See, in particular, World Bank Staff Working Paper No. 375, *The Design of Organizations for Rural Development Projects — A Progress Report* (Washington, 1980); Gabriel U. Iglesias, "Political and Administrative Issues in Regional Planning and Development," and Armand Fabella, "The Regionalization Scheme: An Approach to Administrative Reform," *Philippine Development Journal* (February 1974).

[17] See L.J. Fredericks and R.J.G. Wells, "Planning and Management of Rural Development Projects with Particular Reference to Rice Production Strategies in Peninsular Malaysia" [Paper presented at APDAC Workshop on Project Planning and Management of Rural Development Projects, Kuala Lumpur, June 1980].

[18] Johari bin Mat, "Institutional Capability for Regional Development in Malaysia: Focus on Coordination" [Paper presented at Senior Level Seminar on Institutional Capability for Regional Development: Focus on Coordination, Nagoya, UNCRD, August 1980].

The structuring of roles, authority relationships and leadership positions within the regional framework are important factors in its coordinative capability for achieving vertical coordination with sectoral ministries, planning and monitoring bodies, finance and central personnel agencies and public corporations, as well as for achieving horizontal coordination with their regional and local level subdivisions, local governments and institutions.

Policy

Policy as a management resource is related to structure in at least two ways. First, it is an important factor determining the structure, that is, the legislation creates the organizational framework together with the informal patterns prescribed by social practices and conventions. Second, the structure makes possible the generation of policies, rules and procedures, internally or from the external environment, needed by the organization to perform its functions within its legal/constitutional mandate. Since policies provide the regional framework with the capability to prescribe present or future courses of actions or behaviour, policy as a management resource tends to enhance its capability for deciding or influencing decisions to mobilize, allocate and utilize funds, personnel and physical equipment in the process of coordinating the implementation of regional plans, programmes and projects.

Technology

Technology as a management resource refers broadly to relevant knowledge and practices (e.g., concepts, tools and techniques) essential for the internal operation of the regional framework as an organization (management technology vis-à-vis basic resources), and in particular to specialized and technical knowledge and skills essential in performing its assigned tasks and functions, such as comprehensive planning, growth pole and area-based planning strategies, and the identification, appraisal, monitoring and evaluation of projects.

The level of technological expertise, together with its capability to draw, develop and select appropriate technology from within the regional framework or from the external environment adds immensely to its capability to influence planning and implementation decisions and the behaviour of persons, groups, and institutions involved *per se* in regional development. This aspect does not include hardware technology *per se,* such as computers and other physical resources, except as part of its capability to determine appropriate hardware technology.

Support

Finally, support as a management resource refers to the actual or potential roles and behaviour of persons, groups and institutions which tend to promote the attainment of organizational goals. Unlike the basic resources and the three other management resources, support as a resource is a more dynamic and elusive concept since its enhancement depends to a large extent on the regional framework's capability to perform its primary functions. On the other hand, the regional framework could adopt a deliberate strategy for enhancing support from the internal and external environment;[19] for example, by adopting a more participative planning and implementation strategy involving organization members at all levels as well as the clientele and beneficiaries. Promoting and maintaining linkages[20] with relevant and influential institutions, groups and elites not only increases support which directly affects its management capability to mobilize, allocate and utilize organizational resources (both basic and management), but also enables the regional framework to defend or free its plans, programmes and projects from negative or harmful influences from the external environment.

Mobilization, Allocation and Utilization Capabilities in Terms of Financial Resources

It may be useful at this stage to examine the resource management capability of the regional framework in terms of a critical resource — the financial one. There appears to be a strong correlation between the regional framework's inability to directly control or influence decisions on the allocation and utilization of funds, and its effectiveness as a coordinating mechanism. This refers particularly to its ability for deciding or influencing agencies' decisions within its coordinative ambit regarding the inclusion of programmes and projects in regional plans, as well as programme and project implementation priorities. A series of questions may be posed to ferret out answers that would reflect factors or conditions which tend to constrain its capability as well as identify the appropriate strategy to be used in harnessing management resources to enhance its capability for mobilizing, allocating and utilizing financial resources.

1. Is the regional framework capable of modifying its structure to improve its capability through the budget and allocation process, and to decide or to influence implementation decisions which would ensure greater adherence to national or plan priorities?

---

[19] Environment refers generally to governmental institutions, groups and individuals which directly or indirectly influence the activities of the regional framework in performing its functions of coordinating the implementation of regional programmes, projects and services. It could also refer to non-governmental actors, groups and institutions who have been "coopted" or who can make "claims" over the activities concerned with the coordinated function. See Eric Trist, "Key Aspects of Environmental Relations," in UN, *Appraising Administrative Capability for Development,* "Additional Note 3."

[20] See Milton J. Esman and Hans C. Blaise, *Institution-Building Research: The Guiding Concept* (Pittsburgh: Inter-University Research Programme in Institution-Building, 1966). Esman and Blaise identified four categories of linkages — enabling, functional, normative, and diffused.

2. Is it capable of using its support resources (e.g., through increased participation in the planning process or through its linkages with influentials) in order to modify its policy resources to bring change in existing legislation on financial allocation on the one hand, or to increase its authority in monitoring and reviewing the implementation of regional projects of sectoral ministries and local governments on the other?

3. Can it mobilize fund support from both the domestic and international environments by the adoption of innovative and appropriate approaches and techniques (technology resource) in the promotion of regional government?

4. Is it capable of ensuring better cooperation with regional plan priorities by mobilizing community resources by heightening the ideological commitment of regional programme personnel to some specific regional development goals (e.g., development of depressed areas, marginal farmers and disadvantaged groups), through a deliberate strategy for tapping community resources (labour, savings), and by involving community groups in the planning and implementation process?

Mobilization, Allocation and Utilization Capabilities in Terms of Human Resources

Manpower is another critical basic resource which serves as a basis for appraising the regional framework's administrative capability. Financial resources are generally scarce in developing countries while human resources are abundant. The problems presented by the human resource variable in organizational performance are of different dimensions: for example, the level of technical and managerial competence of personnel; the distribution of qualified personnel in critical parts of the regional system; leadership qualities; and motivation, commitment and other behavioural and social considerations. The human component is perhaps the most vital since it is the most dynamic and unpredictable of the basic resources, and because of its ability to act upon or to transform the more static financial and physical resources.

In assessing the regional framework's administrative capability for mobilizing, allocating and utilizing human resources in performing its regional development coordination and implementation functions, it is important to initially analyse its capability in terms of the four management resources — structure, policy, technology and support. This should be followed by an assessment of its capability to singly or in combination use the management resources to overcome certain institutional and environmental constraints and to enhance its capability to mobilize, allocate and utilize human resources in performing its coordinative functions. In terms of structure, the regional framework's capability for coordination is affected by its composition, authority, decision-making characteristics and leadership pattern. If the structure of the regional framework serves as the major obstacle in accomplishing the performance of its tasks, the analysis should then focus on whether it can mobilize support resources to modify its structure through changes in its basic charter (policy resource) in order to give it more decision-making authority or to influence its decisions regarding personnel (its own or of sectoral ministries) allocation and utilization essential to its coordinating function performance.

The answers to the following questions could reveal the regional framework's administrative capability for mobilizing, allocating and utilizing human resources in the performance of its regional development programme and project coordination and implementation functions.

1. To what extent can it make or influence decisions regarding the recruitment, assignment and transfer of personnel (its own or those belonging to agencies under its coordinative umbrella) essential in performing the various coordinative tasks for regional development programme and project implementation?

2. What is the level of technical and managerial competence of the personnel — its own and that of the sectoral ministries and statutory bodies under its coordinative framework?

3. What is its capability for enhancing the level of competency through training, or through the change of existing policies, rules and regulations?

4. What is its capability for drawing from the domestic and international environment technically qualified personnel, particularly those whose expertise is unavailable in the region or in the country itself?

5. How adequate are its financial resources in terms of attracting qualified personnel or in retaining qualified staff?

6. What is its capability for mobilizing its own manpower and those from agencies under its coordinative authority (e.g., level of commitment, motivation, morale and participation)?

7. What is its capability for mobilizing the community (either private voluntary groups or government-sponsored local organizations) to support regional development programme and project coordination and implementation?

As in the questions related to financial resource management capability, the above list is by no means exhaustive. It simply illustrates some of the relevant questions that may be raised to elicit responses which would reveal the regional framework's capability with regards to these two basic resources. Additional questions should be developed by those who undertake the appraisal. Although the third basic resource — the physical one — is not as critical as the other two in the overall performance of the organization, the same approach used to analyse the administrative capability of the financial and human resources is applicable.

CONCLUSION

The main objective of this paper is to suggest a preliminary approach which is simplified and very selective in focus so that the appraisal of administrative capability is not only feasible but also manageable. Although the suggested approach in appraising administrative capability implies a systems approach, the kind of rigour and complicated analyses inherent in this approach have been deliberately avoided. Similarly, a systematic appraisal of performance capability generally involves the construction of criteria and indicators which are measurable in quantitative or qualitative terms. However, the exactitude and sophistication required by measurement of this nature must be reconciled with the practical problems of the evaluator's capability, the feasibility and manageability of the appraisal and the cost in both time and resources.

Outside of defining these criteria, this paper has avoided construction of an elaborate system of measuring performance. It is suggested that because of the complexity and dynamics of the elements being measured, a less cumbersome analysis (preferably using guided questionnaires and indepth interviews) would reveal some meaningful insights and tentative conclusions. Because of these limitations, it is hoped that efforts to develop more systematic and rigorous measures of administrative performance capability will succeed.

It is hoped that it will serve as a useful, albeit an initial tool, for diagnosing certain deficiencies and strengths in the administrative capability of the regional framework for coordinating the implementation of regional plans, programmes and projects. It could also be a useful approach for recommending ways with which we may enhance and strengthen its administrative capability for plan implementation. With further modifications for improving as well as expanding the area of appraisal, it is possible that more useful analytical systems or approaches will emerge for appraising the administrative capability of the regional framework for coordinating the implementation of regional development.

4

IMPROVING THE IMPLEMENTATION OF DEVELOPMENT PROGRAMMES: BEYOND ADMINISTRATIVE REFORM*

DENNIS A. RONDINELLI AND MARCUS D. INGLE

FEW OF the problems that developing nations have faced during the past quarter of a century have been as complex and intractable as finding effective ways of implementing development plans and programmes. These problems are likely to become even more complex during the last two decades of the twentieth century as developing nations and international assistance agencies more vigorously pursue programmes to promote socially equitable economic growth and extend the benefits to poorer groups in developing societies. Recent national development plans and foreign aid policies underline the importance of decentralized planning and administration and of widespread participation by intended beneficiaries in the design and implementation of development programmes. Indeed, some argue that decentralization and participation are inextricably related in achieving equitable development.

Analysts in the U.S. Agency for International Development (USAID), for instance, contend that "increased popular participation, to be sustained and effective, requires the mobilization of local actors and the institutionalization of their activity." They insist that "decentralization is necessary to increase the scope of decisions, and thus incentives, available to local participants, as well as to build institutions to encourage, structure, focus and stabilize such participation."[1] More equitable development can only occur, they argue, if new

* An earlier version of this paper was presented at the American Society for Public Administration National Conference in 1980. It draws heavily on the authors' previous research on problems of implementation, decentralization and administration in developing countries for the U.S. Agency for International Development. The case material on East Africa is largely derived from Rondinelli's study of decentralization and area development for the Regional Planning and Area Development Project at the University of Wisconsin-Madison, funded through the Office of Rural Development, USAID. Ingle's review of the literature on implementing development programmes for the Rural Development Office helped form insights into various approaches to implementation that are found in development administration theory. Practical Concepts Incorporated, with which both authors are associated, provided generous support to complete this paper. The authors are grateful to all of these organizations, and absolve them from any responsibility for all views and conclusions.

[1] James Wunsch, "Managing Decentralization" (Washington: Office of Rural Development, U.S. Agency for International Development, 1979), p. 25. (Project Paper, mimeo.).

administrative structures and procedures allow those who have been excluded from economic and political activity to participate in development planning and management in the future.

Although decentralization and participation appear frequently as objectives in development plans and policies, implementation has lagged far behind political rhetoric.[2] The difficulties can be attributed to the general dearth of knowledge about programme implementation and more specifically to the lack of attention given to the design of implementation strategies by planners and administrators in Third World nations. Moreover, the theories of development administration that emerged during the past quarter of a century have provided little guidance on either count; development theorists and practitioners are only now beginning to explore the dimensions of the implementation problem. Much of the development administration theory of the 1950s and 1960s focused on macroeconomic planning, societal modernization and national, political and administrative reform. Grand schemes quickly met pervasive and intransigent obstacles, however, and lack of attention to administrative details destroyed the credibility of these approaches during the 1970s.[3]

But implementation has now become a central concern of governments in developing nations and of officials in international funding institutions. Improving the management of development programmes and projects is also likely to be a dominant focus of development administration theory in the 1980s. Nearly all national development plans now recognize that implementation is at the core of development strategy. Nigerian planners, for instance, admit that "implementing a plan is as important as, if not more important than, drawing up the plan. Experience has shown that even with the best planning techniques, there usually exists a gap between plan formulation and plan implementation."[4] Kenya's development plan for 1979-83 makes the improvement of managerial capacity in governmental institutions a major objective, arguing that "performance of many of these [institutions] must be improved if the tasks set forth in this plan are to be accomplished. The development strategy to alleviate poverty places new demands on the nation's institutional network."[5]

International assistance organizations, such as the World Bank, United Nations specialized agencies and USAID, have come to similar conclusions. A recent United Nations report points out that the "process of decision-making on strategy choices for national development should be accompanied by elaboration of their public administration implications."[6] The experience of USAID

---

[2] The policies and problems are outlined in more detail in Dennis A. Rondinelli and Kenneth Ruddle, "Coping with Poverty in International Assistance Policy," *World Development* 6 (April 1978): 479-98.

[3] For review of the literature, see Marcus D. Ingle, *Implementing Development Programs: A State of the Art Review,* Final Report (Washington: U.S. Agency for International Development, 1979) (mimeo.).

[4] Republic of Nigeria, *National Development Plan 1970-1974* (Lagos: Government Printer, 1970), p. 333.

[5] Republic of Kenya, *Development Plan, 1979-1983* (Nairobi: Government Printer, 1978), Part 1, p. 75.

[6] United Nations, Department of Economic and Social Affairs, *Public Administration and Finance for Development* (New York, 1975), p. 46 (ST/ESA/SER.E/1).

officials indicates that "erroneous assumptions about project organization and management or administrative factors have been a major cause of failure, or lack of complete success, of many development projects."[7] And a recent World Bank report concluded that "the main function which has evolved for the Bank is to assist the borrower . . . in identifying, helping to prevent, and solving the problems that arise in the course of implementation."[8]

Despite this strong resolve to deal more aggressively with problems of implementation, little has actually been done to anticipate administrative requirements in the formulation of development plans and policies. Of the 342 pages in the Nigerian plan, for example, only six are devoted to implementation. A recent review of thirty national development plans formulated during the 1970s found that only half had sections addressing administrative and management issues, and that only six of those explored implementation requirements in any detail.[9] Nor is there much consensus among international assistance agencies about how programme implementation can be improved in developing countries. The United Nations report points out that the concept is new and that "in practice, few developing countries have initiated such comprehensive administrative planning."[10] USAID officials frankly admit that "determining the precise application of general development approaches in specific cases remains, despite all our efforts and those of thousands of practitioners and scholars alike, a very murky, difficult, uncertain, complex and intractable business."[11]

Although many studies have been done of Third World governments, little effort has been made by development administration theorists to identify the factors that influence policy implementation and to provide a comparative framework for designing and managing development programmes and policies. Traditional theories of development administration attributed the difficulties of Third World governments to three major deficiencies: ineffective administrative procedures and managerial techniques, weak or inadequate development institutions, and inappropriate or pre-modern governmental structures. The prescriptions of the 1950s and 1960s, therefore, focused primarily on administrative "modernization" and reform. But evaluations of development programmes during the 1970s found that administrative reform alone had little impact on promoting economic and social progress or on alleviating massive poverty. Most prescriptions for administrative reform failed to address crucial questions of distribution and equity, and were themselves deficient in providing strategies for

[7] U.S. Agency for International Development, *Project Assistance Handbook* (Washington, 1978), Vol. 3, p. 6H-1.

[8] Arturo Israel, "Toward Better Project Implementation," *Finance and Development* (March 1978): 27-30.

[9] See Ingle, *Implementing Development Programs*, p. 47, for a list of the plans.

[10] United Nations, *Public Administration and Finance for Development*, p. 46.

[11] U.S. Agency for International Development, *Implementation of the "New Directions" in Development Assistance*, Report to the Committee on International Relations on Implementation of Legislative Reforms in the Foreign Assistance Act of 1973, U.S. Congress, House of Representatives (Washington: Government Printing Office, 1975), p. 4.

implementation. Indeed, the issues addressed by traditional development administration were too narrowly defined to improve implementation capacity; crucial variables such as political will, bureaucratic attitudes and behaviour, cultural norms, economic structure and spatial and physical systems often went unexplored.

This paper reviews the major approaches to development administration in the three decades following the Second World War and their limitations for guiding the implementation of development programmes. It then describes the experience of several developing countries in East Africa that have attempted to implement programmes for promoting decentralized administration and increased participation in development. It identifies major obstacles to implementation of these programmes in Tanzania, Kenya and the Sudan, and some of the crucial variables that impinge on policy and programme implementation in the developing world, to which development administration theory of the 1980s must be addressed.

APPROACHES IN DEVELOPMENT ADMINISTRATION THEORY TO IMPROVING IMPLEMENTATION CAPACITY

The development administration theory of the 1950s and 1960s was reflected in two somewhat different but not mutually exclusive approaches. One, which W.J. Siffin has labeled "tool oriented", contended that programme implementation could be improved in developing nations through the transfer of administrative procedures and techniques from industrialized countries, and especially from the United States, Britain and France.[12] The other argued that political processes and administrative structures had to be thoroughly transformed and modernized before developing country governments would be effective instruments for promoting economic and social progress.

Those who believed that implementation capability would be improved by the transfer of administrative procedures and techniques from industrialized nations followed the Weberian model for building efficient bureaucracies. They sought to create administrative procedures that were objectively "rational", politically impartial, and economically efficient. Advocates of this approach insisted that development administration must be concerned with the "technical procedures and organizational arrangements by which a government achieves movement toward development goals."[13] F.W. Riggs argued that development administration in this sense was concerned with the methods used by governments to attain their development objectives through the implementation of

[12] William J. Siffin, "Two Decades of Public Administration in Developing Countries," in Stifel, L.D., J.S. Coleman and J.E. Black, eds., *Education and Training for Public Sector Management in Developing Countries* (New York: Rockefeller Foundation, 1977), pp. 49-60.

[13] Saul M. Katz, "Exploring a Systems Approach to Development Administration," in Riggs, Fred W., ed., *Frontiers of Development Administration* (Durham, N.C.: Duke University Press, 1970), pp. 109-38.

policies and plans.[14] The United Nations *Handbook of Public Administration* issued in the early 1960s was the embodiment of this approach. It set out prescriptions for creating organizational hierarchies within bureaucracies, establishing a civil service based on skill and merit, improving personnel administration, establishing public enterprises and reforming budgeting, supervision and training procedures.[15]

Administrative and political modernizers, on the other hand, believed that the transfer of administrative procedures and techniques from Western democracies, was necessary but not sufficient. They viewed development administration as "social engineering", and national governments as the prime movers of social change. M. Landau defined development administration as a "directive and directional process which is intended to make things happen in a certain way over intervals of time."[16] Others perceived development administration as a means of improving the capacities of governments to deal with problems created by modernization and change; it would be the primary instrument for transforming traditional societies.[17] Unless the entire political and administrative system was reformed, governments of developing nations could not adequately direct and control social and economic progress.

But traditional approaches to development administration came under heavy criticism during the 1970s. Siffin concisely summarized the weaknesses of the "tool oriented" approach.[18] It attempted to create bureaucracies based on values of rationality, political impartiality, efficiency and democracy that were predominantly characteristic of Western cultures. When the procedures and techniques were transferred to other cultures, they were either misused or found to be irrelevant. This approach also assumed that complex social problems could be solved through modern administrative procedures and techniques. But in many countries the transfer of Western administrative methods simply introduced predetermined solutions and inhibited the development of analytical skills among planners and administrators to deal with unique problems as they arose in their own societies. Moreover, the tools were transferred from well-structured institutions in industrialized societies to loosely organized governments in the developing world, where they could not work as they did in Western countries. Indeed, many procedures and techniques, such as programme budgeting and systems analysis, were transferred before their efficacy had been proven in

4 See, Riggs, *Frontiers of Development Administration,* Introduction, pp. 3-37.

15 United Nations, *A Handbook of Public Administration: Current Concepts and Practice with Special Reference to Developing Countries* (New York: U.N. Technical Assistance Bureau, 1961).

16 Martin Landau, "Development Administration and Decision Theory," in Weidner, E.W., ed., *Development Administration in Asia* (Durham, N.C.: Duke University Press, 1970), pp. 73-103.

17 See for instance, Hahn-Been Lee, "The Role of the Higher Civil Service under Rapid Social and Economic Change," in Weidner, *Development Administration in Asia,* pp. 107-31; and Joseph J. Spengler, "Bureaucracy and Economic Development," in LaPalombara, J. ed., *Bureaucracy and Political Development* (Princeton: Princeton University Press, 1963), pp. 199-232.

18 Siffin, "Two Decades of Public Administration," pp. 56-9.

industrialized nations.[19] In countries where the techniques took hold, they often created powerful technocratic classes that were out of touch with the real problems and needs of people — especially the poor — in their own countries. Finally, the tools of Western administration were concerned primarily with maintenance of functions and thus their transfer did little to improve Third World governments' capacity to promote development.

Similar criticisms have been made of the administrative and political modernization theories. They were ethnocentric and based on philosophies and values that often rendered them useless or perverse in many developing nations. L.W. Pye points out that the literature never yielded a concise definition of political development. It was variously defined as the creation of political prerequisites for economic growth in industrialized countries, the creation of governmental institutions with characteristics similar to those found in European nation states, and reform of legal and administrative structures in the American or British tradition. Some thought of it as mass mobilization and participation in political processes, creation of procedures for orderly political succession, or the sharing of power and authority in democratic fashion.[20]

The institution-building movement, which largely displaced these prescriptions in the 1960s, called for more intensive efforts to expand the number and strengthen the administrative capacity of government institutions. The theory was based on the premise that the poor record of implementation in developing nations was the result of inadequate institutional capability to perform development functions effectively. Thus, development administration was given a new task: to build the institutional problem-solving and innovation capabilities of governments in developing countries. Siffin argued that "the essence of development is not to maintain, but to create effectively. . . . Doing this means, among other things, marshalling substantial amounts of knowledge about organizational design and the effects of alternative organizational arrangements."[21] V.A. Thompson insisted that Weberian models of bureaucracy were inappropriate for the innovative and creative tasks required of development administration. He offered an adaptive model aimed at creating an organizational atmosphere conducive to innovation. Both tool oriented and administrative reform approaches sought to strengthen central government control. But because policies evolve under conditions of rapid change in developing countries, Thompson and others argued that they were not susceptible to central direction. He called for the creation of institutions that would be more conducive to creative problem-solving: nonhierarchical, nonbureaucratic, professional, problem-oriented

[19] See Dennis A. Rondinelli, "International Assistance Policy and Development Project Administration: The Impact of Imperious Rationality," *International Organization* 30 (Autumn 1976): 573-605.

[20] Lucian W. Pye, "The Concept of Political Development," *Annals of the American Academy of Political and Social Science* No. 358 (March 1965): 1-13.

[21] Siffin, "Two Decades of Public Administration," p. 59.

systems in which communications structures were loose and in which decisions evolved from group interaction.[22]

M.J. Esman defined institution-building as "the planning, structuring, and guidance of new or reconstituted organizations which (a) embody changes in values, functions, physical and/or social technologies; (b) establish, foster and protect new normative relationships and action patterns; and (c) obtain support and complementarity in the environment."[23] The aim of the institution-building strategy was to create "viable development institutions"; those with the ability to deliver technical services, to internalize innovative ideas, relationships and practices within the staff of the organization, and to continue to innovate so that new technologies and behavioural patterns would not be "frozen" in their original form. A viable organization would be able to attain favourable recognition within society, be highly valued or regarded by other organizations, and get them to adapt the innovative technologies, norms or methods that it introduced. Thus, the institution-building strategy was concerned not only with strengthening the administrative capacity of individual organizations, but also with forging cooperative relationships among institutions.[24]

Application of the institution-building strategies, however, has usually been limited to ministries in central governments and to large educational and research institutes; the abstractness of the theory and the complexity of executing it made it difficult to apply in most Third World nations. Where institution-building was tried, it was often considered as an end in itself. It did not, therefore, address questions of equity and participation, and the role of the poorest groups lacking access to institutional resources.

Perhaps the most serious shortcoming of traditional approaches to development administration, however, was that prescriptions for modernizing administrative procedures, techniques, institutions and structures were themselves policies and programmes that had to be implemented within existing government institutions. Development administration theorists largely begged the question of how these reforms would be implemented in administrative systems diagnosed as inefficient and ineffective, and therefore in need of reform.

Although debilitating deficiencies in administrative procedures, managerial techniques, government institutions and political structures may, in fact, inhibit the implementation of development policies and programmes in many countries, they do not entirely explain the difficulties that Third World nations have had with implementation. A variety of other factors that condition the amount of change that may be made in institutions, and which therefore, are crucial in

[22] Victor A. Thompson, "Administrative Objectives for Development Administration," *Administrative Science Quarterly* 9 (June 1964): 91-108.

[23] Milton J. Esman, "Institution-Building as a Guide to Action" (Washington: U.S. Agency for International Development, 1969) (mimeo), p. 13.

[24] Ibid.

formulating implementation strategies, have not been integrated into development administration theory or practice. This is illustrated quite clearly when the experience of developing nations with implementing administrative reform programmes is examined and the obstacles are identified. Recent attempts by governments in Tanzania, Kenya and the Sudan to decentralize development administration and planning functions, strengthen local institutions and reorganize the political structure to attain more equitable economic growth, underline the complexity of policy implementation. Experiences in those countries highlight the variety of factors other than administrative variables that affect implementation. Although the policies pursued in East Africa sought to attain quite radical changes, they were based on a conventional assumption of development administration: that reform of administrative procedures, institutions and structures would itself promote social and economic changes in society. Failure to analyse those factors that shape the society in which reform programmes must be administered created obstacles to attaining policy objectives.

ADMINISTRATIVE DECENTRALIZATION AND LOCAL PARTICIPATION IN DEVELOPMENT MANAGEMENT: PROGRAMMES AND POLICIES IN EAST AFRICA

Governments in East Africa have emphasized the importance of administrative decentralization and local participation for equitable economic development since the early 1970s. Tanzania, for instance, has experimented with decentralization and participation for more than a decade. President Julius K. Nyerere, the architect of Tanzania's socialist government, insists that development must mean more than simply increasing gross national product. Tanzania's model for equitable growth required benefits to be widely distributed. Tanzania's leaders attempted to create an economy capable of providing for the basic needs of the entire population and sought to establish a governmental system in which the population would become politically conscious, independent and responsive. Nyerere attempted to fashion a unique form of African socialism, combining institutions for widespread participation in development decision-making and management with those for strong central guidance of the national economy. Tanzania's leaders sought to develop a self-reliant agrarian economy in which all segments of society could participate in productive processes and reap equitable returns for their participation. Tanzania would thus avoid the great disparities in income and wealth between urban and rural areas, and privileged elites and the peasant masses, that appeared in the wake of economic growth in many developing nations that tried to imitate Western industrial societies.[25]

---

[25] A concise summary of the Tanzanian policies can be found in Richard N. Blue and James H. Weaver, "A Critical Assessment of the Tanzanian Model of Development" (New York: Agricultural Development Council, 1977), 19 pp (Reprint; no. 30).

To achieve these goals, Tanzania's leaders decentralized the government in 1972. Local governments were abolished and their officials were absorbed into the central government's civil service. The highly centralized national ministries were reorganized and many of their development planning and implementation officers were assigned to the regions. Regional authorities were given greater responsibility for rural development planning and the powers of district and village development committees were expanded. Teams of technical officials headed by development directors provided administrative support to local development committees.

Administrative decentralization was designed in part to strengthen the ongoing process of "villagization". The creation of *ujamaa* villages was a form of area development in Tanzania through which the widely dispersed rural population could be concentrated in communal production units and be provided more efficiently with government services needed to meet basic needs and increase agricultural productivity. Through *ujamaa* villages, government resources for rural development could be integrated and local organizations could be created for popular participation in development planning and administration. The underlying political and ideological motivations for mobilizing the population to support the national government were reflected in the designation of the Tanganyika African National Union (TANU), the country's only political party, as the organization responsible for implementing the decentralization programme. In most of the country, political party structure paralleled the decentralized government structure, with TANU leaders playing a significant role in village activities.[26]

Three principles were inherent in the reorganization of local administration: that rural development must be managed at the local level, that it must have the participation of the population, and that it must be coordinated by the central government. Thus, the Decentralization Act of 1972 created a four-tier, hierarchically-organized administrative structure, with the President and central ministries at the top, dealing with national affairs and overall guidance of the national economy, and three levels of local administration for planning and implementing regional and community development activities. Regional and district administrations, headed by commissioners, formed the second and third tiers, with wards and villages headed by party secretaries forming the base of the administrative pyramid.

Kenya's economic system remains basically capitalistic, but decentralization of planning and implementation also became the cornerstone of its rural development policy. The national development plan for 1970-74 outlined a programme for delegating substantial responsibility for development to provinces and districts. Provincial and district development advisory committees were set up "to

---

[26] See Diana Conyers, "Organization for Development: The Tanzanian Experience," *Journal of Administration Overseas* 13 (July 1974): 438-48; P. Abraham and F. Robinson, *Rural Development in Tanzania: A Review of Ujamaa* (Washington: International Bank for Reconstruction and Development, 1974) (Studies in Employment and Rural Development; no. 14) (mimeo.); and Helge Kjekshus, "The Tanzanian Villagization Policy: Implementation Lessons and Ecological Dimensions," *Canadian Journal of African Studies* 11 (1977): 269-82.

coordinate and stimulate development at the local level by involving in the planning process, not only government officials, but also the people through their respresentatives."[27] In 1974, the Government further decentralized development functions by making the districts, rather than the provinces, centres of development administration. It would strengthen their technical and administrative capabilities by assigning District Development Officers (DDOs) to local development committees and by providing assistance with industrial, infrastructure, and natural and human resources development through District Planning Officers (DPOs). The staff of the ministries operating within each district were to become members of the development committees along with local officials and members of Parliament.

For the Sudan, decentralization was a necessity in a country that is larger in size than Western Europe and where the ability of the central government to rule from the capital city meets severe physical, political and organizational constraints. With the socialist revolution of 1969, President Gafaar Mohammed Nimeiry and the leaders of the Sudan Socialist Union advocated decentralization as a precondition for political stability and as a fundamental principle of socialist ideology. As one Sudanese official pointed out, decentralization was essential for creating the type of government that Sudan's leaders sought, a "system of government in which power is vested in the masses." For them, "mobilization of the masses for the maintenance of this power in their own hands and for the reconstruction of their own country and destiny" was an integral part of the concept of development.[28]

In 1971, Nimeiry attempted to decentralize by strengthening the authority and decision-making responsibilities of the provinces and by establishing a system of participation for localities. Decentralization was seen as the best way to make administration more responsive to the needs of diverse and physically isolated regions. It would make Sudan's socialist approach to development operable, and mobilize diverse cultural, religious and tribal groups in support of national policy. The People's Local Government Act of 1971 expanded the duties of the Provincial Commissioners and created Provincial Executive Councils to coordinate the work of local officials and central ministry technicians working in the provinces. Provincial planning teams were to be formed throughout the country. Moreover, within each province, the Executive Council could create district, town, rural and village councils to which they could delegate planning and administrative responsibilities. Serious consideration is now being given to regionalizing the entire country and granting a form of autonomy similar to that given to the Southern Sudan in 1972 to the nation's three Northern regions.[29]

---

[27] Republic of Kenya, *Development Plan, 1970-1974* (Nairobi: Government Printer, 1969), p. 75.

[28] See Omar el-Haq Musa, "Reconciliation, Rehabilitation and Development Efforts in the Southern Sudan," *Middle East Journal* 27 (Winter 1973): 1-6.

[29] A more detailed account of the Sudan's attempts to decentralize planning and administration is found in Dennis A. Rondinelli, *Administrative Decentralization and Area Development Planning in East Africa: Implications for U.S. Aid Policy* (Madison: University of Wisconsin, Regional Planning and Area Development Project, 1980), 150 pp.

Administrative Obstacles to Implementing Administrative Reform

The results of these administrative reforms have been mixed; none of the three governments has fully implemented its decentralization and participation policies. Many of the obstacles to reform, ironically, can be attributed to the very weaknesses in existing procedures, institutions and structures that the reforms sought to overcome. Moreover, none of the governments anticipated the constraints and obstacles to, nor engaged in detailed planning for, implementation.

Obstacles to the implementation of administrative reforms appeared quickly in the Sudan after the promulgation of the Local Government Act of 1971. The Act greatly increased the administrative responsibilities of the provinces, but also created serious problems for provincial and local councils, of which inadequate financial resources and the lack of trained personnel were the most pressing. Although the President had transferred many functions from the central ministries to the Provincial Executive Councils, the national budget did not reflect the shift in workloads and responsibilities. As a result, the provinces lacked adequate facilities, equipment, supplies and trained personnel to perform their newly assigned duties. Although the central ministries were required to assign field staff to the provinces, many Commissioners complained that the central ministries did not second staff in sufficient numbers or of good quality to provincial posts. High rates of turnover, resentment on the part of some employees who were involuntarily transferred from Khartoum, and frequent changes in postings made stable administration in the provinces difficult.[30]

An investigation of decentralization conducted in 1975 by the national legislature (the People's Assembly) found that these and other problems were impeding implementation of the Local Government Act. The Assembly committee found that ambiguity in the Act concerning relationships between provincial and local councils impeded the work of both and aggravated problems caused by inadequate manpower and financial resources. Many local councils were unable to perform their functions effectively, even four years after enactment of the local government law. Moreover, the committee discovered that without corporate status for local government, administrative officers were rendered powerless to perform their previous duties. Decision-making and administration were left almost entirely to the rather weak local councils; administrative functions had to be performed in many areas by what the Assembly committee called "part-time persons who may not even be qualified to carry them out."[31] In this atmosphere of ambiguity, the Local Government

---

[30] The experience is described in more detail by John Howell, "Administration and Rural Development Planning: A Sudanese Case," *Agricultural Administration* 4 (1977): 99-120; and John Howell, ed., *Local Government and Politics in the Sudan* (Khartoum: Khartoum University Press, 1974).

[31] Democratic Republic of the Sudan, The People's Assembly, *Final Report of the Select Committee for Study and Revision of People's Local Government,* Translation, referred to hereafter as the People's Assembly, *Final Report* (Khartoum: People's Assembly, 1976), p. 27.

Act had little influence on changing the structure of informal leadership in rural villages.[32]

In 1976, the Assembly's Select Committee for the Study and Revision of the People's Local Government Act concluded that the 1971 law did not really devolve power as much as it deconcentrated it from some central ministries and reconsolidated it in other ministries and in the provincial commissioners' offices. The People's Assembly was told by its Select Committee that "power thus becomes centred in the headquarters of the province and thus the administrative shadow expands at the same time it was meant to be contracted by the establishment of such a tremendous number of People's Local Councils."[33]

To overcome some of these implementation problems, Nimeiry introduced more drastic changes during the late 1970s. He reorganized some central ministries in 1977 and completely abolished others in 1978. He elevated provincial commissioners to cabinet rank and eliminated the Ministry of Local Government to which they had previously reported. In 1979 he devolved nearly all powers, except for a few national functions, to the provinces. Finally, the basis for national budgeting was altered to give the provinces more authority over their own expenditures. Despite these changes, however, decentralization programmes still faced myriad administrative obstacles at the end of the 1970s.[34]

Similar problems — shortages of skilled personnel and financial resources, complex and ambiguous administrative procedures, institutional inflexibility, and weak administrative capacity at the local levels — obstructed implementation of Kenya's programmes of deconcentration. Bureaucratic opposition to decentralization and widespread participation, moreover, limited the attainment of the programme's goals. From the beginning, central ministries tried to maintain control over district and provincial planning and to restrict the scope of participation in the development committees. The Ministry of Finance and Planning (MOFP) made it clear in its early guidance to the provinces and districts that the development committees were to perform only review and approval functions, and not to take part in day-to-day planning. A manual issued by MOFP shortly after the 1974-78 National Plan announced decentralization asserted that "it is utterly fallacious to think that a district action plan can be developed at a meeting of the District Development Committee (DDC)."[35] Ministry officials feared that political manoeuvring would influence the formulation of the plan. "The DDO and the individual sectoral heads should together revise the draft if necessary in readiness for full discussion at the DDC," the

---

[32] See Howell, "Introduction: Local Government and Politics," in *Local Government and Politics in the Sudan,* pp. 1-12.

[33] The People's Assembly, *Final Report,* p. 24.

[34] See Rondinelli, *Administrative Decentralization and Area Development Planning in East Africa,* especially pp. 42-7.

[35] University of Nairobi, Institute of Development Studies, *A Manual for Rural Planning* (Nairobi: Ministry of Finance and Planning, 1974), p. 42.

manual instructed district development officers. "If this 'behind the scenes' consultation is effective, there will be little reason for 'political talks' in the DDC when the draft proposals are put before the full session."[36] The MOFP also saw the participation of members of Parliament and community organization leaders in the revised district planning process as a potential source of political conflict and told the district planners: "The fact of the matter is that the people's representatives should see the DDC as an institution where the heads of departments explain the rationale for their proposals and actions and also as a place where only minor modifications and adjustments that are necessary are made and not as the real planning arena."[37]

Thus, the principles of decentralization and participation in development planning proclaimed in the 1974-78 Development Plan were not always supported by the MOFP or other central government agencies in Nairobi. Administration in Kenya remains highly centralized and province and district development committees play weak roles in development management. The central ministries retain strong control over sectoral plans and budgets and the relationship between national plans and district recommendations is often difficult to ascertain.

The Government also ran into serious obstacles to implementing administrative reforms in Tanzania. Both the critics of Tanzania's strategies and more sympathetic evaluators point out that the government is a long way from achieving its goals of decentralized decision-making, widespread participation and equitable economic growth. The programmes have not always worked as intended. Participation in rural areas, for instance, varies widely among villages and regions. As World Bank evaluations note, the variation seems to be directly related to how well TANU is organized in the area and how intensively it pursues democratic participation. With the abolition of district councils, TANU remains the primary, and sometimes only, channel of political representation for rural people.[38]

Nor has decentralized administration, especially in *ujamaa* villages, always been as efficient as advocates of local management claimed it would be. Organization of communal work in many villages is haphazard, and record-keeping and work-monitoring are nearly nonexistent, so it is difficult to know how much work is actually done on communal land. Nor does the government always know the level of output or rate of productivity in *ujamaa* villages. The steadily decreasing production in Tanzania since the early 1970s, however, seems to support the claims of critics that communal organization is less efficient than private production and that farmers are less motivated to work on communal plots.

[36] Ibid., p. 41.

[37] Ibid.

[38] See Abraham and Robinson, *Rural Development in Tanzania*, pp. 24-54.

Moreover, many families were pressured into moving to *ujamaa* villages, or persuaded by government or TANU officials with promises to provide services and facilities that they were unable to keep. These problems were aggravated by the severe shortages in trained manpower throughout the Tanzanian government, and especially in rural areas, that prevented it from following up on development activities in the villages. Poorly trained and motivated agricultural extension and field agents, and deficiencies in applied agricultural research within the regions, also inhibit increases in agricultural production.[39]

In addition, the rapid creation of large numbers of *ujamaa* villages and the simultaneous decentralization of planning greatly increased demands for social services and facilities that the central government had to satisfy in order to keep the *ujamaa* programme credible and to increase the motivation of rural people to participate. This resulted in severe financial problems for the central government. Since the early 1970s, the government services sector has grown at rates well beyond those of agricultural and industrial production, leading to a deficit in the national budget for 1978-79 of more than US$705 million. Decentralization has been costly and has forced a government dedicated to the principle of self-reliance to depend more and more on foreign assistance to finance national and local development programmes.[40]

BEYOND ADMINISTRATIVE REFORM:
THE CULTURAL CONTEXT OF PROGRAMME IMPLEMENTATION

Experience with the implementation of development programmes in East Africa shows quite clearly that obstacles are pervasive, and that they extend far beyond deficiencies in administrative procedures and organizational structure. Indeed, the complex administrative and organizational problems that arose to obstruct implementation in all three countries were often created by broader "environmental" factors that are rarely considered in the formulation of development plans and the design of policies and programmes. Nor have these variables been well integrated into development administration theory.

·Yet, experience with decentralization programmes in East Africa reveals their crucial importance in determining the success of policy implementation. The most important of these factors in the East African cases have been political will, bureaucratic attitudes and behaviour, cultural traditions and practices, economic structure and spatial and physical systems. Together they formed the "environment" within which programmes must be implemented and managed. They reshape the institutional models, administrative procedures and structural

[39] See Michael Lofchie, "Agrarian Socialism in the Third World: The Tanzanian Case," *Comparative Politics* 8 (April 1976): 479-99.

[40] U.S. Agency for International Development, *Country Development Strategy Statement, FY 1981, Tanzania* (Washington, 1979).

reforms transferred from outside of the society, either remoulding them to conform to indigenous conditions or rendering them useless or perverse. The cultural environment more often changes administrative procedures and institutions in developing nations than the administrative reforms change environmental parameters. Although development administration theory sometimes refers vaguely to the importance of these "contextual variables", it provides little guidance for analysing them in policy formulation and programme design or for coping with them more effectively during implementation.

Political Will

To point out that political commitment and support are essential to programme implementation borders on banality. Yet, in reality, the political feasibility of plans and programmes are rarely tested in developing countries before they are promulgated. Extensive administrative changes were introduced in Tanzania and the Sudan without assessing the depth and breadth of political support. Failure to reckon the strength of political opposition undermined and obstructed programmes during implementation.[41] Little was done in any of the three countries to anticipate and cope with political opposition, or to build political support for decentralization, until after political problems arose. Then, advocates of decentralization had to spend a good deal of their political resources convincing other political leaders of the merits of participative decision-making. Nimeiry has had to exert considerable pressure almost constantly for a decade to obtain support for decentralization from other political leaders and cabinet members in the Sudan, and even after intensive efforts has not convinced some important political factions of its desirability.[42] It took nearly a decade for Nyerere's concept of *ujamaa,* formulated in the 1950s and early 1960s, to be incorporated into national policy, and another decade during the late 1960s and early 1970s to get the policy implemented.[43] Ultimately, both leaders had to resort to coercion — Nimeiry by constantly manipulating his cabinet and finally abolishing some central ministries where strong opposition to decentralization remained, and Nyerere by imposing the control of a single political party over the bureaucracy and local units of administration to obtain their support. Many *ujamaa* villages were created by coercion after the bureaucracy was brought under TANU's control. Where political ideology or coercion could not be brought to bear, as in Kenya, the implementation of decentralization programmes was even less successful.

---

[41] The importance of this factor is pointed up in Dennis A. Rondinelli and Kenneth Ruddle, "Political Commitment and Administrative Support: Preconditions for Growth with Equity Policy," *Journal of Administration Overseas* 17 (January 1978): 43-60.

[42] See Jakob J. Akol, "Old Attitudes Die Hard: Five Ministerial Views," *Sudanow* 2 (December 1977): 13-5.

[43] See Joel D. Barkan, "Comparing Politics and Public Policy in Kenya and Tanzania," in Barkan, J.D. and J.J. Okumu, eds., *Politics and Public Policy in Kenya and Tanzania* (New York: Praeger, 1979), pp. 3-40.

But the weaknesses in political commitment to decentralization should not have surprised those who formulated the programmes, given East Africa's tradition of highly concentrated authority. Under both colonial regimes and independence movements, national and local political leaders benefited from centrism and paternalism. These traditions shaped the attitudes of nearly all officials and much of the population toward the proper role of the national government.[44]

Nor did those who designed the decentralization programmes calculate the depth of political opposition from local elites. Indeed, they saw decentralization as a way of breaking up traditional political influence by bringing younger leaders into community decision-making and by strengthening the role of centrally appointed officials at the local level. But in Tanzania, local elites often joined with small landowners and central ministry officials in obstructing or neutralizing programmes to expand participation in development planning. In Kenya, local leaders often formed alliances with large landowners and central ministry officials or members of parliament to protect the existing pattern of resource allocation and resist changes proposed by district development committees. As L. Cliffe observes of Kenya, "the position of both political leaders and senior government officials depends on a patronage pattern which provides a link between their ambitions, and in turn their ability to deflect resources 'back home', and the aspirations of the local notables on whose organized support they partially depend."[45]

In retrospect, it is clear that political support and commitment to decentralization and local participation in development planning in Kenya and Tanzania were limited to arrangements that would extract greater compliance from localities for central government policies or that would not interfere with existing allocations of resources. Commitment to more extensive forms of decentralization was constrained in both countries and the amount of support that may be mobilized for devolution in the Sudan is still uncertain.

Bureaucratic Attitudes and Behaviour

Adverse attitudes and behaviour of government officials toward the participation of rural people in development planning and administration also underlie many of the obstacles to implementing decentralization programmes in East Africa. Equally as important is the deep distrust that senior government officials have of local leaders and that rural people have of all government officials. East African bureaucracies have supported decentralization only reluctantly, in part,

---

[44] The argument is made in more detail by Jon R. Moris, "Administrative Authority and the Problem of Effective Agricultural Administration in East Africa," *The African Review* 2 (1972): 105-46.

[45] Lionel Cliffe, "'Penetration' and Rural Development in the East African Context," in Cliffe, L., J.S. Coleman and M.R. Doornbos, eds., *Government and Rural Development in East Africa* (The Hague: Martinus Nijhoff, 1977), pp. 19-50.

because of ingrained attitudes toward the sharing of power and the role of government in exercising control. The bureaucracy's resistance to devolution in the Sudan is attributable not only to the unwillingness of central ministries to transfer those functions that provided their base of financial and political influence, but also the deep distrust of local administrators and leaders among technicians and professionals within the central bureaucracy. A recurring objection by central ministry officials to devolution in the Sudan was that local administrators and rural people would not understand their work. They feared that in the field they would not receive the same amount of support that they got from supervisors in Khartoum who shared their professional values.[46]

Indeed, some of the most serious obstacles to implementing decentralization programmes in all three countries arose from the discrepancies between national policy objectives and the behaviour of government officials in the field. The pronouncements of the central government about the need for local participation in development planning and administration were often belied by the attitudes and behaviour of field staff. H.U.E. Thoden VanVelzen's study of Rungwe District in Tanzania vividly illustrates the disparities between the central government's political rhetoric and the attitudes of district officials.[47] Field administrators in the districts maintain an air of superiority in dealing with rural people. They avoid social interaction with villagers and participation in their time-honoured rituals and activities, which they sometimes demean as being primitive and backward. Government officials dress and act differently from rural people, expect and demand deference from farmers and villagers, and attempt to obtain their cooperation through threats and coercion. Even the lowest level agricultural extension agents in Tanzania are usually paid more than most farmers earn, and in addition receive substantial fringe benefits that give them a standard of living well above that of their clients. In both Tanzania and Kenya, local staff are usually assinged by central agencies to posts outside of their home districts and, thus, are not seen by villagers as one of the community, a distinction that many staff officers carefully maintain.

Moreover, the way in which government officials address and deal with rural people makes it clear that they do not expect them to be partners in development planning and administration. Thoden VanVelzen recalls a government extension agent at one village development committee meeting in Rungwe District telling the members: "Remember, you farmers are the chickens and we are the mother hens. If you follow our example you will survive, but if you are not attentive you will perish."[48] The remarks are particularly ironic because most junior extension agents are poorly trained and know little about local agricultural conditions that farmers have dealt with for generations or about the methods they have used

---

[46] See Abdel Moniem al Rayah and Alfred Logune Taban, "Decentralization: Power to the Provinces," *Sudanow* (March 1979): 9-14.

[47] H.U.E. Thoden VanVelzen, "Staff, Kulaks and Peasants: A Study of a Political Field," in Cliffe, Coleman and Doornbos, *Government and Rural Development in East Africa*, pp. 221-50.

[48] Ibid., p. 228.

to survive against constant adversities. This paternalism may simply be amusing to rural people or provide additional evidence that government officials cannot be trusted, but the arrogance displayed by many local administrators often creates resentment or hostility that negates the government's attempts to elicit support for development policy and adds to the uncertainty about government intentions and motivations. Thoden VanVelzen relates the remarks of a community development officer at a local committee meeting in the same Tanzanian districts:

> I am new to this area, so it will be useful if I tell you something about my character. I am not a kind and polite man; I am cruel. If I see that government orders are not obeyed, I will know where to find you and how to punish you. I do not care if you hate me. The only important thing to me is that the orders of the government are fulfilled.[49]

Moreover, the interminable delays and flagrant inefficiencies in providing government services that undermine development administration at all levels cannot be attributed entirely to inadequate administrative procedures or inappropriately structured organizations. The most numerous complaints about government officials in East Africa arise from two seemingly inconsistent sets of behaviour; a slavish conformance at times to complex, detailed and ponderous procedures to accomplish even the simplest and most routine tasks, and the seeming ignorance of or deviation from established procedure at other times. J.R. Nellis notes that both situations are due to the administrators' overwhelming fear of making mistakes, and to the pervasive practice of passing problems on to other levels of administration in order to lighten workloads. He argues that although "the bureaucracy is overbureaucratized and overroutinized, it is at the same time underbureaucratized; meaning that the officials use routine to reduce rather than to expedite work."[50]

Problems are not dealt with, but rather passed from one level or unit of organization to another, because "cases and events that are out of the ordinary contain numerous possibilities for making mistakes; even minor errors are avoided at all costs, and the result is a strict, indeed constricting interpretation of the rules."[51] Yet, complaints are also made of arbitrariness, preferential treatment, failure to follow established procedures, ignorance of the rules and other behaviour that allows bureaucrats to cut through "red tape" when it suits their purposes. In the Sudan, the inevitable long queues in any government office can be circumvented if the client is a relative of, or member of the same village or tribe as the government official in charge, or is recognized by him as being an "important person". The ubiquitous bribe, of course, can obtain preferential service in any East African country.

---

[49] Ibid., p. 231.

[50] John R. Nellis, "Three Aspects of the Kenyan Administrative System," *Cultures et Development* 5 (1973): 541-70.

[51] Ibid., p. 548.

Cultural Traditions and Practices

These obstacles to effective programme implementation, in turn, cannot be fully explained without understanding the cultural milieu in which they exist. Paternalism and deference to authority are extremely strong in East African countries. The behaviour of field staff toward rural people, for instance, is not unlike the behaviour of senior government officials toward the field staff. In Kenya, senior officers attempt to control field staff because they consider them lazy and unreliable. Thus, they give them little discretion in planning or decision-making. Despite the formal structure of decentralization, senior officials are reluctant to delegate responsibility for even routine activities.[52] As a result, nearly all of the attention of the field staff goes to implementing higher level directives; little attempt is made to meet the needs of clients. And even when field officers attempt to comply with the decentralized planning procedures, their initiatives are generally ignored. "The poor experience with plan preparation at the field level," C. Trapman concludes from his study of agricultural development administration in Kenya, may be explained in part by "a lack of support in the past for proposals which field staff have taken the trouble to prepare. This has created a disillusioned attitude toward further efforts in this direction. The same applies to the preparation of estimates annually by district and provincial staff, which are rarely given consideration in annual estimates discussions."[53]

But ironically, the hierarchical structure of government and the overt attempts by high-level administrators to exercise control mask severe deficiencies in supervision and enforcement, many of which are due to deeply ingrained cultural traditions and practices. In the Sudan, for example, government employees at all levels must deal with each other in ways that stress "smooth" interpersonal relations. Conflict and criticism must be repressed. The inability of administrators to dismiss or even severely reprimand incompetent public employees accounts for the lack of discipline and widespread corruption within the civil service that extend down to the lowest levels. One regional minister in Southern Sudan, for example, who was previously a provincial commissioner, describes the case of a clerk in one of the ministry offices who continually files originals of letters, fails to tell his superiors about serious problems, and performs his duties lackadaisically. "He should be dismissed," the Minister contends. "But he has three wives and nine children and if I take disciplinary steps I will become the object of scorn, a *kawaja* (white man) they will call me."[54] Even if charges are brought against incompetent public employees, the disciplinary committee that must be formed under civil service regulations is unlikely to recommend serious punishment, because the traditional Sudanese concept of *malesh* requires that wrongdoers be forgiven and inhibits anyone from taking the initiative at imposing punishment.

---

[52] See Christopher Trapman, *Changes in Administrative Structure: A Case Study of Kenyan Agricultural Development* (London: Overseas Development Institute, 1974).

[53] Ibid., p. 39.

[54] Quoted in Akol, "Old Attitudes Die Hard," p. 15.

The manner in which bureaucrats interact with each other and with their clients is therefore usually more important than the results or consequences of their work. The strong tradition of face-to-face communications heavily burdens middle- and high-level administrators in the Sudan, for instance, who spend an overwhelming amount of their time in personal meetings with other officials, superiors, subordinates and clients, rather than dispatching work through indirect or written communications, which is considered impersonal and rude in Sudanese society. Moreover, face-to-face interaction is necessary because the Muslim concept of *shura* requires mutual consultation to solve problems. Anyone who takes individual initiative is condemned. Thus, decision-making and problem solving are slow, time-consuming and uncertain processes.[55]

High-level administrators are unable to order subordinates to carry out directives, and thus administration in the Sudan, Kenya and Tanzania is highly politicized and organizational control is maintained, if at all, through patronage alliances between senior and junior officers. "Whom one knows and not what one does is regarded as the key to personal betterment," J.R. Moris points out. "Distrust of associates is common and many senior officials employ protective strategies vis-a-vis the younger generation of officials as a matter of routine."[56] Stable alliances are maintained by senior officials by transferring trusted subordinates with them when they are given promotions or new posts.

Economic Structure

A factor that strongly influenced the ability of governments in East Africa to implement decentralization programmes, but which was given surprisingly little attention in policy design, was the economic structure within which the programmes would have to be managed. Decentralization policies in all three countries were promulgated without considering the impact on the economy or the implications of the weak economic structure in rural areas on the ability of local administrations to raise the financial resources to carry out the programmes. Central authorities in all three countries transferred planning and administrative functions to lower levels without providing sufficient financial resources or adequate legal powers to collect and allocate revenues within local jurisdictions. These financial limitations alone raise serious questions about the feasibility of decentralization. But resource shortages at the local level were also aggravated by national economic problems.

---

[55] The cultural dimensions of public administration in the Sudan are described in K.M. Zein, "The Practice of Public Administration in the Sudan: A Study of a District Centre," (Ph.D. diss.) (Rotterdam: Erasmus University, 1978), Chapter 7.

[56] Jon R. Moris, "The Transferability of Western Management Concepts and Programs: The East African Perspective," in Stifel, Coleman and Black, *Education and Training for Public Sector Management in Developing Countries*, pp. 73-83.

Since the mid-1970s, all three countries have faced serious balance of payments deficits, high rates of inflation, rising costs of fuel, and rapid increases in recurrent expenditures. Decentralization policies seem to have intensified rather than alleviated these problems. Even in Kenya, which probably has the most stable financial situation of any of the East African governments, the problems are foreboding.[57] The rising costs of social services demanded by and provided to the *ujamaa* villages in Tanzania have increased recurrent expenditures there to a level far beyond the government's ability to raise domestic revenues. National financial problems in Tanzania have significantly slowed progress on decentralization.[58]

Limited resources for development not only make the decentralization of functions more difficult, but make the value of participation in development planning questionable when local citizens realize they have little or no control over financial resources with which to carry out their plans. The People's Assembly Committee that evaluated the results of the Sudan's Local Government Act in 1976 was blunt in its conclusions: "It became apparent that the insufficiency of funds was the basic cause . . . of weaknesses . . . in the institutions of the People's Local Government and of turning them into empty skeletons," the Committee reported. "It also . . . killed any ambitions or hope to develop present services, let alone to present new services to people."[59] Similar weaknesses were found in the financial and administrative capacity of Kenya's county councils and other local authorities to carry out development programmes.[60]

In most of the poorer rural areas in these three countries, the economic structure is simply too weak to provide adequate tax resources. In the Sudan, the forms of taxation that can be imposed on subsistence economies are extremely limited and consist primarily of personal property and herd taxes that are difficult to assess. Tax collection is generally inefficient and very costly to the provinces because population is widely scattered in villages that are physically isolated from each other and from the provincial capital. The costs of recording, auditing and collection are often so expensive in relation to the amounts collected as to make revenue raising unrewarding to local councils. The problems are even more difficult among nomadic groups.[61]

[57] Cited in U.S. Agency for International Development, *Country Development Strategy Statement, Kenya 1980-1984* (Washington 1979), pp. 14-16.

[58] USAID, *Country Development Strategy Statement, FY 1981, Tanzania*, p. 35.

[59] The People's Assembly, *Final Report*, p. 38.

[60] See W. Ouma Oyugi, "Local Government and Development in Kenya," (Sussex: Institute of Development Studies, University of Sussex, 1978) (Discussion Paper; no. 131).

[61] For details, see K.J. Davey, et al., eds., *Local Government and Development in the Sudan: The Experience in Southern Darfur Province* (Khartoum: Academy of Administration and Policy Sciences, Ministry of People's Local Government, 1976).

Spatial and Physical Systems

Finally, one of the most crucial factors obstructing the implementation of decentralization and participation programmes was virtually ignored in the formulation of policy and is rarely considered in development administration theory: the spatial and physical characteristics of the country in which the programmes are to be administered.

One of the strongest arguments offered for decentralized planning and administration in East Africa is that the countries are large and heterogeneous and that many of the peripheral areas are too physically isolated from the national capital to allow effective central planning and management. Yet, these same physical conditions that make central government ineffective — size of the country, the heterogeneity of regions, distance among administrative centres — are also obstacles to effective decentralization. They are not conducive to national integration and unity, to promoting efficient service delivery, or to allowing communications and interaction among local administrative units within regions.

Physical inaccessibility and lack of communications facilities within rural areas plagued the implementation of decentralization programmes in Tanzania and Kenya from the beginning. In Tanzania, a country of vast size, only about 10 per cent of the less than 34,000 kilometres of roads were of all-weather construction in 1979. Existing roads are well-maintained and those areas that are not directly connected to a paved road are virtually isolated for much of the year. Only a small percentage of all farm families live within a day's walking distance of an access road, making the distribution of government services or information difficult, if not impossible, in many rural areas.[62] Although roads and transportation facilities tend to be better in Kenya, they are not well maintained because of scarcities in equipment and trained personnel. Trapman notes that "accessibility is one of the major problems of providing an extension service to a mass of small-scale farmers, with only a limited number of extension staff, who lack proper transportation facilities and supplies."[63]

Lack of physical infrastructure and low levels of transport and communications access are symptomatic of a larger problem that obstructs decentralized planning and administration in developing countries. The settlement systems in all three East African nations are poorly articulated; that is, they do not consist of large numbers of "central places" of different sizes capable of supporting a wide range of services and facilities. Moreover, existing settlements are not well integrated into regional and national economies. Poorly articulated and weakly linked settlement systems, resulting from overconcentration of public investment in the largest metropolitan centres, create obstacles to the decentralization of planning and administrative functions. Under these conditions, it becomes nearly impossible to coordinate decision-making units and establish effective interaction among localities or with the central government. Moreover, they create enormous

---

[62] USAID, *Country Development Strategy Statement, FY 1981, Tanzania,* p. 31.

[63] Trapman, *Changes in Administrative Structure,* p. 91.

difficulties for local administrators in mobilizing resources, supervising field personnel, distributing services and disseminating information. Unarticulated and unintegrated spatial systems foster political isolation as well. Political linkages between local jurisdictions and higher levels of government, and between citizens and local decision-makers, are crucial for decentralized planning and management. "Without well-developed linkages — which we define as valued and stable networks of communication and exchange of resources — between government and the members of society, public policy cannot be formulated to respond to the needs of the population," J.D. Barkan insists. "Nor can the population be expected to comply with such policies as the state seeks to carry out if its members do not understand the rationale behind these policies and the benefits they might bring."[64]

IMPROVING IMPLEMENTATION PLANNING AND ANALYSIS: SOME BASIC DIRECTIONS AND PRINCIPLES

If programme implementation is to be substantially improved during the 1980s, planners and administrators in developing countries must begin using more effective methods for analysing potential obstacles, identifying preconditions for change, specifying administrative requirements and coping with the environmental factors that influence the management of development policy. Development administration as a field of intellectual and professional inquiry must, therefore, become more concerned with devising and testing the analytical procedures needed for implementation planning and for dealing with the complexities of programme administration. This clearly requires a deeper understanding of the variables that affect programme implementation in developing nations, especially the political, behavioural, cultural, economic and physical factors that were so crucial in the East African cases. It also requires the development of a "grounded" theory of management that is useful and applicable in developing countries.

Although it is beyond the scope of this paper to explore the dimensions of such a theory in detail, the lessons of experience with decentralization in East Africa provide the basic outline for a "strategic" approach to implementation planning. They point to a concept of development administration that is more applied than the administrative modernization and institution-building theories of the 1960s and 1970s, but more broadly defined than the tool-oriented approach of the 1950s. Such a concept of development administration would be less concerned with grand schemes for administrative reform or the transfer of techniques and institutions from industrialized nations, and more with increasing the analytical ability of Third World planners and managers to assess and cope with the administrative and environmental complexities of achieving policy goals. The

---

[64] Joel D. Barkan, "Legislators, Elections and Political Linkages," in Barkan and Okumu, *Politics and Public Policy in Kenya and Tanzania,* pp. 64-92.

elements of such an approach would include: broad reconnaissance as the basis for strategic analysis and intervention; sequenced, incremental action; "engaged planning"; use of simplified management procedures and indigenous resources; and a facilitative style of administration.

Together, these elements form an approach that is quite different from that taken in the design and implementation of decentralization programmes in East Africa. Two of the most glaring problems with that approach were the narrow reconnaissance that was done of the environment in which the programmes had to be carried out, and the sweeping scope of the reforms that were undertaken. Indeed, the scope of administrative reform in all three countries was so badly defined that effective management would have been extremely difficult under any conditions. The success of large-scale government intervention to promote social change is problematical even in industrial societies where leaders have access to far more resources than are available to policymakers in developing nations. A more effective approach would reverse these emphases: it would undertake a broad reconnaissance to analyse environmental conditions, potential obstacles and administrative requirements, and use strategic, sequenced and incremental interventions to establish the preconditions necessary to set economic, social and political changes in motion. Moreover, it would depend on less complex and more clearly defined administrative procedures that use and transform indigenous resources and that attempt to facilitate and guide, rather than dominate and control, administrative behaviour.

Broad Reconnaissance

Planners and administrators in developing countries have sufficient experience with comprehensive macrolevel development planning to discount this approach to formulating implementation strategy.[65] Broadly based but more refined methods of analysis are needed. The ability of planners and administrators to identify and understand all of the potential obstacles to programme implementation is, of course, quite limited in any society. A.O. Hirschman is basically correct in pointing out that all development programmes and projects — no matter how carefully designed — are attended by unanticipated threats to their success that are often met with unsuspected remedial actions. Problems of implementation cannot be entirely anticipated and planned for in advance. Implementation will inevitably remain what Hirschman calls a "long voyage of discovery in the most varied domains."[66]

The problem in most developing nations is not that implementation planning is too comprehensive and detailed, but that it is often not done at all, or done

---

[65] See Dennis A. Rondinelli, "National Investment Planning and Equity Policy in Developing Countries: The Challenge of Decentralized Administration," *Policy Sciences* 10 (August 1978): 203-33.

[66] Albert O. Hirschman, *Development Projects Observed* (Washington: The Brookings Institution, 1967), p. 35.

only superficially. The "long voyage of discovery" is usually embarked upon without maps or charts of the terrain and with only vague notions about destinations. In all three East African countries, for example, decentralization was attempted without assessing the capacity of local administrative units to absorb new functions and responsibilities or the administrative skills of local officials. In the Sudan, for example, functions were devolved from central ministries to provincial councils and commissioners *en mass.* It was simply assumed that capacity for development planning and management existed, or that it would expand as functions were decentralized. Both assumptions, thus far, have been proven false. Similar problems arose with decentralization in Kenya because the postcolonial government simply made local authorities responsible for the same functions they had during the colonial rule. But local authorities had lost the benefits of colonial administrative and technical skills and were subsequently unable to perform many of the functions allocated to them.[67] Although in all three countries, some of the functions decentralized to local administrations are "permissive" — that is, local administrations have the authority to perform them only when they have sufficient resources — many of the functions are mandated, even though local capacity or resources to carry them out may not exist.

There are methods that have been used successfully in developing countries to assess the conditions under which programmes must be implemented. They emphasize broad reconnaissance of the environment and focus on factors that are crucial for successful implementation. One such method of design and analysis is the Logical Framework, developed by Rosenberg and Posner of Practical Concepts Incorporated (PCI) in 1969 and adopted by USAID, the Canadian International Development Agency (CIDA), and more than a dozen developing nations to plan and evaluate programmes and projects. The Logical Framework requires planners and administrators to address explicitly the hierarchy of objectives of a programme, to identify the resources needed to attain the objectives, to define and establish measurable indicators of results, and to delineate and describe assumptions about the controllable and uncontrollable variables that might influence the success of a programme. It provides a procedure for broadly scanning the environment in which the programme will be undertaken and for more systematically identifying the political, social, cultural, behavioural, and physical assumptions about programme design. Moreover, the Logical Framework explicitly recognizes the inevitable uncertainty involved in programme implementation and focuses attention on the actions that must be taken to increase the probability that programme objectives will be achieved. The description of assumptions also allows administrators to monitor the progress of programmes during implementation and to decide when plans must be redesigned to cope with unanticipated events.[68]

[67] Oyugi, "Local Government and Development in Kenya," p. 10.

[68] The Logical Framework, which was developed by Leon Rosenberg and Lawrence Posner of PCI, is described in detail by L. Rosenberg and M. Hageboeck, "Management Techniques and the Developing World" [Paper presented by PCI at the IFAC/IFORS Symposium, Algeria, 1973] and in Practical Concepts Incorporated, *The Logical Framework: A Manager's Guide to a Scientific Approach to Design and Evaluation* (Washington, 1979).

A similar form of analytical reconnaissance was developed by Practical Concepts Incorporated for assessing the viability of institutions in developing countries to carry out new programmes and missions. Adapting and simplifying the institution-building approach, PCI developed an "institutional viability model" for evaluating the capacity of existing organizations to operate efficiently and effectively in new situations or to continue functioning productively with new missions or objectives. Three essential properties of institutions — "image" or the cognitive dimensions of what people think about an organization; "connotation" or the affective dimension of the attitudes clients and staff hold about an organization; and "purchasables" or the money and resources that can be acquired with money — are examined to assess the viability of institutions for implementing new programmes and policies.[69]

Strategic Analysis and Intervention

Because all of the factors that will influence programme implementation cannot be anticipated and controlled in advance, implementation planning must be strategic; that is, it must specify incremental interventions that are manageable with the resources available. Charles Lindblom, the foremost advocate of this approach to policy analysis, describes three fundamental characteristics of strategic analysis and intervention. First, analysis is limited to alternative policies or programmes that differ only incrementally from current policies. This makes the tasks of analysis and implementation more manageable in a number of ways: it reduces the number of alternatives to be examined, focuses analysis on those alternatives with which planners and administrators are already familiar and about which they have some knowledge and information, and permits them to isolate those environmental variables that are most likely to impinge on successful programme implementation. It begins with what is known and attempts to specify interventions that will set other changes in motion rather than beginning with sweeping changes about which little is known or can be predicted. Second, strategic analysis focuses on converting "the problem" into a sequence of problems that can be solved with available resources. This reduces the complexity of analysis, allows better use of information and feedback and permits the reconsideration of goals and means as administrative and environmental problems appear during implementation. Third, the analysis focuses on examination of goals and values in close connection with the means available to achieve them and with empirical investigation of alternatives and their possible consequences.[70] This allows planners and administrators to examine alternatives in light of the values imbedded in

---

[69] Practical Concepts Incorporated, "The P/C/I Model: Some Practical Concepts for Assessing Organizational Feasibility," Report submitted to the U.S. Agency for International Development (Washington, 1974).

[70] Charles E. Lindblom, "The Sociology of Planning: Thought and Social Interaction," in Bornstein Morris, ed., *Economic Planning: East and West* (Cambridge, Mass.: Ballinger Publishing Company, 1975), pp. 23-60.

current attitudes and behaviour, cultural practices and traditions and economic and political structures.

The failure to do this kind of implementation analysis in East Africa allowed policymakers to overlook or ignore a wide range of preconditions for decentralized planning and administration. Strategic interventions to create these preconditions would have made implementation of the reorganization programmes easier and more successful. The failure to build up the financial and administrative capacities of local governments, for example, and to establish supporting institutions at the local level prior to deconcentrating functions obstructed implementation of decentralization programmes in all three countries.

Incremental and Sequential Action

Strategic analysis should identify a sequence of incremental actions that can be taken to implement policies and programmes. Implementation then becomes a series of "successive approximations" toward problem solving that are manageable and more controllable than large-scale, sweeping reforms. The division of large-scale programmes into incremental and sequential tasks can be done in either of two ways: by identifying actions that will gradually overcome deficiencies and create preconditions and requirements for successful programme implementation, or by designing programmes as policy experiments to reduce over a period of time uncertainties and unknowns about programme execution.

Had the first alternative been used in designing East African decentralization programmes, for instance, policy analysts would have delineated specific tasks aimed at overcoming deficiencies in local governments and creating the preconditions that would have allowed lower level administrative units to absorb increasing responsibilities. Government reorganization might have been preceded by intensive personnel training and manpower development projects for local officials in functions that would have subsequently been transferred to them from central ministries. Analysts would then have identified programmes and projects designed to build up the financial and administrative capacities of local governments. Decentralization would have proceeded only as local units acquired the capacity to perform larger numbers of functions more effectively.

The second alternative would have allowed policy analysts to view programme design and implementation as experimental activities. Programmes would have been disaggregated into a series of experimental projects dealing with aspects of decentralization about which relatively little was known: the most appropriate forms of decentralization for provinces or districts with different levels of administrative capacity; the effectiveness of different forms of planning and administration procedures at the local level; the amounts and types of inputs or resources required to make decentralized administration work; and the acceptability of alternative organizational arrangements to the rural population and local leaders. The experiments would have been designed to test alternatives in different districts and provinces to reduce the uncertainties and unknowns about decentralization and participation in rural areas. Pilot projects would then be used to test the results of the experiments under less controlled or a greater variety of conditions, and to adapt, or modify methods, techniques and organizational arrangements proven successful in the experimental projects. A series of demonstration projects would then be designed to exhibit the effectiveness of arrangements tested in the experimental and pilot projects and to increase the acceptability of new procedures and arrangements on a broader scale. Finally, when unknowns and uncertainties were greatly reduced and more information and experience had been gained with implementing these programmes, decentralization would be extended on a larger scale and institutionalized at the local level throughout the country.[71]

Engaged Planning

Moreover, if implementation is to be improved, policymakers in developing countries must begin to practise what Jon Moris calls "engaged planning." Moris argues that policies and programmes often cannot be implemented successfully by existing bureaucracies through routine administration. Special arrangements must often be made to protect and promote new programmes and to guide their institutionalization. He contends that in East Africa "development does not occur under either private or socialist auspices unless someone regularly puts in a large margin of extra 'intelligence' effort of a managerial nature."[72] Either specific individuals with a high degree of motivation to achieve programme goals must be placed in charge of these activities within each organization that has implementation responsibilities, or special implementation units must be created to administer the programmes outside of the regular bureaucratic structure. In any case, Moris argues that:

> Somebody must keep the daily activities of distinct but vertically interlocked services under surveillance, must frame contingency plans, . . . must indulge in bureaucratic politics in order to secure the commitments implied in action programmes, and must be prepared even to break the rules in an emergency.[73]

Semi-autonomous or functional authorities, and "task groups" or field teams of professionals and technicians were needed to assist local organizations with performing the functions transferred from the central government to localities in East Africa, for example, if decentralization policies were to be implemented more successfully. Because the central ministries were reluctant to support

---

[71] See Dennis A. Rondinelli, "Designing International Development Projects for Implementation," in Honadle, G. and R. Klauss, eds., *International Development Administration: Implementation Analysis for Development Planning* (New York: Praeger, 1979), pp. 21-52.

[72] Moris, "Administrative Authority," p. 127.

[73] Ibid.

decentralization, there was the need in all three East African countries for mobile teams of planning, finance and technical experts who were not tied to the civil service system to help build up the capacities of local governments to assume the functions transferred to them. In the Sudan, such teams were needed to provide assistance to local and provincial councils and development committees with project identification, plan formulation, annual budgeting and revenue raising. Assistance was also required to institutionalize those functions once local councils and development committees attained a minimum level of competence.

Clearly, provisions must be made in implementation strategies for "engaged planning" to bring development programmes through the initial stages of dissemination and execution and to institutionalize them in organizations that can carry them on when special implementation arrangements end.

Simplified Management Procedures and Use of Indigenous Institutions

It is also clear from the experience in East Africa that new administrative procedures and arrangements must be relatively simple and uncomplicated, and their purposes must be clearly defined. Complex planning and management methods rarely work at any level of government in developing countries, and especially at the local level in rural areas. Rural people either ignore complex administrative procedures or are exploited by government officials who can use the confusing processes to manipulate them. Moreover, skills and resources for management are in short supply in rural areas and administrative capacity is relatively weak. R. Chambers and D. Belshaw concluded from their experience with the management of rural development programmes in Kenya that "in designing management procedures, the temptation is to introduce more and more requirements and measures, more and more complicated techniques and more and more elaborate relationships. But such an approach quickly leads to a drop in output and· eventually to paralysis."[74]

Ambiguity in the administrative procedures and arrangements used to bring about decentralization in East Africa also led to serious problems of implementation in all three countries.· Public pronouncements in Kenya, Tanzania and the Sudan often implied that the administrative reforms initiated in the early 1970s would create systems of local government. Indeed, the language of the decentralization laws — and even their titles — used the term "local government", whereas in reality leaders in the three countries only intended to create systems of local administration that would be controlled or influenced from the centre. Ambiguity in the political rhetoric led both to confusion and to resentment in some rural areas because the implied promises of local governance could not be fulfilled.

[74] Robert Chambers and Deryke Belshaw, *Managing Rural Development: Lessons and Methods from Eastern Africa* (Sussex: University of Sussex, Institute of Development Studies, 1973) (IDS Discussion Paper No. 15), p. 68.

Equally important, implementation strategies must make provision for using and eventually transforming as many existing institutions as possible in executing development programmes. To the extent that it is feasible, administrative changes should incorporate those indigenous resources and traditional procedures that can be effective in implementing new policies, rather than unnecessarily displacing them or destroying their potential utility. In areas of Tanzania, where decentralization displaced traditional leaders, it sometimes destroyed indigenous authority and informal relationships and eliminated men, who had been effective at mobilizing local resources for self-help projects, from village decision-making. Such programmes may often be administered much more successfully where traditional leaders and groups can be convinced to participate and are given a meaningful role.[75]

Facilitative Administration

Finally, the lessons of the East African experience point up the need for a more facilitative style of administration in Third World nations. An important challenge to development administration is to assist in identifying and testing administrative procedures and mechanisms that rely less on central control and more on incentives and exchange to achieve development objectives. This does not mean that policies should be aimed at weakening or dismantling central government ministries and bureaucracies as was done in the Sudan, but they should seek to reorient the role of central bureaucracies from one of domination and control of development programmes to one of facilitation and support for decentralized implementation. In developing nations, the resources of all levels of government are needed to ensure the success of development efforts. As David Leonard correctly points out in his study of agricultural administration in Kenya, "in a decentralized administrative structure the centre needs to be every bit as strong as in a centralized one, but the reorientation required is one of technical service rather than of hierarchical control."[76]

A wide range of managerial techniques exist to guide and facilitate local decision-making that do not depend primarily on hierarchical control, and that give local groups more latitude in formulating and implementing development programmes. Central agencies can often set off desired development activities simply by using indirect intervention — through prices, subsidies or rewards — that benefit local officials and rural people rather than punishing them for failure to conform to national development plans and central directives. Information dissemination, educational, and persuasion techniques are often more effective

[75] See Peter Rigby, "Local Participation in National Politics, Ugogo, Tanzania," in Cliffe, Coleman and Doornbos, *Government and Rural Development in East Africa*, pp. 81-98.

[76] David Leonard, *Reaching the Peasant Farmer: Organization Theory and Practice in Kenya* (Chicago: University of Chicago Press, 1977), p. 213.

than threats, pressures and punishments in eliciting cooperation and generating innovative approaches to problem-solving.[77]

In brief, an important and exciting challenge lies ahead for development administration in the 1980s to begin formulating a grounded theory that provides the analytical methods and administrative arrangements for improving policy and programme implementation in developing countries. The goals of development policy for the remaining decades of this century have been clearly stated — development must be more equitable, more participative and more effective in reaching the vast majority of the people who have been excluded from the benefits of economic and social progress in the past. Finding ways of improving the implementation of programmes to achieve these policy objectives may be one of the most important contributions to international development in the next decade.

[77] See Dennis A. Rondinelli, "Planning and Political Strategy," *Long-Range Planning* 9 (1976): 75-82.

PART TWO

COUNTRY PERSPECTIVES

5

COORDINATION, INSTITUTIONAL CAPABILITY AND DEVELOPMENT PERFORMANCE IN MALAYSIA

JOHARI BIN MAT

OVERVIEW OF REGIONAL DEVELOPMENT STRATEGIES AND POLICIES

Introduction

REGIONAL PLANNING and development have emerged as one of the major policy instruments towards the attainment of national goals and objectives in Malaysia. Its genesis is due to the realization that spatial dimensions and considerations must be conceived of as an integral part of the planning and development processes. This does not mean, however, that the role of regionally oriented programmes is limited only to spatial objectives. In the Malaysian case, they must also fulfil other national objectives such as the restructuring of society and the eradication of poverty. However, it is no coincidence that poverty in Malaysia is closely associated with geographical space and racial background. The general perception is that a reduction in regional disparities may substantially help bring about overall racial balance and national unity.

The Malaysian Setting: Sociopolitical Background[1]

Malaysia covers a total area of 334,000 square kilometres divided into two major physical parts — Peninsular or West Malaysia, comprising eleven states

---

[1] For general reference, the following books will be useful: *Malaysia Official Yearbook* (Kuala Lumpur: Government Printer, any year); J.M. Gullick, *Malaysia* (London: Ernst Benn, 1963); Gordon P. Means, *Malaysian Politics,* 2nd ed. (New York: New York University Press, 1970); K.J. Ratnam, *Communalism and the Political Process in Malaysia* (Kuala Lumpur: Oxford University Press, 1965); K.J. Ratnam and R.S. Milne, *The Malaysian Parliamentary Elections in 1964* (Singapore: University of Malaya Press, 1967); Karl Von Vorys, *Democracy Without Consensus: Communalism and Political Stability in Malaysia* (Princeton, N.J.: Princeton University Press, 1975); and Wang Gungwu, ed., *Malaysia: A Survey* (New York: Praeger Publishers, 1964); K.C. Cheong, et al., *Malaysia: Some Contemporary Issues in Socioeconomic Development* (Kuala Lumpur: University of Malaya Press, 1979).

and one federal territory; and part of Borneo, consisting of the two states of Sabah and Sarawak. The population in early 1980 was estimated at 13,250,000,[2] of which 11,050,000 (83 per cent) live in Peninsular Malaysia, 1,200,000 (9 per cent) in Sarawak and 980,000 (7 per cent) in Sabah.[3] Of the total peninsular population, 54 per cent are Malays and other indigenous groups, 34 per cent are Chinese, 10 per cent are Indians and 2 per cent consists of other groups. Not unlike most of the neighbouring Southeast Asian countries, Malaysia shares some of the same problems, such as, high dependency on primary exports, high population growth rates (2.7 per cent in 1979) and communist subversion threats.

There are, however, other problems peculiar to Malaysia. The heterogeneous character of Malaysian society results in complex sociopolitical dynamics of many strengths and weaknesses. Malaysian political and economic affairs seem to be dominated by concerns with "racial arithmetics."[4] Consequently, most of its national policies, development plans and activities are tempered by ethnic considerations. Racial differences have expressed themselves in social spheres as well. Many stereotypes have been made or are written about,[5] but these have tended to be exaggerated in order to fit a particular theme or purpose and most of these are now outdated. Certain occupational and locational trends have become evident, and the government has attempted to officially eliminate these socio-economic identifications and inequities. The government's "New Economic Policy" (NEP) incorporated in national plans since 1970, is specifically aimed at solving these socioeconomic problems.

Malaysia is unique constitutionally. Although it is a federation in form, like the United States or Australia, its constitution has many special provisions. The powers of the two states of Sabah and Sarawak are different from the rest of the states.[6] The rationale behind this special arrangement is to accommodate the cultural and level of development differences between the states of Sabah and Sarawak and the Peninsular Malaysian states. The constitution also provides for the status and special protection of several ethnic groups. The cultures, religious and special rights of the Malays and other indigenous groups, as well as the citizenship rights of the Chinese and Indian groups are safeguarded. All these provisions are necessary in order to achieve the workable framework upon which a functioning and united Malaysian nation may be built.[7] The fact that this

---

[2] See *Economic Report 1979/80* (Kuala Lumpur: Ministry of Finance, 1980).

[3] Malaysia conducts official censuses every ten years. The last census was in 1970.

[4] See R.S. Milne and Diane K. Mauzy, *Politics and Government in Malaysia* (Kuala Lumpur: Federal Publications, 1978), p. 4.

[5] For example, some typical statements about Malays and Chinese can be found in Sir Frank Swettenham, *British Malaya* (London: Allen & Unwin, 1948), pp. 136 & 139; and Richard Weston, "A Tragedy of Errors," *Eastern World* 10, no. 10 (1956): 35.

[6] For an in-depth study of the legal and historical aspects of the Federation, see B. Simadjuntak, *Malayan Federalism 1945-1963* (London: Oxford University Press, 1969).

[7] For a good analysis of Malaysia's unique kind of democracy, within its multiethnic context, see Von Vorys, *Democracy Without Consensus*, and Milne and Mauzy, *Politics and Government in Malaysia*.

constitution has worked so far with minimal problems is attributed to the pragmatic and nationalistic sense of Malaysia's leaders. For the last two decades, the
governing party has consisted of a structured coalition of ethnically-based parties.
The procedure and process of working out the coalition's manifesto, and consequently, the nation's policies, are not normal politics. Instead, these processes
are based on unwritten rules of "racial arithmetic" and compromise.

National and Regional Development Strategies

The underlying principle in all five-year development plans in Malaysia has
been "redistribution with growth." This simply means that the amelioration of
existing intercommunal economic disparities was to be achieved through an
enlarged pie and an expanding economy against the deprivation of any ethnic
group. Understandably then, the main thrust or focus of the First Malaya Plan
(1956-60), the Second Malaya Plan (1961-65) and the succeeding First Malaysia
Plan (1966-70) was directed at rural and agricultural development. There was a
more evident change in national priorities, from what formerly were primarily
urban and custodial concerns to rural and more developmental ones. Emphasis
was on modernizing the agricultural sector through improved infrastructures and
social services as well as uplifting the economic well-being of the rural populace
who constitutes the bulk of the country's poor. The First Malaysia Plan, unlike
the previous two development plans, was not narrowly confined just to sectoral
development. The plan was also addressed to solve other socioeconomic problems, notably, the high dependency on primary exports, high population rate
increases and shortages of skilled manpower.

The outbreak of the May 13, 1969 racial riots in Malaysia marked an
important milestone in national development strategies. As a result, the government's efforts to correct the prevailing economic imbalances were made more
specific and pronounced and were incorporated in the Second Malaysia Plan
(1971-75). According to this plan, all future development efforts were to be subsumed under two specific national goals, namely, (a) to reduce and eventually
eradicate poverty by raising income levels and increasing employment opportunities for all Malaysians, irrespective of race; and (b) to accelerate the process of
restructuring Malaysian society in order to correct economic imbalances, so as
to reduce and eventually eliminate the identification of race with economic
functions. The Third Malaysia Plan (1976-80) re-emphasized the direction, goals
and policies of the Second Malaysia Plan. More significantly, it was under this
plan that, for the first time, a whole chapter was devoted to regional development.

Regional development has the special responsibility of helping to achieve the
NEP goals. In particular, regional development has a special strength and role to
play in reducing the incidence of poverty in rural areas and in restructuring
Malaysian society in both its specific and general perspectives.

The above statements define what can be termed as "official" goals of regional
development in Malaysia. They represent statements of the nation's overall
mission and policy. The statements that define the actual direction and activities

of regional development implementation are "operative" goals. They are summarized as follows:

1. To reduce excessive rural-urban migration, especially migration from depressed areas to the already congested core region of Kuala Lumpur-Klang Valley.
2. To revive and strengthen agricultural and industrial development in lagging regions, particularly through the strategy of in-situ rural development.
3. To redirect new development and growth to less developed regions of the country. This would have the effect of redistributing opportunities and facilities throughout the country.
4. To urbanize and industrialize rural and agricultural areas. New physical design of settlements and townships, as well as new administrative organizational procedures, have to be introduced.
5. To resettle and rehabilitate selected frontier areas, that previously were breeding grounds and infiltration routes for communist dissidents. Such strategy would help integrate previously neglected peripheral regions with mainstream national life and activities.
6. To affect greater emphasis on urban growth which will be integrated with overall national regional development and new growth centre strategies.

Malaysia has adopted four strategies to achieve the various goals of regional development. They are: (a) a new land and resource development strategy; (b) an integrated in-situ area and agricultural development strategy; (c) an industrial dispersal strategy; and (d) a deliberate programme of rural urbanization and creation of new growth centre strategies. At the time of the writing of this paper, there are fifteen specially planned regional programmes. These programmes are differentiated from state development programmes which areally and administratively may also be defined as regional development.

Evaluation of Development Performance

Policy Relevance

The Third Malaysia Plan, and the soon to be implemented Fourth Malaysia Plan (1981-85), will continue the NEP's goals and strategies. The relevancy of the NEP to Malaysia's sociopolitical needs has never been questioned even by its most ardent of critics. Disagreements and critical views all focus on the specific translation of policies into socioeconomic programmes and the method of implementing these programmes.

Just as government policies are basically elegant statements of political intent, the NEP is characterized by general statements of intent and goals in the Second, Third and Fourth Malaysia Plans. The projects and programmes that emanate from these plans are all politically and economically relevant, but when implemented, a number of difficulties and inconsistencies have emerged. First, the programme to help the Bumiputras in business and modern sector activities tended to benefit the more "ready" and richer Bumiputras than the needier and poorer ones. Second, significant inroads have been made by the Bumiputras in business activities and professions, but overall and projected trends do not seem to eliminate identification of race with occupation. Third, the concomitant problem of high unemployment among youth and shortage of labour in new growth areas and agricultural plantations reflects some weaknesses and inconsistencies in national labour policy, migration and agricultural development. Fourth, in spite of massive efforts to develop rural and agricultural areas, pockets of poverty areas and groups remain. Finally, the growth of industrial and construction sectors have been higher than expected, while the growth of agricultural and rural sectors, in spite of greater inputs and incentives, have been lower than planned.

Intersectoral Consistency

Intersectoral linkages and developmental complementarity have been attempted through a number of planning and administrative procedures, processes and institutions. Even though Malaysia practises a Federal system of government, centralized planning coordination and development programme implementation are attempted at various levels through different administrative machinery. Theoretically, intersectoral consistency and coordination of development projects are ensured by established procedures and machinery. Just as in any governmental system, however, in reality planning and programme implementation are not rationalized as the original organization charts stipulate. Some intersectoral planning and implementation difficulties may be mentioned here:

1. Intersectoral consistency of planning and development programme implementation has been more effectively enforced at the federal and ministerial levels than at the inter or intrastate levels.
2. In a federal and three-tier system of government, where states and local authorities have defined responsibilities and autonomies, programme competition and duplication are unavoidable. Competition and inconsistencies exist in industrialization and tourism development policies and projects by the different states.
3. Typical intersectoral difficulties occur in programmes that involve the coordination of infrastructural construction and settlement developments as demonstrated in the case of new towns, in recent growth regions without settlers, and in the case of established settlements that are not connected by planned highways. These difficulties occur mainly because of implementation "shortfall".

Efficiency and Impact

The overall economic development performance of Malaysia during the last ten years has been impressive. A number of questions may still be asked, however, about the effectiveness of the country's economic performance and benefits to the people. One must ask whether economic development has benefited all people equally. Has economic growth improved people's quality of life? Has inflation upset economic development performance? Have the NEP goals been achieved through economic growth efforts?

1. Malaysia maintains a free-market economy. In spite of social and distributive policies, the free market forces invariably result in the leading sectors and groups benefiting more from economic and other forms of development than the "less ready" and depressed sectors or groups.
2. Even though economic growth has affected different groups differently, the substantial economic achievements have been able to trickle-down and affect all social stratas and groups. We find that the quality of life of the masses has been affected indirectly by better government services and facilities in education, health, water and electric supplies to nearly all villages and towns.
3. Malaysia was fortunate that domestic inflation averaged only 6 per cent per annum during the 1970-80 period. Inflation, as such, was not high enough to diminish the actual positive effects of economic growth to all sectors of the society.
4. The goals of the NEP were geared for 1990. Current policy implementation trends indicate that substantial inroads are being made by the Bumiputras in certain agricultural and basic industrial sectors. No significant success is anticipated, however, in manufacturing and service sectors.

Besides looking at development performance from the aspect of current economic benefits, it is also important to view development activities from the perspectives of long-term impacts in the social, structural and environmental spheres.
1. As has been earlier alluded, Malaysia's rapid economic growth has not affected all areas and groups of people equally. The feeling of relative deprivation and poverty is deeply felt by the people who have been "bypassed" by rapid growth. It becomes imperative, therefore, that strategies and policies ensure that pockets of depression and poverty will not result from rapid economic development.
2. The achievements of the Federal Land Development Authority (FELDA) in opening new agricultural land and success in new settlement schemes are well known. There are, however, two little-known facts: (a) the cost of developing land and settling farming families is comparatively high; and (b) the total impact of FELDA's effort towards solving the country's overall problems of landlessness and rural poverty has not been very significant.

3. Agricultural diversification has been the major goal of Malaysian develop-
    ment policy. Because of the efficiency and economic lucrativeness of
    export commodities such as rubber, palm oil and timber, not much head-
    way has been made in the direction of agricultural diversification. The
    strategic implications of dependency on a few export crops for national
    income, whatever the current economic benefits, must be carefully
    examined.
4. In striving for rapid economic growth, the negative impacts of industries,
    constructions, etc., upon the environmental system, such as streams, vege-
    tation, water, marine life and the air, have never been seriously considered
    or accounted for in planning and implementing development programmes.

It is important to reiterate two important facts about Malaysian development
performance. First, the economic growth and sociopolitical stability achieved by
Malaysia since its independence in 1957, are most commendable. Second, because
Malaysia is a plural society characterized by ethnic and regional diversities, its
survival is essentially dependent upon the redistribution of economic growth.
Development planning and implementation in Malaysia must proportionately
consider ethnic and regional differences.

OVERVIEW OF INSTITUTIONAL MACHINERY

Various phases of the development of the Malaysian civil administration from
a colonial, custodial machinery to a national and developmental administrative
machinery may be analysed. The early phase was the change from the colonial
model of traditional public administration, mainly geared towards systems
maintenance, law and order and revenue collection to a people and development-
oriented administration. With independence in 1957, and with changes in political
leadership, particularly under Deputy Prime Minister Tun Abdul Razak, the
character and orientation of the Malaysian public service changed to one of
development administration. A development administrative civil service is not
only geared towards maintenance of law and order but also oriented and entrusted with the responsibilities· of managing national change and development.
Some early attempts at administrative changes and reform occurred in the
mid-sixties. These changes were concerned with the adoption of macro and micro
aspects of national development planning, introduction of modern financial procedures and of a programme performance budgeting system. One of the most
important reports, entitled *Development Administration in Malaysia* by
Montgomery and Esman, enunciated the administrative reforms accepted by the
Malaysian government in 1966. It proposed two important recommendations:
(a) the establishment of a Development Administration Unit to help plan and
guide major programmes of administrative improvements; and (b) the improvement of educational and training programmes for all civil service levels in order
to strengthen the professional competence of the Malaysian Civil Service.[8] Many
changes that have occurred in government ministries and departments and the

improvement of skills, knowledge and competence of civil servants in general, may be attributed directly or indirectly to the implementation of the Montgomery and Esman report recommendations.

Another important document that has directed administrative reform is the *Training for Development in West Malaysia* by the Development Administration Unit, the Prime Minister's Department and the Staff Training Centre.[9] This report made a comprehensive survey of the training facilities and programmes in West Malaysia and consequently proposed a comprehensive strategy and plan for the training and career development of public servants. Establishment of the National Institute of Public Administration (INTAN) and extensive training programmes resulting from this report have provided for today's civil servants.

Currently, there exists a special organization within the Prime Minister's Department, established in 1977, called the *Malaysian Administrative Modernization and Manpower Planning Unit* (MAMPU). Two major tasks of the MAMPU are to carry out administrative modernization and reform and to coordinate planning and development manpower in the country. It also provides consultant management services to government organizations.[10] The MAMPU, in a way, succeeds the earlier Development Administration Unit (DAU), but with the additional functions of providing consultancy services and undertaking manpower planning. This agency plays a very crucial role in administrative modernization, rationalization and reform of public organizations at district and ministerial levels.

A well-known and effective method of rural development implementation introduced in Malaysia was the utilization of the *RED Book and Operations Room System*. The RED book stands for the Rural Economic Development Plan document that is jointly developed by the Village Development Committee and the District Office. The book or plan identifies and records in detail all the proposed infrastructural and economic development village programmes both for current year and five-year plans. The Operations Room is a centre where all plan documents are deposited and project implementation progress is monitored and recorded. Operations Rooms are maintained by all villages, district offices, states, ministries and the Prime Minister's Department. The success of planning, coordination and implementation in Malaysian rural and economic development through the years may be partly attributed to these systematic management procedures.

---

[8] J.D. Montgomery and Milton J. Esman, *Development Administration in Malaysia: A Report to the Government of Malaysia* (Kuala Lumpur: Government Printer, 1966).

[9] *Training for Development in West Malaysia* (Kuala Lumpur: Development Administration Unit and Staff Training Centre, 1969).

[10] See Abdullah Sanusi Ahmad, "Administrative Reform for Development in Malaysia — Focus on Grassroot Organization" [Paper presented at Expert Group Meeting on Administrative Reform for Decentralized Development, United Nations Asian and Pacific Development Administration Centre, New Delhi, 17-21 September 1979].

Within the administrative structure, the *Yang Di Pertuan Agong* (King or Supreme Sovereign) is the Supreme Head of Malaysia. He has authority over every government action, although he acts on the advice of Parliament and the Cabinet. The Prime Minister's appointment and dissolution of parliament are at his discretion. As fountain of justice, he appoints federal court and high court judges upon the Prime Minister's advice, and in accordance with prescribed federal constitutional procedures. The *Agong* is also Supreme Commander of the Armed Forces and head of the Muslim religion in Melaka and Penang.

The Federal Parliament is the supreme legislative authority in Malaysia. Parliament controls government finances. Federal taxes and rates according to federal law may only be raised under the authority of Parliament. Parliament also serves as a forum for criticism and focus for public opinion on national affairs. The *Yang Di Pertuan Agong* appoints a cabinet which consists of a council of ministers, to advise him in the exercise of his functions. It consists of the Prime Minister and an unspecified number of ministers who must all be members of Parliament.

All federal government policies are implemented through various ministries and departments. They are the main instruments for effecting government policy after passage of the necessary legislation through Parliament. There are at present twenty-three ministries. There are operating departments and agencies under the various ministries which actually plan and implement development programmes. Even though all statutory bodies and public corporations have some degree of legal and functional autonomy, these bodies and corporations are under the minister's control for purposes of coordination and supervision. Ministries and agencies are staffed by personnel who have been recruited and appointed by the Public Services Commission.

Excluding the Federal Territory, there are thirteen states in Malaysia. Area size and population of the states range from 102,000 ha for a population of 1,049,000 in Penang to 12,441,000 ha for a population of 1,278,000 in Sarawak. Each state has its own written constitution and legislative assembly. Every state legislature has powers to enforce matters not reserved for the Federal Parliament. Although legislative subjects are set forth in federal lists, concurrent lists, and state lists (which either federal or state legislatures may enact), residual power lies within the state. Rulers or state governors act on state government's advice under the direction of the State Executive Council or Cabinet, just as the *Yang Di Pertuan Agong* acts on the Federal Cabinet's advice. The state legislative authority is the State Legislative Assembly. In other words, the ruler or governor acts on the elected State Legislative Assembly's advice.

In Peninsular Malaysia, each state is divided into districts, each under a District Officer. There are seventy-four districts in all. Each district is subdivided into *mukims* headed by a *penghulu* (chief) or *penggawa* in Kelantan. A *mukim* normally consists of a few neighbouring *kampung* or villages. Each *kampung* is headed by a *ketua kampung* or village headman.

At the substate level, there are two other types of spatial-functional authority or administrative units. One substate administrative hierarchy is the municipality or local authority. The other intermediate administrative functional unit, which

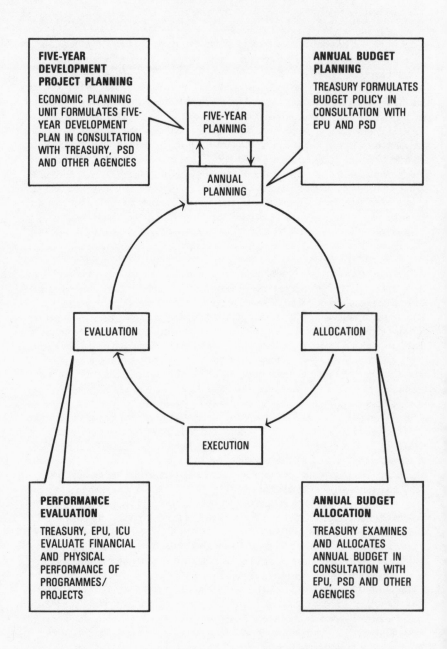

Figure 5-1. Agencies Responsible for Planning, Budgeting
and Implementation Management

has recently become popular, is the specially created regional development authority. In terms of development implementation and delivery of services, these three types of intermediate level administrative organizations and institutions are very important and significant.

COORDINATION IN THE PROCESS OF ANNUAL PLANNING, BUDGETING AND IMPLEMENTATION MANAGEMENT: A SYSTEMIC PERSPECTIVE

Overall Planning Structures and Processes

Figures 5-1 and 5-2 describe the development planning procedures and structures from the perspectives of concept, responsible agencies and overall structural framework. From the perspective of concept, five-year and annual planning should be integrated with financial allocation, execution or implementation and performance evaluation. These activities are interrelated processes that form a continuous cycle. Integrated functions should be attempted as much as possible in practice.

Figure 5-1 identifies the planning, budgeting and evaluation agencies and their activities. It, however, only describes the situation and practices at the federal level. Responsibilities of five-year development and annual budget planning are divided between the Economic Planning Unit (EPU) and the Treasury. All perspective development planning, such as the NEP and the five-year plans, and annual development planning are the functions of the EPU. Annual operating and development budgeting, as well as estimation of costs of five-year plans, are the tasks of the Treasury. Basically, anything that concerns development and planning is the EPU's responsibility, and everything concerning financing or budgeting is the Treasury's responsibility. It is also an established practice at the federal level that planning, policy formulation and budgeting activities be undertaken by the EPU and the Treasury in consultation with the Public Services Department (PSD) and other pertinent ministries and agencies. Execution or implementation of policies and programmes is the task of the operating ministries and agencies. Even though the Implementation Coordination Unit (ICU) is the major central agency responsible for implementation coordination, other agencies involved in programme performance evaluation include the Treasury, the EPU, the Social and Economic Research Unit (SERU), the MAMPU and operating ministries themselves.

State planning, budgeting and evaluation are undertaken through a different administrative structure and process. Development planning is the main responsibility of the State Planning Unit (SPU). Budget planning is done by the SPU with the help of the State Financial Officer. Programme performance evaluation is conducted by the State Development Office. In the case of the SPU and the State Financial Officer, all of these agencies and their activities are coordinated by the State Secretariat, whereas in the case of the State Development Officer, these are coordinated by the *Menteri Besar* (Chief Minister) and the ICU.

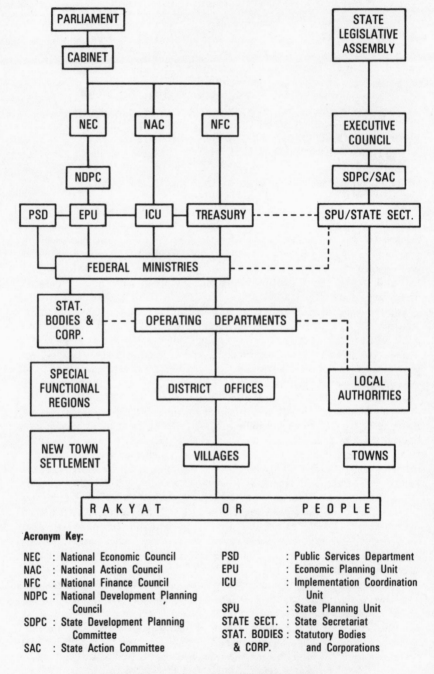

Figure 5-2. Development Planning and Implementation:
Multi-Level Structures and Linkages

Acronym Key:

NEC : National Economic Council	PSD : Public Services Department
NAC : National Action Council	EPU : Economic Planning Unit
NFC : National Finance Council	ICU : Implementation Coordination Unit
NDPC : National Development Planning Council	
	SPU : State Planning Unit
SDPC : State Development Planning Committee	STATE SECT. : State Secretariat
	STAT. BODIES : Statutory Bodies
SAC : State Action Committee	& CORP. and Corporations

Both five-year and annual development planning and budgeting are done during a prescribed period of the year. It is essential that programme identification and cost estimates be completed early in the year for necessary legislative and budgetary approvals by the Parliament and the State Legislative Assemblies before the beginning of the following financial year. There is no statutory stipulation in the Federal Constitution that requires states to plan their development programmes together with the Federal Government or to submit their plans to the EPU, the Treasury or the PSD for approval and inclusion in national five-year or annual plans. Absence of these legal stipulations is especially true of projects which states plan to implement with their own resources and personnel or with operating expenditures that are financed by state funds. In practice, however, because of administrative traditions and since most state projects are directly funded by federal grants or loans, all of the SPUs closely follow the planning and budgeting instructions and schedules provided by the EPU and the Treasury.

Figure 5-2 provides a macro systematic illustration of Malaysian planning and implementation structures and processes. As earlier explained, the Parliament is the highest legislative body that approves plans and authorizes expenditures at the federal level, while the State Legislative Assembly is the highest approving body at the state level. The main executive body in the Federal Government is the cabinet, and in the states it is the Executive Council (EXCO). The National Economic Council (NEC) is the main Cabinet Committee that scrutinizes and approves all development plans and programmes. The highest executive planning group is the National Development Planning Council (NDPC), which is a committee of officials headed by the Chief Secretary to the government. The NDPC is serviced by the EPU, which is the main arm of the Federal Government that undertakes the collation of data, analysis of needs and formulation of national plans and programmes. As indicated in the figure, these planning activities are done in consultation with the Public Services Department (in personnel needs), the Treasury (in finance) and the ICU for policy and programme coordination.

The State Development Planning Committee (SDPC) scrutinizes and approves all development programmes in the state. The SDPC is serviced by the SPU in the State Secretariat. SPU activities are supplemented with the help of specially created federal and/or state regional development authorities, local authorities and the district offices. The planning capacities of these intermediate organizations vary from good to weak. One planning channel and process not evident in Figure 5-2 is the special status and function of the State Development Officer (SDO). The SDO is administratively supervised by the ICU, but in the states he works under the *Menteri Besar*. The SDO identifies and plans social and community development projects, and he controls all the funds that come from the ICU in the Prime Minister's Department.

Three types of substate or intermediate level planning and administrative structures may be identified, namely, the District Office, the Local Authority and the specially created functional Regional Authority. The Local and Special Regional Authorities have their own planning units and plan all aspects of their development projects. The Local Authority submits its plans to the State Secretariat, the SPU, the SDPC, the EXCO and to the State Legislative Assembly for scrutiny and approval. The Federal Special Regional Authority submits its plans to the Ministry of Land and Regional Development, the EPU, the NDPC, the NEC, the Cabinet and to the Parliament for scrutiny and approval. The District Office conducts limited planning in areas of social and community development for the State and SDO. Projects in agriculture, health, education, infrastructure, etc., are planned by the district and state operating departments concerned. They normally submit their plans to the SPU and to the pertinent federal ministries for scrutiny and approval. Districts have District Development and Security Committees, but their main responsibilities are to examine and coordinate all proposed projects planned in the districts. To ensure these limited planning and coordinating functions, District Development and Security Committees have been established to oversee planning, while District Action Committees ensure coordinated implementation.

The lowest tier of the planning machinery is the Village Development Committee. The Village Development Committee is chaired by the Village Headman or *Ketua Kampung*. The Village Development Committee consists of representatives and leaders of different interests in the village. During the heydays of the RED Book system in the 1960s, Village Development Committees were full partners in the bottom-up planning process. Requests by the *rakyat* (people) for development projects are identified through the village committees and forwarded to the District Office for feasibility study and decision. District plans are later linked and integrated at the state level, forming the total State Development Plan. The proposed state plans are channelled upward to the EPU and the NDPC for integration and inclusion in the national five-year or annual plan.

Two observations need to be noted in this brief analysis of the overall development planning procedures and structures. First, the planning, budgeting and implementation practices at the federal level are more integrated and clearly defined. The same cannot be said of planning and budgeting at the state level, especially in cases of overlaps and conflict of planning and programming of state and federal projects and in federally funded state projects. Second, even though the District Office is the main administrative institution and organization that implements development projects in all states, the District Office has limited planning capacity or authority. All these observations indirectly indicate some procedural and structural weaknesses in Malaysian development planning and implementation.

Integration of Intersectoral Programmes and Projects

The administrative machinery that facilitates the integration of intersectoral programmes theoretically exists at all government levels. At the grassroots level, the coordinating machinery is the Village Development Committee. Other integration and coordination levels are at the district (through the District Development Committee), the state (State Development Planning Committee) and in a number of locations at the federal levels. An important level where sectoral programmes may be integrated is at the ministries themselves. Ministries must coordinate and integrate all activities of departments and statutory bodies under their control, and have organized planning and coordination committees for these purposes. Other loci where sectoral programmes are integrated are the EPU, the ICU and the NDPC. It may also be assumed that some form of integration is enforced by the Treasury and Public Services Departments when they review financial and manpower needs and the implications of sectoral and state programmes.

In terms of formal design and functions, all the centres and coordinating organizations mentioned earlier are entrusted with the task of rationalizing and coordinating the planning and implementation of development projects and programmes. At the federal level, to a substantive degree, some success has been achieved in ensuring that both sectoral and area development projects do not conflict, duplicate and are not haphazardly identified and implemented. As all systems in public administration reality, however, there are numerous occasions when prioritization and inclusion of projects in the annual or five-year plans are the result of such extra-administrative intervention as local or national political interests. There is also the typical problem of agencies having pet projects in which they have been working on or that they plan to undertake. The problem of amending or integrating such projects into a rationalized state or national plan is a serious one, particularly when such agencies have high powered "patrons". Theoretically, and speaking in general terms, however, priority issues and project approvals may be resolved at various levels.

Conflicts during planning may be viewed from three perspectives, namely, an interdepartmental, an interlevel and an interjurisdictional view. The procedures and processes for resolving these conflicts are different, depending on the case. Conflicts between departments within the same ministry are resolved during the ministries' high level Planning and Coordination Committee meetings. These meetings are chaired by the Secretary-General of the ministry concerned. Since ministries are expected to produce an integrated and rationalized development plan, it is incumbent upon them to resolve interdepartmental conflicts before submitting development plans to the EPU for consideration by the NDPC. Conflicts between departments of different ministries are more difficult to resolve. In theory, the role of the NDPC, through the help of the EPU, is to eliminate all administrative and developmental duplications and wastage so that a comprehensive and rational development plan for the whole country may be presented to the Cabinet and Parliament. Normally, by the time proposed programmes are presented to the Cabinet, except for politically related issues and conflicts, all issues of developmental duplication and irrationality should have been resolved beforehand.

Interlevel conflicts normally take the form of problems arising between states and the Federal Government, between local governments and state governments or between district departments and ministries. If the conflict occurs within the same line organization or ministry, it may be resolved administratively. If it is between agencies within different line organizations, the probable solution is through a third party organization or committee specially created to solve such problems. Generally, in the planning area, however, conflicts within the state are resolved by the State Planning or Action Committees or by the Chief Minister through the Executive Council. Problems at the federal level are resolved by the NDPC or the Cabinet. Problems between states and the Federal Government are resolved through the special National Councils within the various functions, such as finance (National Finance Council), land (National Land Council), local government (Local Government Consultative Council) and public administration (Federal-State Relations Annual Meetings).

Interjurisdictional conflict occurs between different areas of functional authority, for example, conflicts between the Regional Development Authority and the District Office or the State, or conflicts between local authorities and the state or district administration with respect to land use, provision of services or administrative functions, such as town plan approvals, health law enforcements, safeguarding, environmental quality, etc. In clear cases, conflicts may be resolved through state machinery, such as the State Action Committee or through the Chief Minister's office. When cases involve legal definitions, these are referred to the law courts. Generally, most planning, implementation and interjurisdictional problems may be resolved through the state and federal planning and coordination machinery.

Budget Formulation

The Budget Division of the Treasury is responsible for working out the budget. The Malaysian budget consists of operating and development expenditures. The former is budgeted yearly whereas the latter, although disbursed annually, is based on approved five-year plans. The EPU is responsible for calling in bids for five-year plan development proposals from all the ministries, state governments and statutory bodies. Selection and compilation of development proposals are carried out once every five years and during the mid-term review period. Preliminary screening is done according to a set of criteria based on national objectives. The initial selection report prioritizes the development proposals before submitting them to the NDPC for deliberations and to the Cabinet and Parliament for final approval. A list of all the approved development projects is sent to the pertinent ministries and agencies for inclusion in their respective annual treasury budgets.

The Budget Division requests and examines bids for annual operating budgets from agencies as well as for their annual financial requirements for approved five-year plan development projects. Government agencies submit their requests for development projects not included in the five-year plan to the EPU. These requests are considered by the NDPC and its sub-committee on estimates headed by the Treasury budget director. Development projects approved by the NDPC are included for implementation in the five-year plan. The Budget Division concerns itself with the annual financial allocations required for these new development proposals.

Malaysia presently adopts the Programme Performance Budgeting System for all of its annual budgetary estimates. The operating and development expenditures and the revenue estimates are listed according to ministry, department, programme and activity. The approved budgets are listed according to vote head, subhead, ministry, department, programme, activity and others. In reality, budget examination by treasury officials and debates on budget estimates by members of Parliament are still oriented towards the old line-item and agency-based activities. True programme performance analysis and decision-making are not in operation.

Implementation Management — Monitoring and Evaluation

The Government has identified three major central agencies under the Prime Minister's Department responsible for three types of evaluation. Thus, the EPU, being responsible for economic planning, formulation of the Five-Year Plans, and allocation of the national development funds, should also be responsible for evaluating the need for specific programmes and projects and undertaking feasibility studies. The ICU is generally responsible for coordinating all development efforts and giving direct feedback to the Government. As such, it is responsible for programme and project monitoring. Finally, the Socioeconomic Research and General Planning Unit (SERGPU) is responsible for post-evaluation, which entails in-depth research of the socioeconomic impact of development programmes and measures.

While the evaluative role of the three central agencies is clearly stated, it must be borne in mind that the three types of evaluation are also undertaken by all operating ministries and agencies within the administrative system, from federal to village level. This is accomplished through various councils and committees. Further, central agencies like the Ministry of Finance (the Treasury), the PSD and the MAMPU are also involved in the evaluation process through examination of the annual budget and special studies conducted from time to time. Their representatives are members of many planning and evaluation committees at the federal level as is the case with the EPU, ICU, SERGPU and some of the major ministries.

The most important planning, implementing and evaluating agent at the state level is the State Action Committee (SAC). This agency is a replica of the National Action Council (NAC) at the central level, where the Chief Minister is Chairman and the membership consists of all state EXCO members and state and federal department heads. At a lower level, each district within a state has a District Development and Security Committee, while each village within the district has a Village Development and Security Committee. The former is comprised of all departmental heads at the district level, including the chief of the mukim *(Dato Penghulu)* and some village chiefs *(Ketua Kampung),* with the District Officer as Chairman. The latter is chaired by the village chief and is comprised of leading villagers. In both cases, evaluation is undertaken in conjunction with development planning and monitoring of implementation activities.

Assessment of the Systemic Coordination Process

Development procedures and practices in planning and budgeting are well established in Malaysia. Different organizations and procedures have been instituted to ensure rational planning, budgeting, implementation and evaluation of development programmes and projects at different levels. Part of Malaysia's socioeconomic achievements may be attributed to these arrangements. In practice, however, the procedures and structures of these administrative systems have an inevitable number of weaknesses and inconsistencies. Some assessments are as follows:

First, the division of planning and of financial budgeting into the EPU and the Treasury, respectively, may potentially be a structural weakness from the viewpoint of overall functional arrangements for development planning and budgeting. This may develop into a situation where the EPU plans for programmes that the Treasury underfinances or does not wish to finance. Major conflicts and problems of this nature have not yet been experienced, however, due to the NDPC's and Cabinet's influence in ensuring that what is planned and approved is fully budgeted and financed.

Second, planning, budgeting, implementation and evaluation efforts at the federal level are better coordinated, despite their weaknesses, than at the state level. An underlying problem at the state level is that programmes and projects implemented in states are financed and managed by different sources and authorities. These "cross-authorities" and powers present problems to integrated planning, budgeting and evaluation of state district development programmes.

Third, these "cross-authorities" at the intermediate and local levels of implementation result in administrative inefficiency and in duplication of development efforts. The problem at the district, regional and local levels is the proliferation of unintegrated government services, agencies and operations, rather than their lack. It is urgent for government efforts at the local level to be rationalized and integrated.

Fourth, indigenous organizations are particularly weak and underdeveloped partly due to the proliferation of local level government sponsored institutions. The weakness of local institutions and agencies, including the district office, inhibits bottom-up planning as well as more active local participation.

Fifth, planning, budgeting and implementation coordination problems at the local and national levels will exist as long as planning continues to focus on sectors rather than on integrated space, functions and activities. Although Malaysia should continue the federal administrative system, it is imperative that better coordination methods are instituted.

COORDINATION IN THE PROCESSES OF ANNUAL PLANNING, BUDGETING AND IMPLEMENTATION: CASE OF THE IMPLEMENTATION AND COORDINATION UNIT OF THE PRIME MINISTER'S DEPARTMENT

Brief Description of the ICU

The predecessor to the Implementation and Coordination Unit (ICU) was the Implementation, Coordination and Evaluation Unit (ICEU). The ICEU was created in 1970, through administrative decision by the Prime Minister (Tun Abdul Razak). Its tasks then were to identify the specific factors and causes that were slowing down programme and policy implementation and to suggest ways of expediting them. The Prime Minister was particularly concerned that national development programmes be successfully implemented as planned and scheduled. The ICEU enjoyed substantial clout, authority and effectiveness under the Prime Minister's patronage at the time. In turn, the Prime Minister and the Cabinet relied on the ICEU's assistance to evaluate and accelerate federal and state development implementation efforts. Thus, the ICEU came to be recognized as a critical administrative development agency throughout the country. The ICEU was substantially changed with the reorganization of the Federal Cabinet on 5 March 1976. Not only did it undergo a title change to that of ICU, but its size was also diminished and its major functions were curtailed. The division responsible for public corporations coordination became the Ministry for the Coordination of Public Enterprises and eventually separated from the ICU. The division responsible for development programme evaluation was transferred to other agencies that were instituted within the Prime Minister's Department, such as the General Planning Unit and the MAMPU. During that same time too, the reorganized Ministry of Land and Regional Development was given responsibility for coordinating regional development programmes.

The functions and objectives of the ICU as it exists today are as follows:

1. To monitor and evaluate the implementation of all economic and social policies and programmes aimed at achieving the New Economic Policy (NEP) objectives.
2. To coordinate all ministry and government department policies, initiate new policies and change existing ones in order to facilitate achievement of the NEP objectives.
3. To develop and maintain a continuous, dynamic and effective administrative system at federal, state and local levels.
4. To further improve the administration's capacity and capability for plan implementation through administrative reforms as well as to develop cost and efficiency consciousness in all government activities.
5. To foster and encourage the public's attitudes and values consistent with the times and in line with national development needs for change and progress.[11]

The secretariat for the National Action Council (NAC) is provided by the ICU. The NAC working committee meets fortnightly to hear briefings from the various government agencies on their efforts at implementing the NEP. The ICU is responsible for monitoring decisions made at these briefings and ensuring that the responsible agencies promptly carry out these decisions. This action committee system is also used at the state and district levels, and minutes from meetings held at both of these levels are sent to the ICU for information and for further action, if necessary.

The ICU has been made secretariat of the *Seminar Ekonomi Bumiputra* in an effort to encourage Bumiputra participation in commerce and industry, as well as to study, monitor and coordinate actions taken on all resolutions passed in line with the NEP. The ICU is also responsible for various aspects of community development. In particular, it monitors achievements in Malay business participation and coordinates efforts towards the eradication of poverty and social restructuring. Recently, the ICU has been given new functions and responsibilities. Among these are the activity coordination of two of the country's largest public corporations, i.e., the National Corporation (PERNAS) and the Malaysian International Shipping Corporation (MISC), and there are also moves to place the Petroleum Development Unit under the direct ICU supervision.

Coordination Procedures and Techniques

Coordination functions are carried out at various levels and through several methods and techniques. In this regard, it is evident that the ICU has utilized a number of monitoring, evaluating and coordinating methods and procedures on development plans and projects which may be summarized as follows:

First, the ICU has a high degree of influence and leverage in ensuring that development activities are carried out according to projected plans and schedules through its formal administrative position as NAC secretariat. The NAC meets regularly with the specific purpose of discussing the progress of critical project and programme implementation. Normally, each briefing session is preceded by the presentation of papers prepared by the ICU. Consequently, the ICU's assess-

[11] It is evident that objectives 3, 4 and 5 seem to duplicate the functions mandated by the MAMPU. One explanation for this is that the ICU was instituted a year prior to the establishment of the MAMPU in 1977. The ICU and its predecessors (ICDAU and ICEU) have also always had the dual objectives of coordinating implementation and improving administrative capacity (or modernization, in the MAMPU's terms). Since the establishment of the MAMPU, however, the function of "improving administrative capacity" has been minimized by the ICU. Such function is presently subsumed under the section called "social development and administrative modernization" within the ICU. This section carries out additional monitoring of social programmes at the district level and works in conjunction with the MAMPU at proposing administrative improvements.

ment and evaluation, as well as recommendations for improvements or policy changes, are very influential during the discussions and decision-making process of the NAC and even the Cabinet itself.

As mentioned earlier, NAC members are also members of the Cabinet. The NAC may use the presentation and briefings to evaluate the capabilities and performance of the administrative machinery and professionals involved in development programme implementation. It is important thus, for most agencies to perform well during the briefings and presentations to the NAC. The agency's reputation and its future prospect for obtaining more projects, funds and personnel depend on good performance during these presentation sessions.

Briefings given to the NAC are conducted according to two formats. The earlier approach was to call upon agencies, often at the request of the Prime Minister or a senior cabinet member, to present a detailed review of the implementation progress of all programmes, or certain critical programmes, undertaken by agencies concerned. Recently, the briefing format has been improved. Presentation or briefing of implementation are focused on "programmes" rather than agencies, and all relevant departments and agencies have to attend such briefings in order to evaluate their contribution and performance in helping to achieve the programme goals. This latter approach is called the Goal-Programme-Agency-Matrix.[12]

Even though the NAC must meet once a month, the sessions have recently been less frequent. What has increased are the less formalistic but more action-oriented briefing and presentation sessions chaired by the Prime Minister or Deputy Prime Minister. During busy weeks or critical phases of national development implementation, say at the end of the Third Malaysia Plan period, there were two or three briefing sessions weekly.

Second, ICU has upgraded and modernized the National Operations Room technique, since it was initiated in the 1960s, through use of a high powered fourth generation computer. Data on all major ongoing projects in the nation have been fed into the computer, providing the Government with information on: (a) financial allocations given to each ministry, programme and state; (b) the current stage of progress in implementation and money utilized for each project; (c) reasons for any delays; and (d) the number of beneficiaries catered by the project.

A scanning process built into the system enables the basic data on projects in any particular area of concern to be immediately screened for purposes of discussion and decision by members of the NAC or by agencies briefing the NAC. The data are updated every quarter in order that the latest situation in terms of project progress and implementation may be known, thereby allowing for effective monitoring and coordination.

---

[12] See Mohd. Iwaz Karim, "Decision Support Systems and Project Monitoring in Malaysia" [Paper presented at the Sixth Annual Conference of the Society of Management Information Systems, San Francisco, Cal., 11-13 September 1974].

Third, ICU also achieves its coordination function through indirect means, such as participation in planning, budgeting and development evaluation meetings. It is normal for ICU staff to go to states and to operating agencies and explain the current procedures and concerns with regard to the process of monitoring and coordination of development activities. These indirect approaches enable ICU to make its role more acceptable as well as make its tasks and responsibilities clear to the agencies, ministries and corporations which ICU has to coordinate. Another aspect of the ICU's activities is the existence of State Development Officers (SDOs) in all thirteen Malaysian states. The special task of these SDOs is to represent the federal government's interests, and help the states and the ICU to monitor, coordinate and evaluate development implementation at the state level. The role of the SDOs is also to help monitor and assess the states' political and administrative situations. Such information is essential if intervention is necessary in order to ensure that development implementation in the states is carried out as planned and scheduled, as well as to ensure that development efforts produce the desired equitable impacts.

Fourth, unlike most coordinating agencies in other countries, by virtue of its history and unique location within the administrative machinery, the ICU has financial allocation of its own. This financial allocation for special projects facilitates the ICU to plan and directly supervise implementation of projects and activities that are of critical interest to the country but which cannot be effectively undertaken by the existing line agencies. Among these projects are activities that aim at social restructuring, rural community and political development, and some special large programmes and corporations which the Prime Minister closely monitors and supervises. The ICU may be allocated $2 billion for programmes such as rural roads, entrepreneurial development, rural community development, urban poverty eradication, etc., proposed in the Fourth Malaysia Plan of 1981-85.[13]

Effectiveness of the ICU as a Coordinating Agency

The ICU is strategically located within the total Malaysian planning and coordination machinery framework. As NAC secretariat and having responsibility over the Operation Room with the large computer, the ICU has major political access to and leverage with the top-ranking administrative and political authorities. Thus, in terms of physical and strategic location and administrative access, the ICU is an ideal agency for coordination. The ICU was not created through any Act of Parliament or such legal statutes. It existed previously as the ICEU in 1970, and in its present form since 1976, through the administrative

---

[13] This proposed $2 billion allocation is different from financial allocations made to sectoral departments such as Public Works, Rubber Industries Smallholders Development Authority (RISDA), State governments, etc. These funds are to be channelled through the SDOs who operate state community development projects, minor rural roads, applied nutrition programmes, Bumiputra entrepreneurial development, urban poverty eradication and the like.

decision and action of the Prime Minister during that time. Whatever authority or responsibility it has now is based on the prestige and the position of its main patron, the Prime Minister, and the main organization that utilizes its information, namely the NAC. In terms of reality of authority and influence, with or without legal or formal document, the ICU has sufficient clout and accessibility to be able to undertake whatever monitoring, evaluation or coordination function it is instructed to do. Furthermore, this apparent authority is continuously reinforced by the Prime Minister, who continuously uses the ICU as his main source of information and as the "trouble-shooting" agency in monitoring and coordinating development activities and programmes of all ministries, states, agencies and public corporations.[14]

Except for special projects and programmes that are under its direct responsibility, the ICU is not endowed with powers of resource allocation. Such powers and authority are entrusted to the Treasury and, indirectly, to the EPU. The function of the ICU, administratively, is mainly to ensure that development plans and programmes are implemented to meet the goals and missions of the NEP.

The ICU and its equivalent predecessors, such as the ICEU and ICDAU, have been in existence for nearly a decade now. Despite changes in its detailed functions, terms of reference or methods of monitoring and coordination, the ICU's special role and responsibility are well understood and appreciated by all government ministries, departments and agencies. In fact, government departments or agencies cannot call themselves effective without having submitted to the ICU and being evaluated by the NAC and ICU for their effectiveness and efficiency in programme implementation.

In terms of functional specialization and activities, it is evident that the ICU is particularly concerned with the implementation of programmes that will lead to the achievement of NEP goals. The other activity that ICU undertakes, which receives the most publicity and touristic exposure, is maintenance of a massive development information system through use of sophisticated computer technology at the National Operations Room.

Through its years of existence, the ICU has acquired experience and developed its own monitoring and coordination systems and processes. The general quality of ICU personnel is high. Although most of the staff are young, averaging in the early thirties, most are well-qualified and experienced in various functions and levels of public administration. All the managerial and professional staff have first degrees in various fields. From an impressionistic survey, the majority of the ICU personnel are fully aware of and sensitive to the nation's important goal of achieving the NEP's twin objectives.

---

[14] Even though Malaysia operates on a federal system of government, the ICU, as an important arm of the Prime Minister's Department, is able to receive the necessary cooperation of states and non-federal agencies in its request for data on projects that are being implemented at any particular time. There is no legal provision that obligates states to cooperate fully with the ICU, but because of the special status and influence of the Prime Minister and his agencies, most states make efforts to meet the ICU's requests.

The procedures and techniques of monitoring, evaluation and coordination were highlighted earlier. The ICU also produces quarterly progress reports on development programmes implemented by the ministries. These reports are reviewed by the NAC and by the ministries concerned so that corrective or follow-up action may be taken by responsible agencies and department heads. When major implementation problems emerge, the NAC or the Prime Minister himself will call for special briefings and case analyses, upon which necessary action is taken.

A number of observations should be noted upon evaluation of the ICU's own effectiveness and performance. First, it is important to note that the ICU attempts to coordinate development implementation as a continuous process at multi-levels. Consequently, both direct and indirect approaches to coordination are necessary. With respect to this, ICU's performance has generally been good. Second, effective programme monitoring and coordination requires various kinds of information. At this particular juncture, ICU is only able to monitor four aspects of programme implementation, namely, financial allocations, implementation progress and utilization of funds, reasons for delays and number of beneficiaries reached. Important information on the effect and impact of implemented development programmes is nonexistent. While the ICU has successfully monitored and coordinated infrastructural and economic projects, it has been rather weak in monitoring projects of a social character, such as those dealing with social restructuring or Malay participation in modern sector activities. A major cause of this weakness is the lack of reliable procedures and of social data base models that would allow an agency like the ICU to effectively monitor and evaluate the progress and impact of social development programmes.

Generally, it may be concluded that the ICU has been able to play the main government agency role of monitoring, coordinating and evaluating development programmes implemented in all sectors and areas of the country. The success of the ICU is not based on strong or formal legal authority. Its success is based more on the outcome of its historical reputation as the agency through which the Prime Minister acts and coordinates policy and programme implementation, its critical task assignments in the massively developing country of Malaysia, its role as keeper of wide ranging and important information within the Operations Room, as well as the fact that the ICU has "operatives" (the SDOs) in the field (states) and substantial resources of its own to ensure the effective direction and impact of certain important sociopolitical programmes.

One weakness which should be mentioned is that in Malaysian administrative culture, senior officials do not readily accept directional command from others who are, in terms of the administrative seniority/hierarchy, lower than they are. The effectiveness of the ICU is inhibited by the fact that the ICU director-general is "lower" than all of the ministry and big department secretaries-general. The continued effectiveness and clout of the ICU is due mostly to the patronage, continued support and concern of the Prime Minister and Deputy Prime Minister. To ensure the ICU's continued influence, with or without the Prime Minister's patronage, it would be helpful to upgrade the administrative seniority and status of the agency's director-general.

SYNTHESIS

Growth of the Malaysian economy according to 1970 prices was quite rapid, even by developed countries' standards. The 8 per cent per annum GNP growth, however, belies two important phenomena which have been the major weaknesses of Malaysian development planning and implementation. First, while growth of the industrial, construction and service sectors has exceeded ambitiously planned targets, the traditional agriculture and rural sectors have remained stagnant. The stagnation of rice agriculture and rural economy occurred in spite of large governmental inputs and help to these sectors. Some authorities argue that stagnation of the agricultural and rural sectors is not "real", but more the phenomenon of slower growth compared to fast growing industrial and urban oriented sectors. It may also be argued that agricultural and rural stagnation is the result of inequitable coordination of government inputs and implementation efforts. Governmental inputs and help are indeed substantial, but the processes and methods of distributing the help are inadequate and do not reach farmers and rural populations. As has already been alluded to, there are possibly administrative and structural implementation difficulties at the state and local levels in need of serious examination and adjustment.

It is evident that development planning and implementation may be accomplished in an integrated and coordinated way within the context of the formal administrative machinery and procedures. Partly because of the comparatively small physical size and centralized federal government system, development implementation has been achieved consistently and with minimal conflicts. In spite of the existence of coordinated planning and implementation on one dimension, and developmental performance, on another, it may not be validly concluded that there is a causal relationship between these two phenomena. To a great extent, Malaysia's developmental performance is strongly related to its resource endowments and economic growth orientation. Beneath Malaysia's high economic growth, there still remain poor and underdeveloped social groups and regions. A number of factors may be pointed to in explanation of this situation. One factor is historical-geographical in nature, but more influential is governmental emphasis on economic growth based on free-market variables. The New Economic Policy enunciated since 1970 attempts to redress the developmental inequities.

The Malaysian planning, budgeting and implementing machinery is well defined and specialized in practice. In reality these three functions are interrelated and must always be coordinated in order to be effective. There are a number of occasions, however, when agencies responsible for specialized functions are in conflict with one another. Conflicts are not due so much to situations where one agency usurps another's role, but rather because one agency's decision or activity is not in agreement with another's. There are complaints about development targets decided by the EPU being overly ambitious, lack of proper fund allocations from the Treasury, slow disbursement of funds from the Treasury's Finance Division, or that the Public Services Department was not consulted about manpower capacity considerations. Thus, in spite of the formal and clear stipulations regarding planning, budgeting and implementation processes and procedures, these are less clear when applied in reality. This is not a problem unique to Malaysia, but one which exists in other developing and developed countries as well. Despite the ideal formal systems, there are always situations when those in charge of financial and personnel organizations are not in complete agreement or sympathy with plans proposed by operating agencies. Or conversely, the situation may be one where the planning and operating enthusiasm of operating agencies tends to underestimate financial allocation and limited manpower resource problems. In their growing awareness of the need to achieve social development equity, Malaysia must increase manifold its efforts at restructuring the society as well as affecting equitable distribution of economic growth and well-being. This requires innovative planning and policies, and concerted implementation efforts. Concerted efforts mean coordinated and rationalized social development planning, budgeting and programme execution, as well as sincere support from private and industrial sectors. Recently, Malaysia's Deputy Prime Minister publicly complained that the private sector was not only slow in coordinating its efforts towards realizing Third Malaysia Plan goals, but that it was particularly unresponsive about efforts to restructure Malaysian society. To be really effective in development, therefore, coordination must also involve activity integration with the private sector.

A general weakness in Malaysian implementation is expenditure "shortfall", which refers to the inability of ministries, departments or agencies to fully spend their monetary allocations according to projected schedules and amounts. Strangely enough, even central level coordination focuses on how much money is "not spent", rather than on whether the money has been used effectively, whether programmes funded are benefiting target groups or whether the programmes are relevant to people's needs. This managerial misdirection is partly due to the complacent attitude that "money is not an issue" in Malaysian development. As a result of this attitude, a number of programmes have failed due to early ineffectiveness, and lack of impact or post-hoc analysis and evaluation. It is about time that the government ascertains cost and impact effectivess of projects before allocating funds.

The strengths and weaknesses of Malaysia's coordinating machinery may be seen from institutional as well as noninstitutional contexts. Institutionally, Malaysia's primary coordinating agency, namely the ICU, has the advantages of being situated within the federal administrative organization, directly under the Prime Minister, and of having administrative clout and influence under his patronage. Other advantages that the ICU enjoys are its clearly established and accepted role, access to and utilization of a modern computer system and continuation of programme monitoring and coordinating traditions via the operations room technique.

The noninstitutional variables that affect implementation coordination efficiency include (a) lukewarm state and statutory body support (especially submission delays of quarterly reports) and the inability of obtaining relevant data from the private sector; (b) an incomplete and unclear policy framework that makes monitoring and data analysis difficult and controversial (especially with reference to asset ownership by the Bumiputras, and their participation in modern sectors); (c) an administrative culture that takes significant cue from positional seniority as well as general reluctance on part of professional service colleagues to discipline or be strict with one another; and (d) the common kind of "political intervention" by individuals who have no legal authority to intervene. In the Malaysian case so far, constraints in monetary resources have not been the real major cause of development implementation problems.

It has also become evident that planning, budgeting and implementation coordination problems are generally less acute at the central or federal level than at the substate, district or regional levels. At the substate level, where actual development implementation is carried out, there currently is a high level of responsibility and authority conflicts between the District Office, Local Government and Regional Development Authorities. Thus, there seems to be a need for some kind of function and power delineations so that the efforts of these three offices are not duplicated or in conflict with one another.

One of the factors that has contributed to the lack of coordination of development planning and implementation in Malaysia, particularly at the state and regional levels, is the proliferation of semigovernmental agencies and public corporations during the last few years. It is imperative that the actual roles and effectiveness of such entities as public corporations be analysed, and if need be, some of these should be dissolved.

Studies about programme implementation at the local level indicate the weakness and impotency of local institutions and organizations, in particular nongovernmental ones. It is imperative for effective rural and urban development, therefore, that local organizations and institutions undergo reorganization in order for them to play more active roles in development planning and implementation. Where necessary, government-sponsored local level institutions should be diminished in order to allow indigenous institutions to grow.

Because of the unique nature of Malaysia's federal government system, the politico-administrative structure of the society is very centralized. The need in Malaysia is not additional centralization, coordinative organization or structures, but more decentralized coordinating focal points and systems. One method would be to decentralize functions and responsibilities. But to be more effective, this effort must be supported by delegations of authorities to districts, regional bodies and agencies. Institutions should be strengthened by giving them planning personnel and authority. District officers should also be better selected and trained. The District Office should be restructured and strengthened with better qualified and trained staff, allocated with special funds and mandated with the responsibilities for development planning and coordination at the district level.

6

DECENTRALIZATION, COORDINATION AND DEVELOPMENT IN THAILAND

CHAKRIT NORANITIPADUNGKARN

INTRODUCTION

THE PURPOSE of this paper is to present an overview of development performance and institutional capability in Thailand, with particular reference to coordination in planning, budgeting and implementation. Coordination is posited to be one of the most critical factors affecting the level of performance in development.

Thai development strategies will first be explained, followed by a description of the administrative system and coordination. Discussion of coordination will be divided into two parts: the overall and the specific systems. References to regional development will be made, where relevant, throughout the paper.

NATIONAL DEVELOPMENT AND REGIONAL POLICIES

Historical Review of National Development Strategies

Thailand's first national economic development plan, initiated in 1960, focused on construction and rehabilitation of major infrastructures in the country, i.e., large-scale multipurpose dams, main interregional and interprovincial highways and other communication networks. The development of electricity and other principal sources of energy, as well as the expansion of education and public health facilities were directed towards large communities.[1] These were expected to provide a rapid increase in private investment and national economic output. Results were encouraging, since the gross domestic product grew at a rate of about 7.2 per cent annually and per capita income doubled by the end of the plan in 1966.[2]

---

[1] National Economic Development Board, *The Six-Year National Economic Development Plan 1961-1963-1966* (Bangkok: 1963).

[2] National Economic Development Board, *The Second Economic and Social Development Plan 1967-1971* (Bangkok: Government Printing Press, 1967), p. 13.

Although initially no reference was made to regional disparities, this thought was soon in the minds of the national elite and the Prime Minister. During inspection trips, the Prime Minister became aware of the backwardness of his homeland, the Northeast region, which has long been neglected by previous governments. Communist threats to subvert the region prompted him to take more immediate action. He first set up a regional development committee in the Northeast and served as chairman, and later other regional committees were also created. Furthermore, the Prime Minister intended to augment special resources for regional development in greater amounts than earlier planned.[3]

As a result, in addition to the amounts of money regularly spent in the regions by line departments, the second five-year national development plan of 1967-71 provided a special fund exclusively for regional development.[4] There was also a chapter in the plan stating regional and local government guidelines which aimed at "spreading development benefits to people throughout the Kingdom."[5]

Regional development planning was to be adopted as a blueprint for spending funds reserved exclusively for that purpose. At that time, there was also an attempt to introduce provincial planning in the fifteen Northeastern and in some Northern provinces. However well-intended the second development plan appeared to be, both regional and provincial development plans failed to achieve their purposes largely due to inadequate policy and financial supports.

A national perspective on regional development was utilized in the third development plan of 1972-76. Although the desire to achieve more equity seemed increasingly serious, regional development committees as well as the regional development fund were abolished. One of the objectives stated by the third plan was the need to achieve "social justice", and the phrase "to reduce income disparities and differences in living standards of the people" was heard.[6] This objective was expected to be implemented by means of (a) agricultural production acceleration, (b) employment provision to rural people through construction of farm-level irrigation, rural roads and village development, (c) reduction of the birth rate and (d) development of additional urban and industrial centres. Project initiatives and financial expenditures to support regional and provincial development were supposed to have been the exclusive responsibility of the central government's line departments.

The main goals of development strategies have presently been expanded to include economic restructuring, management of natural resources, environmental conditions and national security, all of which are critical issues of modern times, and need more attention from government agencies. Several previous goals have

---

[3] Northeast Regional Development Committee, *Northeast Development Plan 1961-1966* (Bangkok: Aksornprasert Press, 1961), pp. 41-6.

[4] National Economic Development Board, *The Second Economic and Social Development Plan 1967-1971.*

[5] Ibid.

[6] National Economic and Social Development Board, *The Third Economic and Social Development Plan 1972-1976* (Bangkok: Government Printing Press, 1972).

also been maintained as important elements of the present national economic and social development plan of 1977-82. These goals are economic growth, economic and financial stability, reduction of income disparities and manpower development. Each goal is followed by a set of development strategies, but there have been attempts to integrate strategies, as some may serve several development objectives. The regional policy objectives mainly directed towards "reduction of income disparities and better delivery of social services" are:

1. Decentralization of industries in order to expand employment opportunities and establishment of regional centres and special programmes for depressed areas in all regions.
2. Immediate decentralization of basic economic services (public utilities, transportation, communications and electric services) in order to support production in rural areas and improve the quality of life.
3. Pricing policy revisions on public utility provisions in order to promote better income distribution and give a fairer deal to rural producers.
4. Immediate decentralization of social services (education, public health, social welfare and nutrition) in order to reach more rural areas and reduce social service disparities between urban and rural areas.[7]

In carrying out these strategies, the various line departments are responsible for project identification, formulation and implementation. But their channels have been inadequate in serving regional needs.[8] Thus in 1977, a bottom-up development planning scheme focused on a province was introduced for diffusing development and implementing projects to serve immediate local needs. In 1979, a new village development scheme was inaugurated for developing about 5,000 impoverished and remote villages over a three-year period. The scheme requests Tambon councils to identify their own needs, prepare their own projects and implement their own programmes.[9] Both schemes present a new hope of redistributing development benefits to various regions of the country.

Overall Evaluation of Development Performance

Project initiation and choice as well as preparation and implementation are highly relevant to development performance. When the National Economic and Social Development Board collected statistics for 1973, it was evident that Thai development had forged ahead despite having undergone some rough times.

---

[7] National Economic and Social Development Board, *The Fourth Economic and Social Development Plan 1977-1981* (Bangkok: Karn Satsana Printing Press, 1977).

[8] Prime Minister's Office; "Regulation concerning Provincial Economic and Social Development Plan B.E. 2520 (1977)," dated 2 July 1977.

[9] The Secretariat Office of the Cabinet, "Letter No. Sor Ror 0202/10649 dated 22 June 1979, Re: Appointment and Functions of the New National Rural Development Committee."

Development performance was affected by the impact of international economic and political events upon the Thai economy, a present decade phenomenon which has had worldwide negative and positive repercussions.

Performance of the third five-year national development plan which ended in 1977 was as follows:[10]

(a) Economic stability and growth. Since 1973, Thai economic stability has been tremendously affected by world price increases in major commodities, particularly food items and raw materials, in addition to successive increases in oil prices. The average rate of price level increases jumped to 11.4 per cent per annum during 1973-77, compared to a 3 per cent increase during 1966-72. Also, worldwide economic stagnation decreased domestic investment, which accentuated the unemployment problem in industrial and service sectors. The output growth rate, which had been increasing at a high and sustained rate, began to fluctuate drastically and decline annually.

The economic growth rate also fluctuated and dropped to 6.2 per cent from the previous ten years' (1960-70) average of 7 per cent. This was largely due to declining agricultural output, which was affected by drought, flood and price changes.

(b) Income disparities. While the overall growth rate may be considered satisfactory, it nevertheless resulted in further income disparities among various income groups and regions of the country. This income disparity may be partly attributed to past development strategies aimed at economic efficiency and general income and production growth rates. Those who had had access to economic and social infrastructural facilities provided by the government benefited most. Conversely, those in remote areas which had received little government attention benefited less due to the ruling out of public investments in their areas on the basis of national efficiency criteria.

Although the third plan added additional measures to alleviate the problem of income disparity, most production expansion, diversification and productivity increases took place mainly in the central region. Meanwhile, the economy of other regions experienced relatively slow growth and little structural change. Hence, in terms of living standards, income, and job opportunities, most of the people living in periphery regions are still dependent upon traditional agriculture. This form of production is seasonally oriented and output increases are largely achieved through expansion of newly cultivated areas rather than through actual productivity increases. Moreover, the income disparity problem is accentuated by agricultural prices, scarcity of production factors, and an increasing debt burden on the part of rural farmers.[11]

[10] National Economic and Social Development Board, *The Fourth Economic and Social Development Plan 1977-1981.*

[11] National Economic and Social Development Board, *Development Performance during the Third Economic and Social Development Plan* (Bangkok: The Cabinet's Secretariat Office Printing Press, 1977), pp. 56-8.

There is also some evident imbalance in industrial development. In the past, rapid growth in the industrial sector strongly stimulated general economic growth. Most industrial activities are concentrated within the metropolitan Bangkok area, however, and are basically import-substitution industries with low labour content, dependent on imported raw materials. These industries have little relationship with rural agricultural and natural resource development programmes.[12] This structural imbalance in intersectoral and interregional production distribution, has largely contributed to the acute income disparities.

(c) Employment generation. Planners have become especially concerned about the labour force and employment in a country with high birth rates and a proportionately high rural agricultural population. Success in the expansion of nonagricultural activities and of government services, and prolonged education in formal institutions as well as the export of labour enabled the country to maintain a relatively stable employment rate. The unemployment rate ranges from 4 to 6 per cent. It is believed that the country may fare better if advanced technology is introduced to eliminate widespread underemployment or seasonal unemployment in the agricultural sector. Generation of employment in the country should be practicable provided it is not highly susceptible to internal and external factors such as political unrests, instability and change, inflation and economic recession.

(d) Preservation of natural resources and ecological balance. For about ten years now, there has been a notable increase in the rate of destruction of Thailand's natural environment due to (i) slash-and-burn cultivation practised by the increasing numbers of hill tribes, immigrating from neighbouring countries; (ii) increasing shortages of available farmland; (iii) extensive land use by capitalists (these groups illegally occupy national preserves and turn them into plantations throughout the country); (iv) enlarging urban populations and industries that occupy and utilize fertile land around cities for nonagricultural purposes; and (v) lack of effective measures for the development and conservation of water resources. The present government's awareness and concern over these problems have not resulted in adequate solutions.

The problem of population imbalance between the primate city of Bangkok and the rest of the country has been aggravated. Much has been said and written about this problem, but there has been little effective accomplishment. Consequently, Bangkok is a largely inconvenient place, overcrowded and highly polluted. More than 10 per cent of the nation's population live in Bangkok in an area equal to 1/322 of the country's land area.

Major Issues of Development Performance

The following discusses how Thai development administration fares in the major issues of policy relevance, intersectoral consistency, efficiency and impact, which are considered key criteria in measuring development performance.

[12] Ibid.

(a) Policy relevance. Economic growth and equitable income distribution are still badly needed. Due to both favourable and unfavourable conditions which affected production, imports and exports, the nation's economic growth as a whole increased but at a lower rate than planned. The problem of inequity, however, has remained unsolved and appears to have become more acute. Instead of decentralizing development, the trend has been to the contrary. This has not totally been the fault of major development policies adopted by the plan, but rather the kind and quality of projects formulated by the line departments. These pay little attention to poorer sectors of the country, and yet they have passed the central planning agency reviews and received financial support from the Government.

Because the Government's policy is to give top priority to the construction of major infrastructure in the most productive regions, industrial and commercial sectors expand very rapidly. These sectors, in turn, have significantly contributed to large-scale employment and helped diversify the country's economy.

(b) Intersectoral consistency. There have been very few linkages made across sectors when programmes are planned in this country, although some policy statements suggest that such relationships are necessary. Once the national development strategies and policies are adopted, it is the duty of the line agencies to prepare their own programmes and projects, and to independently request for budget allocations. Once the budget is approved, programmes or projects are implemented by their own field agencies, without consulting other sectors or departments. Thus, projects are conceived within very narrow perspectives and responsibilities are delegated within limited areas of specialization. Each agency does things its own way and when necessary, independently attempts to establish linkages with other projects which have been completed. There is always a time lag for departments to conceive of projects which may link with other projects. Integrated and interdepartmental project formulation is still rare. The region, the province or the district which should be able to integrate most government efforts in their respective areas have not been able to do so.

(c) Efficiency. In the past, because of government red tape and the unreadiness of some sector agencies in preparing plans or implementing projects, a substantial amount of funds could not be spent. In some sectors, the underspent amount is as large as 40 to 45 per cent of allocations.[13]

It is very difficult to determine exactly the cost effectiveness of project implementation since no systematic evaluative measure exists. But by crude observation, a lot of waste is incurred by rigid rules, centralized decision-making, the leisurely manner of handling matters, incompetent personnel and frequent transfer of officials. Substantial amounts of money are spent in duplications and overlapping of organizational functions with unclear lines of responsibility.

Policies to increase agricultural productivity have met with little success not only because most agricultural production still relies heavily on nature, but also

---

[13] National Economic and Social Development Board, *The Fourth Economic and Social Development Plan, 1977-81*, pp. 24-7.

because the Government has not been able to provide effective measures for a large number of farmers in the country. National preserves and soil fertility are undergoing wide destruction due to the Government's inability to devise protective meausres. Rural students are poorly trained, and what they learn is soon forgotten or of little relevance to the real-life situations they must confront. Due to insufficient water supplies, people are unable to utilize toilets promoted through projects. Public property deteriorates rapidly due to inadequate maintenance and lack of a civic consciousness. Some of the projects mentioned in the national development plan have never been implemented.

(d) Impact. Thailand's development plans have brought about great change in the centre and other large cities in the country, where the standard of living has been substantially upgraded. They have also contributed to the improvement of basic and important facilities of the society, in the expansion of industrial, commercial, financial and service activities and in the level of modernization. These have helped the country keep pace with world development.

On the other hand, the high cost of living poses serious threats to the lower-middle class and low income groups. These groups barely earn sufficient income to cover rising expenditures. Farmers are among the groups which suffer most. Although the birth rate has declined, the ratio of farmers to size of land is increasingly unfavourable. Prices of agricultural products drastically fluctuate from year to year and from season to season, which indicates that the income of rural people is very unstable. Their income is also diminished by middlemen, who always make greater profits.

Due to the world economic situation, even the nation's more developed industrial and commercial sectors suffer frequent setbacks. They are subject to unanticipated changes and greater risks. Perhaps the policy of self-reliance has to be emphasized more in the near future. Heavy concentration of investment in Bangkok has not only resulted in a high level of development, but also population congestion and housing problems. There is a shortage of public utilities, transportation facilities are lacking, slums are burgeoning and cost of living is high.

In rural areas, where little attention and investment have been given by the Government in the past, people suffer periodic damages due to drought, flood and pests, which have resulted in indebtedness and land losses. Some rural people are migrating to Bangkok, while others are settling in national preserve areas.

If determined initiative is not made by the Government to remedy spatial and economic inequities, these imbalances may result in additional hardships and economic stagnation. The most serious difficulty of the Thai government seems to be the implementation of ideas. Many government policies have not been sufficiently supported in the implementation process. Consequently, even good ideas at the policy level become ineffective and are overlooked when translated for implementation.

OVERVIEW OF INSTITUTIONAL MACHINERY

Historical and Cultural Background

The Thai national bureaucracy was established by the reform of 1892 during the reign of King Rama V. The *Kin Muang* feudal system was replaced by a centralized monarchy, whose objective was the strengthening of the country's defensive capabilities by unifying the loosely integrated subregions. This unifying effort was essential to cope with external threats posed by the two major Western powers — Great Britain and France — which had already colonized all the Thai neighbours, such as Burma, India and China to the North and West, Laos (now Lao People's Democratic Republic), Cambodia (now Democratic Kampuchea) and Vietnam (now Socialist Republic of Viet Nam) to the East and Malaysia to the South.[14]

Based on functional differentiation, twelve ministries patterned after the Western model were established. Governors and their lieutenants, were sent to the provinces as field agents. At that time, a system of regional government called *Monton* (circle) was established, whereby provincial governors were made responsible to the *Tesa* (chief executive) of the circle. With the King's half brother, Prince Damrong, at the helm, the Ministry of the Interior was largely responsible for the systematization of regional and provincial administration.[15]

With the expectation that upon their return they would occupy key positions, princes and nobles were sent abroad to receive modern education. The Royal Page School founded by King Rama IV, which initially limited enrolment to children of the dynasty and nobles, was not sufficient to produce government officials to man posts in the capital and provinces. Thus, Chulalongkorn University's Institute of Public Servants was created. A medical school was also founded and eventually received continuous support for expansion. Additionally, in 1929 a new law governing the civil service was promulgated and the Civil Service Commission was established.[16] As early as 1892, during the reign of King Rama V, a major tax reform was initiated. The expanded bureaucratic system had made modern focus of levy and new organizational arrangements necessary.

˙ In 1933, there was a coup d'état which succeeded in changing the country's governmental system from an absolute to a constitutional monarchy. The Institute of Public Servants became a part of the full-fledged Chulalongkorn University, and another new University of Moral and Political Sciences was set up mainly to produce government officials with a basic knowledge of law and jurisprudence, plus some other social science subjects. These two universities have

---

[14] Chakrit Noranitipadungkarn, *H.R.H. Prince Damrong Rajanubhab and the Ministry of the Interior* (Bangkok: Thammasat University Press, 1963).

[15] Ibid.

[16] *History of Civil Service Commission* (Bangkok: Aksornsarn Press, 1964) [A book published in commemoration of the Sixtieth Anniversary of the Secretary-General of the Civil Service Commission, Luang Sukhum Nayapradit].

produced many thousands of senior level civil servants, while rank-and-file officials were recruited as high school graduates. Later on, specialized professional and vocational education became more available and has become a major factor enabling the country to pursue new welfare and development functions.

During the years immediately following the Second World War, foreign assistance provided for many of the modernization programmes affecting the Thai administrative system. Among these, the Institute of Public Administration was created with the expressed purpose of producing graduates in addition to being responsible for in-service modern administrative science training of government officials. A Public Administration Service team came to review the Thai budgetary system, followed by an International Bank for Reconstruction and Development team sent to evaluate and recommend ways to better utilize scarce government resources. Those missions turned out to be the starting point for the first national development plan and accordingly, the former Economic Council was reorganized as the central planning organ.[17]

At about the same time, a super-Ministry of National Development was formed, whereby several existing departments concerned with development were consolidated. These departments, for example, had been the Royal Irrigation Department, the Highways Department, the Cooperatives Department and the Land Development Department. Subsequently, a first-of-its-kind Planning Division was created to serve this new ministry. In addition, at least two national level development boards were created to help accelerate development capability, i.e., the Board of Investment and the Board of Tax Supervision. Foreign assistance programmes, coupled with the national aspiration for development, enabled many government officials to receive training abroad in many fields of study, including development administration, economic development and planning. Furthermore, numerous foreign advisors were sent to Thailand to assist departments improve their project formulation and implementation practices.

In effect, the prestige of the Thai bureaucracy was due to its long history, its Royal affiliation and its major involvement in commercial ventures. This has continued to be the case until diluted by the emergence of more diversified business interests after the Second World War. The patronage system so widely used in personnel administration in the old days has gradually given way to a more tenable merit system. The rapid economic change of recent years, however, has diminished the prestige and influence of the Thai bureaucracy whose low salaries have been outrun by the rising cost of living. The private sector on the other hand has been experiencing rapid expansion, and as a result an increasing number of capable, competent officials and other trained personnel have been drawn into the private sector. An additional difficulty for the bureaucracy results from its highly centralized nature. The top level, highly-educated officials, many of whom lack experience in the peripheral regions, have been increasingly concentrated in Bangkok and other large cities.

[17] *Technical Papers* (Bangkok: EGAT Graphic Arts Section, 1970) [A book published in memory of the late Secretary-General of the National Economic and Social Development Board, Prayad Buranasiri].

Administrative Framework

The Thai administrative system comprises three administrative hierarchies — the central, the provincial and the local. Thirteen ministries compose the central administration. Each ministry is a composite of departments divided into divisions and sections. The central administration is the headquarters for the various line agencies which direct all field operations either directly or through provincial administrations. There are as many as 131 departmental units operating programmes throughout the provinces.[18]

The nation is subdivided into seventy-one provinces, plus metropolitan Bangkok. Provinces consist of three to twenty districts and each district consists of several communes (Tambon), further subdivided into villages. Provincial administration is subdivided into districts which are the lowest level of government.[19] Provinces and districts, being administrative units, also have a number of field officers found together under the direction of governors and chief district officers. Both the provinces and districts as jurisdictional bodies have clear territorial boundaries. Province size varies from 403 square kilometres of Samutsongkram to 22,991 square kilometres of Chiengmai, and provincial populations range from 81,617 in Ranong to 1,886,192 in Nakornrajsima. The average province size is 7,198 square kilometres and the average population distribution is 649,489.[20]

Governors are appointed from among the senior officials of the Ministry of the Interior, and district officers from within the Department of Local Administration of the Ministry of the Interior. These officials are subject to periodic transfer. By law, they have been given authority to supervise the officials of agencies operating within their respective areas.[21] They may order, advise or stop the actions of the functional officers by requiring them to perform their duties according to the law, the resolutions of the cabinet, the orders of the Prime Minister and the policies of the respective ministries and departments. They are also empowered to control local self-governmental units. In addition, the governor must oversee the operations of public enterprises located within his province. The governor and the chief district officer, however, have very limited power to appoint, transfer, punish or reward functional officers within their province or district, respectively. Commune and village leaders are nonofficials. They are elected personalities who are nominally paid by the government.

There are at present four forms of local administration which are autonomous self-governing agencies — the Changwat Administrative Organization (CAO),[22]

---

[18] Voradej Chantarasorn, "The Growth of Public Organizations in Thai Administrative System," (unpublished).

[19] Revolutionary Party, "Pronouncement No. 218," dated 1 October 1972, Nos. 48-55.

[20] Department of Local Administration.

[21] Revolutionary Party, "Pronouncement No. 218," Nos. 56-63.

[22] Changwat is the Thai name for province.

the municipality, the sanitary district and the special authorities of the Bangkok Metropolitan Administration, and the City of Pattaya Administration. The fifth form — the Tambon Council, which consists of village membership and is destined to be one of the local self-governing bodies — is not yet a jurisdictional body.

The Changwat Administrative Organization performs some functions in the provincial rural areas, while the municipality is responsible for such functions in urban areas. The sanitary district takes charge of semiurban areas, while the Tambon Council is delegated the responsibility of some limited functions within its own commune.

The Changwat Administrative Organization and the municipality each have separate executive and legislative bodies. Members of both legislative bodies are elected by people living within the areas. Although theoretically they should be elected, Changwat Administrative Organization executives are now appointed by the Ministry of the Interior. Municipal executives are first elected as members of the municipal council by the people at large within an area, and then are selected among themselves as members of executive committees. One of them is called mayor, and the others are deputy mayors.

The sanitary district is governed by a commissioned body consisting of government officials and elected personalities. The chief district officer is ex-officio chairman of the sanitary district. The Tambon Council is an elected body with a schoolmaster acting as secretary, while the assistant district officer, and the district community development officer act as advisors.

Presently, the Bangkok Metropolitan Administration differs only slightly from the rest of the municipalities.[23] It performs more functions, maintains some kind of relationship with the ministries and is subject to close surveillance by the central government. The City of Pattaya Administration is a special case in that it is experimenting with the city-manager type of municipality.

Institutional Machinery for Development

In order to present a closer view of the organizational structure of the Thai Government at the central, provincial and district levels, Figure 6-1 is provided to show how each level of government comprises clearcut functional units. As may be observed, the structure portrays a rather strong executive system, in which the Prime Minister keeps at least three resource allocation staff agencies on hand — the Budget Bureau, the Civil Service Commission and the NESDB — but he also has about fifteen agencies linked with his office.[24]

---

[23] Government of Thailand, "The Bangkok Metropolitan Administration Law of B.E. 2518 (1975)," dated 20 February 1975.

[24] Revolutionary Party, "Pronouncement No. 216," dated 1 October 1972.

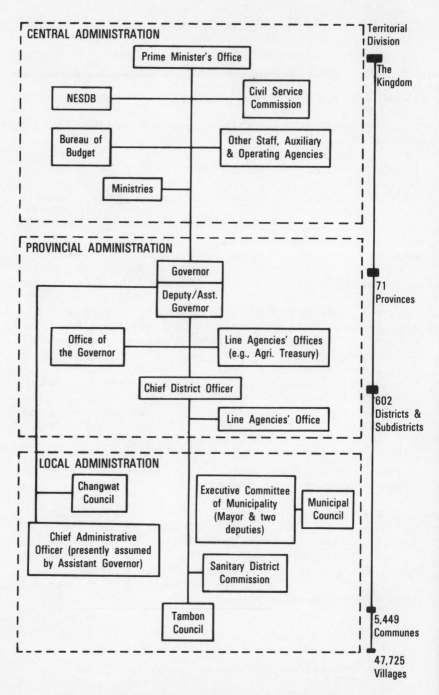

Figure 6-1. Administrative Structure of the Thai Government

All three forms of government (the central, provincial and local administrations) are responsible for the various aspects of development functions. Under the present system, however, the central administration has more role and privileges. The provincial administration has no decision-making power on development, except for some minor matters, while local administration only has small amounts of funds for development purposes. Both practitioners and academicians have long advocated reforms which would give provincial and local administrations more authority and funding for development, but so far these have not materialized.

In addition to the regular government units mentioned above, many public enterprises have been created under different laws and operated under the supervision of the most available ministries. These public enterprises have been established with a variety of motives, such as, the provision of social and merit goods, ownership of natural monopolies, prevention of competitive practice and external diseconomies, economic growth, decontrol of private enterprises over important sectors, revenue-earning, administrative convenience and historical and accidental motives as well.[25]

Many top Thai public enterprise management posts and boards are vested in the hands of high-ranking active and retired civil and military officials. Hence, their attitude and manner of operation have been largely influenced by bureaucratic procedures with which they have been acquainted. Most public enterprises depend largely on government subsidies and monopolistic privileges, and many cannot compete efficiently and effectively with business enterprises.

DEVELOPMENT PLANNING AND COORDINATION

Development planning encompasses the processes of planning, budgeting, implementation, monitoring and evaluation. Currently, Thailand has two approaches to development planning — planning from the top-down and from the bottom-up — but these are not well integrated. The interrelationships between the various processes of development planning, as well as the relationships between the various government levels concerned, will be described in this section with the intention of presenting a picture of the entire process.

Coordination in Planning

Prior to the introduction of the first national economic development plan, the departments were the operating agencies independently responsible for identifying activities or projects to be implemented in their own spheres of concern, calculating costs of implementing them, preparing annual budget requests and

---

[25] Chakrit Noranitipadungkarn, *The Role of the Public Enterprise in Development: Asia and Pacific Region* (Bangkok: Prae Pittaya International Press, 1979), pp. 325-27.

formally submitting them for funding to the Budget Bureau through the ministries. Departments in the Thai administrative system are rather self-contained and have been vested with the authority to initiate, control and administer their own activities. The ministries and the Economic Council, as it was called at the time, did not have the capable body for reviewing those activities, nor did there exist a tradition or the courage to reject the department's proposals. As a consequence, when coordination was necessary, it had to be done on an *ad hoc* project basis.

There also were weekly cabinet meetings of all the ministers to deliberate major decisions and to perform coordinating functions between ministries. But these were only effective when initiative was taken to prepare interrelated positive programmes for the cooperation of several departments which in the past were very few in number.

When the first economic development plan was introduced in 1960, the National Economic and Social Development Board (formerly National Economic Development Board) was revamped so as to constitute a more effective central planning agency. As central planning agency, it was expected to integrate the development efforts of all the agencies of the Thai Government. The NESDB was empowered to screen all the development projects from the line departments before they were forwarded to the Budget Bureau for financial support, or to the Civil Service Commission for manpower increases. In its embodiment of national objectives and policy measures, the NESDB was the focus of development integration.[26]

Effective development planning processes proved to be very difficult for the entire government system. The Thai Government achieved only partial success in its attempts to upgrade planning methodology from project-to-project to sector programming approaches in later years. The regional division of the NESDB is responsible for only part of the regional and provincial development programmes at those levels with regards to provincial development, development of growth pole centres, specific area development and backward village development. It accomplishes this by suggesting measures and by reviewing the project proposals of others.

In formulating the middle-range plan, the NESDB attempted to bring together the various agencies which were in the same economic and social sectors to deliberate national and sectoral objectives and major policy measures as well as to propose some important programmes and projects. It attempted these functions by setting various interagency committees, which were represented by officials from the agencies concerned. It failed, however, to form a comprehensive committee for all activities in every sector. Some committees were appointed by the cabinet or by the Prime Minister and his deputies. The NESDB also tried to set up cross-sectoral committees to deliberate on major issue areas, such as regional, urban and rural development, water resources and energy development. Guidelines and policy measures are only partly followed by the implementing

---

[26] Government of Thailand, "The National Economic and Social Development Law B.E. 2521 (1978)," Articles 6, 12, 13 and 14.

agencies, as they are usually occupied with ongoing programmes.

Since there were frequent changes in government policy and in the economic and social conditions of the country, the NESDB at one time had hoped to introduce the annual plan at the national level. It did this by asking line agencies to submit to it in advance all development projects and identify the stages of work and amount of annual funding necessary. The line agencies could not comply with such requests, since they only had a few detailed projects on hand. When they submitted budget requests to the Budget Bureau, they did so according to the line-item budgetary approach. This did not differentiate regular and development budgets, nor did it show a complete picture of any development project. There were also other problems, viz.: (a) inconsistencies between the fiscal and crop year and the construction season; (b) the NESDB's inability to work within the planning cycle, as the required techniques are complicated; and (c) bureaucratic red tape and the line agencies' unpreparedness to perform their work within a time limit consistent with the annual plan.[27]

Since 1977, there have been new attempts to coordinate development planning at the provincial level in accordance with two new strategies which provide direct funding to the provinces: a provincial development scheme and a new village development scheme. Committees with corresponding officials are set up at the national, provincial, district, tambon and village levels. Five-year and one-year development plans are formulated within which all local projects are included. The Changwat Administrative Organization, the municipality, the sanitary district and the Tambon Council, must prepare plans for funding requests. The Provincial Planning Committee is expected to integrate the plans with national and regional development policies in order to achieve provincial development goals.[28] The Central Committee on Provincial Development also has to comply with the policy of attempting to coordinate the line agencies' projects to be implemented in each individual province with local government projects.

In an effort to better organize development plans, the Government promoted a planning coordination mechanism at the ministerial level by establishing a Policy and Planning Office in addition to the NESDB. The functions of this office have been to develop an integrated ministry plan as well as to monitor the performance of respective programmes. It was hoped that an office of this kind would also be able to recommend policies and have some say within the ministries in resource allocations. The Office of Policy and Planning of the Ministry of the Interior and the Ministry of Agriculture respectively, have indeed produced ministry plans which, however, so far consist of mere collections of proposed projects of various units under their jurisdiction. The ministerial committee of the Ministry of Agriculture and Cooperatives has even been given the authority to rearrange the departments' budgets.

[27] Snoh Unakul, "Annual Planning in Thailand," *Economic Bulletin for Asia and the Far East* 20 (June 1969): 68-80.

[28] Prime Minister's Office, "Regulation Concerning Provincial Economic and Social Development Planning B.E. 2520."

Coordination at the departmental level is unsystematized with each division pursuing its own development pattern. For those divisions where the planning interests of the director-general of the department extended, he frequently attempted to call meetings of the division directors in order to consult them on planning and implementation.

Planning coordination as practised at the provincial level, however, has not been consistent. The Provincial Planning Committee was created, subsided and was recently revived. Legally, it must prepare an integrated provincial development plan, but in practice, it is unable to do so because it does not have the necessary information and planning capability. In addition, tradition does not allow it to get too involved in other agencies' affairs. The NESDB has the responsibility of integrating provincial development plans with the national economic and social development plan. Thus, it attempts to operate within various committees at the national level and orders its regional development centres to assist the province in adopting annual development plans. Despite its efforts, the NESDB recognizes its limitations.

Coordination in Budgeting Process

The director of the Budget Bureau has been granted considerable authority under the Budgetary Procedure Law of B.E. 2502 (27 October 1959) to supervise and coordinate preparation of the annual budget. He arranges for the format of the budget cycle, the conditions of compliance and the timing schedule. He is also authorized to make budgetary analyses and submit recommendations to the Government.

Under the Budgetary Procedure Law, the various departments are made responsible for preparation of budget requests. The departments usually compile the requests from their respective divisions, which are supposed to initiate development projects. The regional, provincial and district field offices may make their needs known to their superiors in Bangkok, but the decision to include them rests solely on the directors-general of the departments. The Ministry has a limited role in screening and changing requests made by their departments. After funds are authorized by parliament, the departments are the ones who request fund release from the Budget Bureau and from the Ministry of Finance. The NESDB, the Bank of Thailand and the Ministry of Finance have representatives in the committee which determines budget expenditure ceilings for the respective ministries.

Theoretically, all projects to be financed must obtain prior approval from the NESDB, but in practice, this may be overruled by cabinet decisions. Although ceilings must ideally be sent to the ministries before budget preparation, the ministries in fact send in their budget requests before the ceilings are approved by the cabinet.

With respect to this, some comments may be made regarding the integration and coordination of project finance and the extent to which these contribute to better performance of development at the field level. First, in the Thai context, very few integrated projects have been identified or formulated by the agencies. Most attempts have been at stating sectoral policies and activities to be undertaken by a given sector. Each department is free to prepare its own projects, choose the location and schedule its operations. The Budget Bureau scrutinizes requests department by department, as they are submitted. It is very likely that the foundation activity will come after the supportive activity. This has resulted in large amounts of funds being wasted from year to year. The classic example is found in the urban area, where construction of roads, footpaths, drainage, laying of water pipes, telephone lines and traffic lights are often installed at different times, even though they are under the infrastructural sector.

Secondly, even in the case of integrated programmes, budgets for component projects are separately requested and reviewed by different divisions of the Budget Bureau, resulting in parts of the requested budget being cut and/or reduced and leaving the integrated programmes unfinished. Furthermore, there is no agreed upon rule on how programmes or projects should be financially supported in case they should be inherently integrated. Thirdly, new projects which require additional personnel recruitment must request for this several years in advance. Even when the Civil Service Commission has approved personnel increases, oftentimes the Budget Bureau does not have sufficient resources to pay for additional positions until some years later. The Budget Bureau also has difficulties reviewing such proposals, because they are not well prepared and are often subject to vague conditions in the future. Fourthly, since the departments in Bangkok are responsible for requesting funds and distributing them to subordinate units, procedures involved in making the money available to provinces provide little guarantee that it will get there in time to meet their needs. For example, delays in getting fuel for bulldozing activities may interrupt necessary subsequent work in a land settlement project during a particular year. Fifthly, funds to provinces are delayed two or three months after the new fiscal year begins and unspent funds are usually transmitted during the last month of the fiscal year. These delays make funds unavailable for construction before the rainy season. When funds become available, it is difficult or impossible for agencies to implement and complete projects on time and within the expense ceiling provisions due to congestion during the remainder of the fiscal year. Many energetic officials have been frustrated with delays in the flow of funds and are discouraged from working more effectively and efficiently. Within the two new schemes of provincial planning and new village development, funds are more rapidly available because they do not have to go through the regular line department channels. The central committees allocate funds to each province directly.

Coordination in Implementation, Monitoring and Evaluation

Implementation of development projects at the regional and provincial levels is usually done in a separate manner, since provincial or other units are only the field units of the central government. Almost all programmes and decisions on fund allocations are initiated by the line departments in Bangkok. Vertical coordination is thus, carried out within projects by these line departments with two or three hierarchical steps. Line departments send guidelines and materials as well as operating expenses to field units as they see fit. If funds available are limited, they will reduce funding to their field offices. If the field offices are not satisfied, they may request more funds, but most likely, these will not be granted. Field units have to carry out tasks according to existing resources under the conditions mandated. There are coordinating committees at the ministerial or departmental levels, which are mainly appointed for coordination tasks during the stages of implementation. These committees largely solve problems rather than supervise tasks, but their effectiveness varies greatly according to the situations.

The provincial governor with his office staff is the coordinator at the provincial level and chief district officer at the district level, under this system of supervision. They have limited opportunity to coordinate central government projects, especially field unit projects outside the provincial administration whose officers report directly to their superiors in Bangkok. At the provincial level there are several coordinating committees, all of which are chaired by the provincial governor. Membership in these committees consists of the relevant provincial functional units, while officers in charge of programmes concerned act as their secretaries. These committees include a provincial committee, a provincial community development coordinating committee, a provincial land reform committee, a provincial development planning committee, a provincial anti-profiteering committee, a provincial land committee, a provincial land consolidation committee and a provincial forest protection committee. They are under jurisdiction of different laws and regulations and rarely are able to operate satisfactorily due to the following reasons:

Firstly, members other than those from the core office usually pay little attention to programmes, on account of difficulties in implementing their own activities under those programmes without sufficient manpower, equipment, travelling expenses, gasoline and, sometimes, moral support. They are entitled to rewards primarily or solely for service in their own line agencies. Secondly, they have a different understanding of the nature and approach of the projects of other departments in which they are asked to participate, partly because committee members usually differ in educational background, age, working experience and work styles and attitudes.

With regards to the system of progress reporting, each agency is required to submit various types of periodic and special reports to their superiors in Bangkok, such as monthly, bimonthly, quarterly, midyear and annual reports. The Prime Minister's Office, the ministries and the departments all have inspectors-general for assisting the chief executives in watching the work progress of the economic and social development projects of the country. Reports sent to Bangkok must be reviewed and analysed by someone's unit, but oftentimes this task is performed so slowly that the effectiveness of such efforts is greatly diminished. Few reports are used effectively for project planning and implementation improvements.

Presently, attempts have been made to introduce an effective monitoring and evaluation system for these two provincial schemes, but thus far none are in use. It may be concluded that monitoring and evaluation techniques and their utilization need to be developed in the country.

NESDB AS A COORDINATING AGENCY

As mentioned previously, the NESDB has been expected to play a vital role in the integration of the country's development efforts. Its effectiveness, however, depends on the extent of time for direction which the national leadership will have, on the degree to which other resouce allocation agencies such as the Budget Bureau and the Civil Service Commission will be able to jointly work with it, and on the acceptance granted by the line ministries and departments. In this section, we will discuss the role and the effectiveness of the NESDB.

The Legal Basis of the NESDB

The NESDB has its secretariat office. Both were created under the Law of National Economic and Social Development and are under the Prime Minister's Office's supervision. The law has been revised several times during the last two decades in an aim to increase the role and authority of the NESDB to successfully integrate the government's development efforts. According to the latest law, the following functions are expected to be performed by the NESDB: (a) offer opinion on economic and social development issues to the cabinet; (b) review proposed drafts of the National Economic and Social Development Plan and other NESDB secretariat's proposals before submitting them to the cabinet; and (c) coordinate the preparation and the implementation of development programmes and projects between the NESDB secretariat and other government agencies and public enterprises.[29]

The NESDB secretariat performs several staff functions aimed at increasing the capability of the nation's leadership to integrate the nation's resources for the acceleration of national development. These functions are to: (a) survey, study and analyse economic and social situations and make recommendations on the objectives and policies for national economic and social development; (b) review development programmes and projects of government agencies and public enterprises for the purpose of making them integrally consistent with the overall national development plan according to available resources and need priorities; (c) study and plan the use of available national finance, manpower and other resources as well as those which may be obtained from other sources; (d) annually prepare proposals in accordance with budget fund allocations and in consultation with line agencies and public enterprises; (e) study and recommend the guidelines

---

[29] Government of Thailand, "The National Economic and Social Development Law B.E. 2521."

to be followed by agencies and public enterprises in formulating development programmes and projects to be submitted for foreign assistance or loans in accordance with the national economic and social development plan; and (f) monitor and evaluate the performance of development projects of all the line agencies and public enterprises and make recommendations for the improvement, acceleration and abolishment of development projects where deemed appropriate.

The Effectiveness of the NESDB[30]

According to the law, the NESDB has the privilege of jointly recommending budget ceilings for each ministry when the scrutinizing committee comprised of representatives from the Budget Bureau, the Ministry of Finance and the Bank of Thailand, meets each year. The law also requires that all line agencies submit development projects for review and appraisal by the NESDB before sending them to the Budget Bureau for funding.

Inclusion of the NESDB in the recently instituted scrutinizing committee gives the NESDB a better position than in the past of at least influencing the general direction of development. In the past, it was very difficult for the three organizations — the NESDB, the Budget Bureau and the Civil Service Commission — to coordinate with one another, because each has its own governing board with its own policy guidelines. With the co-option of the NESDB into the budget scrutinizing committee, it is hoped that government investment will be better geared to support development plans which have been adopted. It remains to be seen whether the Civil Service Commission would be included in the committee in the future.

Although the NESDB is a staff unit of the Prime Minister, who acts as chairman, in the past it did not have sufficient support in contrast with the line ministries' power, who as cabinet members could seek special favours or fund transfers. Politicians could also rely on decisions made by the Prime Minister or cabinet, bypassing development plan guidelines, to stabilize the Government's position through political bargaining.

During the reign of General Kriangsak Chommanand as Prime Minister, more attention seemed to be given to the role and recommendations of the NESDB as well as to the implementation of national development plan projects adopted. The NESDB still attempts to maintain close contact with the Prime Minister, briefing him on development movements. In the past, the Prime Minister's ideas and those of the technicians were often in contradiction. The same can be said of the present Prime Minister who does not seem to view the national plan as the expression of his own policies.

The NESDB used to consist of many bright young men during the first few years of renovation and introduction of the first national economic and social development plan. The realization that technical recommendations had not been

---

[30] Hereinafter the NESDB signifies the secretariat office of the Board itself.

followed by the line agencies or the cabinet caused many to leave the NESDB and work for the line agencies or universities. Nowadays, the NESDB is fostering a new breed of young planners. It also recruits more graduates at both the M.A. and B.A. levels from Thai universities. At present, about 80 per cent of the staff are locally trained, and about 20 per cent are foreign trained. Approximately 80 per cent are economists, while the rest are political science and social science graduates. Many require more years of experience even though they are active and enthusiastic about development planning.

It is felt by the staff, however, that the direction of planning widely acceptable to Thai society is yet unclear, and thus different divisions of the NESDB try to pursue their own kinds of activities. They also feel that under the situation, good teamwork among themselves has not yet been established. This has partly been shown by the inadequacies in coordination among units which share very little information among themselves.

COORDINATION IN PROVINCIAL PLANNING

The province is the key regional area for development at the present time in Thailand. In this section, therefore, we will refer to the Provincial Development and Planning Scheme which was adopted three years ago as a new bottom-up approach to planning and development. This is in addition to the numerous activities and projects of the central government's line agencies which have regularly and increasingly been operated by their provincial field offices. It is also in addition to the subsidies which the central government has regularly given to local self-government units from year to year.

It is the Government's policy of this scheme to decentralize development planning and implementation to the local levels. This will not only be a way to stimulate more people's participation in the development process to help solve people's real needs, but it may also be a means to effectively help narrow down the disparities in the socioeconomic status of people in the country. In implementing this policy, 1 per cent of the central government's annual budget was earmarked for this scheme, and it has been hoped that this amount will increase once the administrative capability of local units has been tested. Under this scheme, two levels of coordinating committees were established, i.e., the Central Committee on Provincial Development at the central level and the Provincial Planning Committees in the provinces. The former has in turn appointed the subcommittee on plan harmonization, the subcommittee on plan supervision and four subcommittees on monitoring and evaluation for each of the four regions, i.e., North, Northeast, Central and South.

The Method and Procedure of Coordination

There are two basic regulations issued by the Prime Minister's Office to systematically coordinate this scheme and to explain plan operations and execution. The regulation on provincial economic and social development plans requires establishment of two committees with duties and authority and contains planning, implementation, and monitoring and evaluation procedures. The second regulation on the disbursement of funds specifically stipulates the method of fund utilization for development as well as financial responsibilities and authorities of the officers concerned.[31]

These regulations are supplemented by letters of explanation or verbal advice made by respective officials. The following are the regulation procedures:

(a) *Problem identification.* In preparing provincial development plans, regulations require that local problems and needs be derived from the following sources: (i) resolutions made by authorities such as commune, sanitary districts and municipalities and opinions of provincial council members and district officers; (ii) plans of the Changwat Administrative Organization, the municipality or the sanitary district; and (iii) any other source with prior approval from both the Provincial Planning Committee and the Central Committee on Provincial Development.

(b) *Project formulation and approval.* Projects are to be identified by local government units, reviewed by the Provincial Planning Committee and approved by the Central Committee on Provincial Development about a year in advance. Approved projects are incorporated in the multi-year development plan and upon being notified about the provincial budget ceiling, they are selected from among a list of approved projects and put in the annual provincial operations plan.

(c) *Criteria for national level fund allocation.* At the national level, the Central Committee on Provincial Development uses the criteria in Table 6-1 for allocating the fund among the provinces.

(d) *Criteria for provincial level fund allocation.* At the provincial level, the Central Committee on Provincial Development stipulates that 80 per cent of the fund has to be allotted for Changwat Administrative Organization or rural projects, while 20 per cent is destined for municipal and sanitary district projects. Each province is also expected to formulate additional subpolicies consistent with national guidelines. Provinces are allowed to devise their own screening procedures.

(e) *Method of implementation.* The regulation on disbursement of the fund requires that: (i) projects of less than one million baht (US$50,000) in value must be carried out by the local governments themselves; and (ii) projects exceeding one million baht must be subcontracted to outsiders. In any case, dispensing of the fund must be determined by regulation.

---

[31] Prime Minister's Office, "Regulation concerning Provincial Economic and Social Development Planning B.E. 2520," and "Regulation concerning the disbursement of fund of Provincial Development Plan B.E. 2522," dated 1 December 1978.

Table 6-1. Criteria for Fund Allocation

Criteria Factors	FY 1979 (per cent)	FY 1980 (per cent)
Population	40	
Urban		5
Rural		15
Agricultural Areas		
Irrigated	5	5
Rainfed	15	10
Other Infrastructure*		
Rural Roads	–	10
Rural Electricity	–	10
Rural Clean Water	–	10
Per Capita Income	20	15
Disaster Areas	10	10
Security Areas	10	10

NOTE: * In 1980, this and agricultural area categories are called "development level" by the CCPD secretariat.

SOURCE: Regional Planning Division, NESDB.

(f) *Reporting procedure.* Implementation agencies are responsible for reporting work performance every three months to the Provincial Planning Committee. This is done to ensure the effectiveness of projects which have both been financed and implemented.

The Effectiveness of Provincial Planning

Hopes for a provincial plan, with its own identity, encompassing all development project operations within an area have met with little success. This is due to application of the concept which ultimately must face various problems dealing with capability, attitude and the work system.

Firstly, the Provincial Planning Office, which acts as secretariat to the provincial governor, has limited capability to formulate specific provincial guidelines or to succinctly identify the economic, physical, social and resource conditions of the province. It has limited vision and time for accomplishing this due to the present structure which burdens this office with a variety of tasks unrelated to planning. Secondly, there are several lines of communication from Bangkok to the provinces. At present the provinces receive guidelines from the Prime Minister, the various ministries and central committees, the Policy and Planning Office of the Ministry of the Interior and the NESDB. The province has to adapt itself to policies which are sometimes contradictory and inconsistent with one another. Thirdly, the Provincial Planning Committee still lacks experience and the will to carry out the work effectively. Provincial functional units have limited time and resources to devote to their main job. It cannot spare much time or efforts and funds to cooperate with the provincial committee, because its superior expects it to effectively accomplish tasks which the former assigns to the latter. Fourthly, local government units (the CAO, the municipality and the sanitary district) do not have a planning unit or officer responsible for the work, thus, they are unable to produce meaningful development plans. Innovative projects are rare and many are criticized for not reflecting people's real needs. Lastly, despite the favourable psychological impact emerging from the introduction of the Provincial Planning Scheme, it nevertheless has limited influence on social change. This is because most resources are still in the hands of the line agencies, which plan their projects from the national or their own agencies' perspectives. The provincial authorities and people would benefit much more if the line departments in Bangkok would also change their attitudes and cooperate with one another more fully.

PROBLEMS OF COORDINATION

Introduction of development planning in Thailand indicates the desire of the leadership to consolidate government efforts in order to attain the most benefits from wise spending of public funds. Development planning is expected to promote consistent, continuous and smooth interrelationships between development activities, and minimize losses and conflicts through a well-consolidated system. Development success or failure depends on how the coordinating mechanisms work. In this section, we will identify the major problems associated with each stage of development planning: (a) planning, (b) budgeting, (c) implementation and (d) monitoring and evaluation, respectively.

Coordination Problems in Planning

The NESDB has attempted to integrate the programmes and projects of the line agencies and coordinate them with the sectoral programmes according to general policy guidelines. Although interagency committees usually agree on policy guidelines, many line agencies have not been able to submit concrete programmes or project proposals as anticipated. This is partly because most ministries and departments do not have long-range policies and plans. These are decided on the eve of the annual budget requests by agencies responsible for such activities according to the rules and regulations. When new policies are conceived, many times they are approved in principle by the cabinet, and this facilitates subsequent budget requests. By then the NESDB, which is a screening agency, cannot make any change recommendations, even if the programmes are inconsistent with the plan guidelines.

Provincial authorities and the NESDB would like to see that the coordination of all provincial development programmes implemented within their plan serve unified development objectives. Each line agency presently designs its own projects in Bangkok, and lack interagency project coordination. This lack of project coordination results in duplication of efforts and inefficient use of limited resources in some areas, while other areas are neglected. Each project initiating agency is limited in its area of responsibility as well as in its scope of project planning. Another problem inhibiting planning coordination is that each new government aspires to identify itself with new public projects and terminates those projects identified with the former regime, even though they might prove to be beneficial to the people.

Coordination Problems in Budgeting

Government funds are scarce, yet every agency wants to expand its activities and new organizations are created every year. The Budget Bureau cannot strictly use development plan guidelines in allocating funds due to short-term policies and orders executed by the Prime Minister and his cabinet which might not be in agreement with the line of policies of the national plan. In addition, guidelines stipulated in the development plan are so broad that they may accommodate a variety of things. Development policies also are subject to change when the situation changes. Thus, the Budget Bureau has to adopt its own guidelines every year and only partially take into account development plan guidelines.

The line item budgetary system poses a serious problem for financing development projects because budget analysts cannot see how parts of the budget requests of even one department fit together as complementary projects. Each item is liable to be reviewed separately and cut as the analysts see fit. The result is that many projects cannot be effectively implemented and must often be postponed until the following fiscal year due to insufficient funds.

The Budget Bureau is comprised of three budget review divisions, each composed of several subdivisions. Each subdivision reviews requests from certain departments only within the same sector. Thus, it is difficult for them to associate the budget of a department in one sector to the budgets of departments in other sectors. Unless integrated programmes are introduced, budget approvals will not be as satisfactory as they should be. In addition, coordination between budget and manpower is difficult because the nation has limited funds for personnel employment. It cannot readily comply with every agency's requirement, even though the manpower increase may have been approved by the Civil Service Commission. There must be an unavoidable time lag.

Since there are many line agencies and national committees distributing funds to provinces, districts, communes and villages, they do so independently. The result is that some communities might receive a greater number of projects and a substantial amount of development funds, while others do not get any support at all. Even within the same community different standards might be employed in allocating different funds to the community. Unless there is a policy clearance centre, this problem will continue. Under the present system of budgeting, provincial governors have no way of knowing exactly how much funding must be allocated to their provinces because there is no system to integrate such data. The same is true for the district, commune and village levels.

Coordination Problems in Implementation

Since strong vertical relationships exist between the headquarters and provincial or district offices of all the line agencies, little horizontal coordination during programme implementation is accomplished among these field offices. Field officers receive mandates and accompanying resources from their respective superiors, and carry out their own projects themselves. They will seek cooperation from others only when they have problems which they themselves cannot solve. Little communication is shared among agencies, since they consider that their business is not the business of others, and it is as well thought to be a waste of time and energy.

Field officers also have problems of communication with their superiors in Bangkok due to geographical distance. When they have operational or administrative problems which must be solved within a short period of time, the distance and red tape delay their actions and often disrupt their time schedules.

In the Thai Government, there are many agencies with similar responsibilities such as in occupational or agricultural promotion, in land settlement, infrastructural construction and water resource development. Local governments also have many functions similar to those of the central government. No clearcut line of responsibility exists.

Coordination Problems in Monitoring and Evaluation

Formerly, when field officers spent funds and utilized all materials appropriated by the headquarters, they were obliged to submit reports on the outcome. Even prior to that, several agencies required their field officers to periodically report to them even though there was not much that the headquarters could do to help alleviate problems. The use of such reports is rather limited, and there is great doubt about their validity and reliability as they are not subject to any verification procedures.

It is also difficult for the Provincial Planning Office to monitor and evaluate the performance of the field officers whose superiors are in Bangkok. Great conflicts would likely ensue if the Provincial Planning Office attempted to do so even if the governor, who has legal authority to supervise them, would dare to order the Provincial Planning Office to carry out such tasks. Some officials would claim that it is not others' business to encroach in their departments, while many officials may not be sufficiently competent or specialized to evaluate their own work and less capable of ascertaining the performance of themselves.

CONCLUDING REMARKS

Review of Thailand's development administration in the foregoing sections suggests that there have been continuous improvements in governmental development planning and administration. While there have been development planning attempts to integrate intra- and inter-ministry and sectoral efforts, however, administrative unit improvements entail an increase and proliferation of many new units. Old departments are further subdivided into more specialized units and many are eventually elevated to divisional and departmental status. Additions are also made within existing agencies and agencies are created when new ideas are conceived, instead of accommodating new functions into old units or reorganizing old units to serve new requirements. Thais prefer to work independently and to avoid confrontation with one another, for fear of mutual encroachment and criticism of each other's affairs. Departments and divisions are now professionally specialized and have become strong decision-making centres for their own activities, preferring to operate independently or through their own established field units. Because of this distinctive character, the NESDB had found it difficult to improve the planning process. It has never had sufficient support from the national leadership to enforce the implementation of policies stated in the plan.

Provinces and districts are at the lower levels of Thailand's highly centralized administrative system which controls initiative and funds from Bangkok. Since each project is independently planned in Bangkok, the opportunity for provincial bodies to effectively coordinate with one another is limited.

To date, there have been few integrated projects or programmes introduced, even within the same sector. Where they do exist, they are loosely formulated and separately financed and administered. Under this system, the Budget Bureau itself finds it difficult to see the interrelatedness of work which complements one another. This is especially the case when parts of programmes are separately handled by line agencies. The organizational structure is compartmentalized and subject to strong directive from different agencies, therefore, it poses problems of coordination.

The Provincial Development Planning Scheme which has been recently introduced as a bottom-up approach with funds directly channelled to the provinces appears to be promising in its potential for reaching the poor and reducing economic and social disparities between rich and poor. These objectives have never been realized before in Thailand. This scheme entails a new set of coordinating committees whose membership consists of the usual representatives from all the agencies concerned. While the planning and implementation are to be done at the provincial level and lower, the responsible organs still lack expertise and administrative resources to adequately undertake the mission. Naturally, they are subject to improvement. The time schedule is also very tight for provinces to comply with one another since little time is given for coordination. Improvement of their capabilities will strengthen the effective coordination and integration of development efforts.

Channelling the fund directly to provinces appears to facilitate consolidated area development, but this procedure is not yet well institutionalized, and is subject to change in the future. It is also subject to political intervention and weak administrative apparatus and support. Furthermore, methods of coordination are undeveloped, i.e., the art of formulating and implementing integrated programmes, the techniques for handling effective meetings, placement of qualified persons for the right jobs and adoption of new authority relationship patterns among those bodies concerned. Perhaps because of the unsatisfactory coordination techniques presently employed, the line agencies tend to be conservative in adapting to the idea of working with others.

In order to improve the effectiveness of development planning and coordination, the present organizational structure must be dealt with first, as it is characterized by extreme disintegration and proliferation.

It has been proposed that a supreme policy harmonization body be appointed with the Prime Minister as chairman, the secretary-general of the Prime Minister's Office as secretary; and the secretary-general of the NESDB, the Budget Bureau director, the Civil Service Commission secretary, the governor of the Bank of Thailand and the Ministry of Finance under-secretary as key members, under whose jurisdiction all other committees should be. This committee would be responsible for rural development. But since provincial development encompasses both rural and urban aspects, it is felt that such a committee could be responsible for provincial, not only rural, development. In order to increase the provinces' capabilities for carrying out integrated planning, a field office of the Policy and Planning Office of the Ministry of Interior, which would be solely responsible for planning must be created. There should be only one planning committee at the provincial level, and a development committee at the district level must also be instituted. There must be a clearer line of responsibility drawn between central and local governmental bodies.

The budgetary system must be decentralized. Small changes in budget items should only necessitate provincial approval. This would help the implementing agencies cope with time problems, expedite work and thus, help conserve government resources. Above all, this would increase the implementing official's morale. All projects submitted for approval to the Budget Bureau must show implementation areas and budget needs according to province. This would facilitate analysis and consolidation of projects at the provincial level. A programme budget must be introduced to facilitate review and analysis by the Budget Bureau and the parliament. More integrated projects must be encouraged in order to help solve coordination problems. In preparing the five-year development plan at the national and provincial levels, policy statements alone are insufficient, programme planning must be agreed upon as well during that time.

Finally, training of all the officials involved ultimately could help improve coordination and development quality. Frequent transfer of officials within the Thai system is a problem. Planning officials are poorly recruited and not given the opportunity to develop expertise. Therefore, the recruitment and transfer systems could also stand improvement.

7
ORGANIZATION FOR LOCAL LEVEL DEVELOPMENT: THE CASE OF BANGLADESH

SHAIKH MAQSOOD ALI

INTRODUCTION

BEFORE INDEPENDENCE, Bangladesh was a part of the former Pakistan (1947-71) known as East Pakistan. The other part of Pakistan, known as West Pakistan, was separated from East Pakistan by the Republic of India by over 1,000 air miles and over 3,000 nautical miles. From the very beginning these two wings of Pakistan differed significantly on the question of the country's future direction of political, economic and social development. In the East, the society was relatively more egalitarian with a rising middle class trying to break the backbone of the moneylenders and landlords in collusion with the peasants. Indeed, they had successfully introduced a series of social legislations[1] in the 1930s which had made the abolition of the *Zamindari* (landlord) system in East Pakistan almost inevitable. After partition, they wanted to carry these social reforms further. In contrast, the West Pakistan power elites preferred a centralized government administration based on the *status quo,* somewhat in line with the prepartition vice-regal system,[2] sustained by an economic system based on capitalistic growth processes[3] with substantial military and financial assistance from Western countries. The tension between the two wings continued until East Pakistan became independent in 1971.

After independence, Bangladesh had to critically re-examine the entire political, administrative and socioeconomic framework that it inherited from Pakistan. In the political field, after a process of trial and error of about six years, it has finally opted for a democratic, presidential form of government. This is being increasingly supported by greater decentralization of administrative and financial powers in favour of local government institutions. Such transition in the

[1] A.S.M. Rab and A.K. Fazlul Haq, *Life and Achievement* (Karachi: Ferozsons, 1966).

[2] K.B. Sayeed, *The Political System of Pakistan* (Oxford: Oxford University Press, 1967).

[3] Mahbubul Haq, *The Strategy of Economic Planning* (Oxford: Oxford University Press, 1966).

field of economic development has been more difficult. During the initial post-independence years (1972-75), the Government repeatedly spoke of socialism. After 1975, it claimed to have become more pragmatic. In 1978, the formulation of Bangladesh's Second Five-Year Plan[4] was postponed in favour of a transitional two-year plan. For the 1980s, the direction of development is appearing with greater clarity: Economic development has to be essentially rurally based with relatively greater emphasis on distribution and on the target groups, such as the landless and marginal farmers. The crucial question, however, remains: Bangladesh is a small country with a large population and an extremely low income but is dominated by the middle-class. How can Bangladesh come out of the vicious cycle of poverty with relatively greater emphasis on distribution? Planners in Bangladesh are desperately searching for an answer to this question.

Any study on the political or socioeconomic development of Bangladesh should be analysed in the background of the transitional character of the country over the last eight years. This means that we cannot start our present study on the assumption that a stable planning process is already in existence in this country and then investigate the relative merits, or demerits of the system with focus on coordination. In analysing the process of coordination, we have to keep in mind the transitional character of the planning process itself.

The First, Second and Third Five-Year Plans of Pakistan (1955-70) were formulated under the direction of civil and military elites operating within a highly centralized political framework. People's participation in the determination of the objectives and strategies of these plans was minimum. A group of Harvard University economists was hired to assist in providing decision-makers with the necessary analytical rigour to their plans. The Harvard economists helped the Pakistani government in the formulation of their plans until 1970. The main characteristics of the five-year plans so formulated in Pakistan were: (a) greater emphasis on economic growth relative to improved distribution of income in favour of the poorer section of the community; (b) greater emphasis on development of import-replacing and export-promoting industries relative to agriculture; (c) greater resource allotment in favour of growth centres around a few big cities (like Karachi and Lahore); (d) acceptance of the private sector as the engine of growth and complementary public sector development; and (e) recognition of the need to reduce the heavy dependence on foreign assistance over a prospective twenty-year plan by increasing domestic savings and investment ratios during that period through increased productivity. By the end of the 1960s, it appeared that this pattern of growth was benefiting the relatively better-off sections of the society and, therefore, the system came under severe criticism.

After independence, the First Five-Year Plan was launched in July 1973. The main weaknesses of the plan were as follows:

1. The economists who prepared the plan were mostly Western-educated professionals. They spoke of socialism on an *ad hoc* basis without giving a

---

[4] The First Five-Year Plan of Bangladesh covered the period 1973 to 1978.

comprehensive framework for their ideas and beliefs. There was little or no participation in the plan from other social scientists — political theorists, sociologists, etc.

2. There was also a communication gap between the planners and the politicians. The planners claimed that most decisions about development were made within the party to the exclusion of the planners.[5]

3. In 1973, the planners assumed (a) that Bangladesh would remain a multi-party state as prescribed by the constitution, and precluded the emergence of a one-party state; and (b) that the political cadre would control and direct the bureaucracy from outside the administration. In 1975, the politicians changed the constitutions and opted for a one-party state, and control and direction of administration from within by the political cadre.

Such a change in the constitution was unacceptable to those who preferred a representative democracy. Further in 1975, the Government was changed through an uprising.

In addition, the plan itself was in trouble for the following reasons:

1. The oil price hike of 1973 disrupted the cost estimates of the plan.
2. In 1974, the country faced severe drought and floods leading to famine conditions, particularly in the Northern districts of Bangladesh.
3. The nationalized public sector enterprises could not improve their performance as expected[6] (most of these industries had to be subsidized).
4. The inflow of foreign assistance also fell short of expectation.

As a result of all these cumulative factors, the savings and investment assumptions of the planners proved to be wrong, and the prices of strategic inputs, essential goods and services rose rapidly.

The military government that came into power in 1975 thought that the answer to these policy questions should best be provided by the representative political leaders. Therefore, during 1976-78, a series of steps were taken for the restoration of democracy in the country. In 1977, elections were held for reviving local governmental institutions all over the country. This was followed by a general election in which a very large number of political parties participated. Simultaneously, it was decided that the formulation of the Second Five-Year Plan of Bangladesh should be postponed for two years in order to facilitate participation of the political government in the national plan. Accordingly, it was decided that a transitional Two-Year Plan and not the Second Five-Year Plan should be formulated in the intervening period (1978-80). The transitional Two-Year Plan emphasized a Gross Domestic Product growth rate of 5.6 per cent per year with

[5] Nurul Islam, *Development Planning in Bangladesh* (London: C. Hurst, 1977), pp. 47-52.

[6] There is also the opposite view that the performance of the public sector in Bangladesh has not been so bad. See Rehman Sobhan and Ahmed Muzaffar, *Public Enterprises in an Intermediate Regime: A Study of Political Economy of Bangladesh* (Dacca: Bangladesh Institute of Development Studies, 1980).

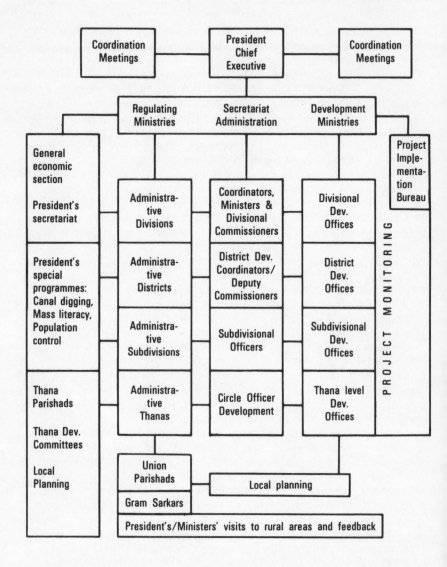

Figure 7-1. Linkage Structure of Administration and Planning in Bangladesh

simultaneous emphasis on food production, and reduction of population pressure. It took cognizance of the President's nineteen point programme developed during 1977-78. This programme was framed around the concept of basic needs-oriented planning to be implemented by mobilizing people at the grass roots.

MULTILEVEL PLANNING AND COORDINATION

Figure 7-1 shows the linkage structure of multilevel planning and administrative coordination in Bangladesh. At the apex of the administrative structure is the President, who is assisted in his function as Chief Executive by a Council of Ministers. The ministers are individually responsible to the President for the functioning of the ministries under them. These ministries are broadly divided into two groups: regulatory and developmental ones. Developmental ministries are mainly responsible for the preparation of sectoral development projects and for processing them with the Planning Commission, the Ministry of Finance and other related ministries. The Executive Committee of the National Economic Council examines the projects and the National Economic Council (NEC) grants them final approval. After approval from the highest level, these projects must receive a number of sanctions — administrative, financial and technical — from the respective ministries and agencies before their execution.

Development ministries like agriculture, water and power, resources development, industries, transport, and communication, have their own field agencies for the execution of these projects. The offices of these field agencies correspond to those of the administrative units. A division consists of four to five districts, a district consists of two to five subdivisions, and a subdivision consists of about ten Thanas. Below the Thanas, are the local government institutions of fifteen to twenty Union Parishads, each of which consists of ten to twenty villages. These villages are now being organized into Gram Sarkars.

Traditionally, the district is considered to be the main unit of administration and development at the field level in Bangladesh. The Divisional Commissioner acted mainly as an appellate with inspectorial authority in revenue and general administration. The District Officer, previously known as the District Magistrate and Collector and now known as the Deputy Commissioner, historically acted as the eyes, ears and hand of the Government within the district.[7] The main functions of the Deputy Commissioner are as follows:

1. The collection of revenue and administration of land laws. He exercises this function under the supervision of the Commissioner and the National Board of Revenue.
2. The maintenance of law and order. The Criminal Procedure Code empowers him to take preventive measures against any breach of law and order.

[7] A.M.A. Muhith, *The Deputy Commissioner in East Pakistan* (Dacca: National Institute of Public Administration, 1968), p. 9.

3. The administration of criminal justice. He has jurisdiction over a limited number of cases but he is magistrate over severe offences under specific sections of the Criminal Procedure Code.
4. The coordination of development work. He coordinates all development activities within his area, helps eliminate bottlenecks, supervises development project implementation and tenders general advice and guidance for the success of these projects.
5. The fostering of local government institutions and supervision of their work.
6. The administration of laws and regulations bearing on people's day-to-day life. This category represents miscellaneous functions such as licensing of arms, trades and motor vehicles, administration of flood and famine relief, inspection of factories and labour establishments, supply of essential consumer goods and rationing of food.[8]

From the description of the functions of the Deputy Commissioner, it may appear that his power is wide and pervasive. This, however, is far from the truth. The Deputy Commissioner's power in Bangladesh is strictly regulated by law and is rather limited in contrast to the responsibilities he is given. Even in British India, it was observed that the "lot of the District Officer like that of a comic opera policeman, is not a happy one. He is expected to see that nothing goes wrong in his district, but he has little power outside the Magistrate and Collector fields to see that things go right."[9] A Committee, therefore, recommended that the "existing District Officer become the Head of the Government in his District."[10]

In 1960, the Provincial Administration Reorganization Committee recommended that the following powers be given to the Commissioner and the Deputy Commissioner:

1. The power to solicit reports directly from any division/district level officer of their area.
2. The power to inspect all works and projects and to suggest to the Director concerned, measures for accelerating progress.
3. The power to inspect any office within the area and to suggest measures for improving its working in dealing with the public.
4. The power to call for tour diaries from heads of other offices.
5. The power to secure the services of officers from all departments for specific duties in cases of emergencies, i.e., floods, famines, etc.

---

[8] Ibid., p. 2.

[9] Rowland's Committee, *Report on District Administration* (Dacca: NIPA, 1962), p. 86.

[10] Ibid.

6. The power to grant casual leave to other department heads upon intimation of the Directorate heads concerned.[11]

There was also opposition to giving increasing powers to the Commissioners and the Deputy Commissioners.[12] First, the Commissioner and Deputy Commissioner posts were reserved for officers of general cadre services, while the heads of the development departments were technical people. The latter resented any increase in power of the former group over them. Second, the Commissioner's and Deputy Commissioner's paternalistic role was also resented by the people's representatives. They wanted all officials, including the Commissioners and the Deputy Commissioners, to be responsible, responsive and accountable to the people.

In spite of this opposition, certain factors helped to increase the Deputy Commissioner's coordinating role during the 1960s. These were:

1. The country was under martial law since 1958, and political parties were disbanded and later revived only to a limited extent.[13] This gave prominence to the Deputy Commissioner within the district.

2. A set of local government institutions was set up within the country under the authoritative control of the generalist administrator at the district and Thana levels.[14] The technical department officers concerned were made *ex officio* members of the development committees representing the local people and were headed by the generalist administrators — the Deputy Commissioner, the Subdivisional Officer at the district and the Thana levels.

3. In accordance with the recommendation of the First Five-Year Plan, the Deputy Commissioner was given an Additional Collector of Revenue to relieve him of some of his revenue collection responsibilities. A District Development Coordination Committee was created and the Deputy Commissioner also got an Additional Deputy Commissioner to assist him in the field of development administration.[15]

4. Under the Basic Democracies Order of 1959, the Union Council was made responsible for the preparation and execution of local development projects. Under the Second Five-Year Plan of 1960-65, the Government launched a Rural Works Programme[16] for constructing roads, irrigation, drainage channels, etc., with the help of funds available through the U.S.

---

[11] The Provincial Administration Reorganization Committee Report, 1960, quoted in Qauzi Azhar Ali, *District Administration in Bangladesh* (Dacca: NIPA, 1978), p. 45.

[12] Author's interview of selected technical officers and people's representatives.

[13] K.B. Sayeed, *The Political System of Pakistan*.

[14] Government of Pakistan, *Basic Democracies Ordinance*, 1959.

[15] Government of Pakistan, *The First Five-Year Plan of Pakistan* (Karachi, 1957), pp. 101-3.

[16] Government of Pakistan, *The Second Five-Year Plan of Pakistan* (Karachi, 1961).

Public Law 480. The Union Council prepared these programme projects and the Thana Council recommended them to the district authorities for approval. To assist in this process, the Circle Officer (Development) post was created at the Thana level in 1962. The Subdivisional Officers controlled the Thana Council[17] as representatives of the Deputy Commissioner. In his absence, the Circle Officer (Development) controlled the Thana Council. There used to be monthly meetings at the levels of union, Thana, subdivision and district to review progress, identify problems and devise solutions in implementing projects. In the 1960s, therefore, the Thana became an effective unit for local planning and development supported by the district and subdivisional administration.

However, the funds allotted for local planning and development remained small. These constituted only around 5 per cent of the total planned expenditure. The bulk of development funds was spent by the sectoral departments. Here again, there was significant improvement, but for different reasons. During the old Pakistan days, this region was given less money for investment on the basis that its absorptive capacity was low, in terms of both project formulation and implementation. The people of this region contested this accusation and maintained that development project preparation and implementation were not a problem if the central government would make sufficient money available. They could even show that in the 1960s, when some more money was actually available in contrast to the 1950s, performance in the project implementation field improved significantly. It is said that this was accomplished mainly through a process of improved informal coordination between the different development agencies.[18] The process of this improved informal coordination may be described as follows:

1. Prior to the 1960s, most senior officers in this region were non-Bengalis. After the 1960s, senior Bengali officers gradually started moving in to the decision-making positions at the provincial level. It is claimed this increased the commitment of the provincial administration to the development of this region.
2. Many development departments in those days were inadequately staffed and were not in a position to formulate viable projects. However, because of a higher degree of commitment to this region's development, the officers of development departments, the planning department and even the Ministry of Finance, cooperated among themselves in utilizing the available expertise to the maximum extent so that money available to this wing for development was not returned to the Central Government for alleged lack of absorptive capacity.

[17] The Subdivisional Officer was the Chairman and the Circle Officer (Development) was the Vice-Chairman of the Thana Council.

[18] Author's interview of a number of selected officers. The author also worked as Subdivisional Officer during 1961-62.

However, there were a number of difficulties in implementing projects in this region, such as:

1. The fiscal year started in July. It coincided (as it still does) with the onset of the rainy season (June-August) when construction work was hardly possible.
2. The central government did not release the allotted development funds at that time. Only one-fourth of the fund was available during the first quarter of the fiscal year and only an amount equivalent to the actual expenditure of the first quarter could be released during the second quarter. Similarly, only an amount equivalent to what was actually spent in the second quarter could be released in the third quarter. The remaining amount was released during the fourth quarter. Since very little could be spent during the first quarter due to heavy rains and to the time required after observations for various sanctioning procedures, only a small portion of the fund was made available to this region during the second and third quarters. On the other hand, there was a sudden availability of more funds during the fourth quarter. There was, therefore, a built-in danger for a significant amount of unspent money to be returned to the central government.[19]

To minimize the shortfall of development activities in this area on account of the above hazard, a number of informal mechanisms were devised, such as:

1. Instead of merely sending the files to the departments (administrative and finance) concerned, the officers from the project locations themselves would sometimes go to Dacca and get sanction through informal contacts.
2. At the project locations, the different officers cooperated voluntarily in such matters as site selection (this required agreement from the local Deputy Commissioner, the Civil Surgeon, the Superintendent of Police, etc.), the movement of strategic materials within the project site, and at times, even in the use of materials purchased with the money available for one project for the use of another project (for which adequate funding was not available on time), subject to later adjustment. The district administration rendered all possible help to the technical officers for final completion of the projects.[20]

As a result, the development performance of this area increased significantly during the 1960s. The development expenditure which was only around Tk320 million (Tk15 = US$1) in 1957, jumped to around Tk600 million during 1960, and to about Tk2,000 million per year in the late 1960s.[21]

[19] Department of Finance, *The Economic Survey of East Pakistan, 1962-63*. Also based on author's interview of a number of officers in the Ministry of Finance.

[20] Author's interview of a number of officers concerned.

[21] Department of Finance, *Economic Survey of East Pakistan, 1962-63* and *1968-69*.

After independence, it was expected that such informal coordination between the various officers would continue in the project implementation field, but a number of new factors emerged which made coordination more difficult at the multilevels. First, during the immediate post-independence period, civil administration was found shattered as a result of the aftermath of war. Many civil servants were stranded in Pakistan, many were in hiding, many junior officers and freedom fighters demanded government jobs and higher posts for having participated in the independence war. Second, the local members of parliament were made responsible for the distribution of relief goods, and they tended to become real administrators of their areas. Third, the technical department officials united more effectively in their demand for equal status with their generalist counterparts. Fourth, there was also widespread demand for equal pay and equal work status among other civil servants as well as for reduction of the gap between the highest and lowest pay ceilings. Finally, there was a demand for a change in the attitude of civil servants towards the people. It was believed that Bangladesh had become a democratic state replacing an administrative state and, therefore, the whole civil service had to be restructured before the problems of administrative coordination within the new perspective could be effectively handled.

The period 1972-79 was, thus, characterized by a number of steps taken by the Government to adjust its administration to the new situation. The constitution of Bangladesh provided that the parliament make laws regulating the appointment as well as the conditions of service.[22] An Administrative and Services Reorganization Committee was set up to examine the service structure and suggest appropriate reorganization of services.[23] A National Pay Commission was set up to examine the existing pay scales and suggest their rationalization. The recommendations of the Services Reorganization Committee and the National Pay Commission created some problems. Therefore, a new Pay and Service Commission was set up in 1975.[24]

As a result of the Committee and Commission recommendations, the service structure in Bangladesh has been reorganized into one unified service divided into fourteen functional groups (replacing a number of cadre services) and over 2,000 pay scales have been amalgamated into fewer scales.

The introduction of these reforms was time-consuming because it had to be accomplished through the democratic process. A series of representations were made to the government from the various services by government servants with respect to the position of their services, as well as by many individuals with respect to their fixed pay-scales. There were even cases lodged against the government in the courts of law. These had to be heard and dismissed. Although these steps were expected to create better coherence and performance within the

---

[22] *Report of the Services Reorganization Committee* (Dacca, 1973).

[23] Ministry of Finance, *Report on Introduction of National Scales of Pay* (Dacca, 1974).

[24] Ministry of Finance, *Report on Introduction of New National Grades and Scales of Pay* (Dacca, 1977).

Bangladesh civil service in the long-run, in the short-run these created a number of problems in the planning and administrative coordination field. For example, as a result of the pay scale revision, the salary of some departmental heads at the district level (and also at the subdivision and Thana levels), like the officers of the education, agriculture, health and livestock departments, increased relative to the generalist administrators. These officers were, therefore, no longer willing to accept the traditional coordinating role of the generalist administrators.[25]

The situation appeared somewhat confusing. On the one hand, there was a secular weakening of the traditional coordinating and leadership roles of the generalist administrators at the field level. On the other hand, the need for a coordinator at various field levels increased as the number of development agencies were augmented with more decentralization of power in their favour. It was, therefore, not surprising to find that in 1976, the Cabinet Division issued a circular reasserting the traditional leadership and coordinating roles of the Commissioners, Deputy Commissioners, Subdivisional Officers, and Circle Officers (Development).[26] These officers were empowered to supervise the activities of all the departments functioning within their respective jurisdictions, to call for reports with respect to any development project and to write performance evaluation reports on any officer functioning within their areas.

In spite of this circular, the Deputy Commissioner, the Subdivisional Officer and the Circle Officer (Development) continued to find it difficult to coordinate the development activities in their areas for the following reasons: First, the pay scales of some departmental officers remained above those of the generalist administrators and, therefore, these departmental officers were reluctant to attend coordinating meetings called by the Deputy Commissioner, Subdivisional Officer and the Circle Officer (Development). Second, at the Thana level, a Thana Development Committee was set up with chairmen from the various Union Parishads as members, chaired by one of them. This Committee was responsible for administering about 80 per cent of the total development funds that were made available at the Thana level. Of course, these projects processed by the Thana Development Committee had to be approved by the Thana Parishad, presided by the Subdivisional Officer with the Circle Officer (Development) as vice-chairman. Frequently, the members of the Thana Development Committee resented this control of the Thana Parishad over the Thana Development Committee. Also, when the Subdivisional Officer was absent during Thana Parishad meetings, it was difficult for the Circle Officer (Development) to provide leadership, given his diminished status. Third, the Circle Officer (Development) was not only vice-chairman of the Thana Parishad, he was also chairman of a number of other development committees, such as the Thana Agricultural Development Committee, the Thana Seed Committee, the Thana Irrigation Programme Committee, the Thana Deep Tube-Well Site Selection Committee and the Thana Project Implementation Committee; but for reasons explained above, the frequency of these meetings also lessened.

[25] Author's interview of selected technical officers.

[26] Cabinet Division, Circular No. CD/DA/73-170(1000), dated 27 February 1976.

During 1979-80, the Government turned its attention to the problem of organizing the people at the village level besides trying to improve the existing level of coordination in development programmes. The Ministry of Local Government, Rural Development and Cooperatives had already provided, under Section 86 of the LGRD Ordinance of 1976, the scope of such village organizations. On 30 April 1980, the President of Bangladesh declared that Swanirvar Gram Sarkar would be organized in all the 68,000 villages of Bangladesh by December 1980.

Simultaneously, the Government tried to change the attitude of civil servants so that they might work with the people as their partners in development. A pioneering venture in this field is the "Own Village Development Programme" of the Cabinet Division (executed in cooperation with the National Institute of Public Administration).[27] Under this programme, mid-level officers were given the option to work in their own villages at government expense. Since these officers go as volunteers and social workers, they have to work with the people and help them set up their own organizations for development work. The programme started on 24 February 1977. By now, over 800 officers have participated in this programme.

Furthermore, during 1979-80, the President of Bangladesh launched some special programmes, like canal digging, mass education, family planning and population control, to be implemented on the basis of mass mobilization.[28] The President considered these programmes so important that he termed them "revolutions" and asked all agencies at the multilevels to coordinate their activities toward that purpose.

One significant by-product of these programmes was the reinforcement of the district administrators' coordinating roles, as these executives — Deputy Commissioners, Subdivisional Officers, and Circle Officers (Development) — had to play a crucial part in organizing the masses and officials into work teams, and they were ultimately responsible to the President for the successful completion of the programmes.[29]

As far as the role of coordinator at the regional and subregional level is concerned, Bangladesh seems to be moving rather carefully for the time being, and has opted for a compromise solution. Since April 1980, Members of Parliament have been appointed as District Coordinators within each of the twenty districts.[30] However, they have not been given the coordinating function for all development activities within the districts. For the time being, at least their coordinating role remains primarily limited in five main areas: (a) Agriculture,

---

[27] Shaikh Maqsood Ali, "Public Servants as Change Agents, an experiment with OVD Programme," *Administrative Science Review* 9 (March, 1979): 1-24.

[28] These programmes are being coordinated through the General Economic Section in the President's Secretariat.

[29] Author's interview of selected district officers.

[30] Resolution No. ED/SA IV-51/80-112.

(b) Education (adult literacy), (c) Family Planning and Population Control, (d) Livestock, and (e) Fisheries. They have been given the status of Deputy Ministers so that they may have direct access to the ministers in charge of these sectors and, thus, bring problems identified in the field for immediate attention at the highest level. In other fields, the Deputy Commissioner performs coordinating functions. It is expected that the Deputy Commissioners and the District Development Coordinators will understand each others' roles and cooperate in the interest of improved performance at multilevel development activities.

In order to encourage local participation for development programme formulation and implementation, several Development Boards were constituted: one in each division (Dacca, Chittagong, Rajshahi and Khulna), and three in less developed areas (known as Chittagong Hill Tracts Development Board, Offshore Island Development Board and Hoar Development Board).[31] The functions of these Boards were: (a) preparation of projects for regional development; (b) approval of projects up to Tk1 million (Tk15 = US$1; for Hoar development the limit is Tk0.25 million); and (c) execution of approved projects.[32] Formerly, Divisional Commissioners were the heads of the Divisional Development Board. Now these have been reconstituted, with Ministers from that area as chairmen of the Boards.

It is expected that these Development Boards will attain greater importance in the future and that the Divisional Commissioner will assume a more developmental than appellate-*cum*-inspectorial role. Simultaneously, the districts and Thanas will be effective planning and implementation units respectively, and planning at these multilevels have to be integrated with the national plan. It is also noted that the people's representatives (ministers belonging to the area) have already taken over the coordinating function of the Development Boards. As the government functionary, the Divisional Commissioner renders him all possible assistance. At the district level, the people's representatives (District Development Coordinators) have assumed coordinating functions in specific areas. In other areas, the Deputy Commissioner still remains the coordinator, but he works in cooperation with the District Development Coordinators. At the Thana level, there are indications that the coordinating function may eventually be handed over to the people's representative. Already the Thana Development Committee, controlled by the elected chairmen of the Union Parishads, is playing a crucial role in processing area development projects. The critical question in the field of regional development planning and coordination in Bangladesh is how these multilevel planning efforts may be further consolidated and integrated. Two types of efforts are being made in this direction: (a) at the national level, the Second Plan proposed some institutional and procedural improvements, such as the setting up of the Policy Planning Council and the Policy Coordination Committee, and the preparation of annual development programmes for two

---

[31] Planning Commission, *Two-Year Plan 1978-80*.

[32] Ibid.

years, etc.; and (b) at the microlevel, attempts are being made to organize the people into viable organization of their own *(Gram Sarkar)* and to integrate these with the Union Parishads and the Thana administration with a built-in coordination process in the system.

DEVELOPMENT PLANNING AND COORDINATION AT THE GRASS ROOTS: ORGANIZATION OF GRAM SARKAR

As was pointed out, Bangladesh inherited a top-down planning process at the time of independence. By the late 1950s, the main defect of this system had become clear: the growth process benefited the relatively well-to-do more than the poor and disadvantaged. There was, therefore, widespread demand for a more balanced growth process. However, it was not known to the planners how this could be achieved in the context of the then prevailing reality of the situation. It goes to the credit of Akhtar Hamid Khan, a former member of the British-India civil service (who had resigned from his job), to have successfully highlighted the main problems of rural development, and to have developed a mechanism for trying to solve at least some of these problems. According to him the main problems of planning and development in this country could be identified as the shortage of food, unemployment, and the alienation between the different groups of people. The solutions to these problems could be found in the progressive development of agriculture, increased employment, and popular participation.[33]

Khan believed that the real constraint to agricultural development was not people's ignorance, but the absence of an administrative infrastructure and an economic infrastructure in rural areas. In order to find out how these infrastructures could be built in Bangladesh, he studied models of rural development in India, Japan, Taiwan and China. He devised what came to be known as the "Comilla approach" in Comilla Kotwali Thana of the present Bangladesh. Under this approach, (a) a two-tier cooperative system (with a village cooperative federated at the Thana level) was organized and a Thana Training and Development Centre (TTDC) was built within the Thana as the administrative infrastructure for rural Bangladesh; and (b) a network of water works programmes, such as the building of small dams, and irrigation and drainage channels, were initiated through the local cooperatives. It was believed that the above would lead to capital accumulation and prepare the ground for intensive agricultural development.

However, the programme had to work under a number of structural bottlenecks. These were: First, the existing economic development fostered by central planners was urban based. In this system, rural areas were to finance urban development through (i) adverse terms of trade against agricultural products

---

[33] Akhtar Hamid Khan's lecture at the National Institute of Public Administration, 1979. Also see: Akhtar Hamid Khan, "Framework for Rural Development in Bangladesh and a Plan for 250 Cooperatively Organized Thanas" (Bogra, 1979).

relative to manufacturing output; and (ii) movement of cheap labour from rural to urban areas on account of increased pauperization of the rural poor. Second, the administrative structure was paternalistic and centralized. It served mainly the interests of organized groups within urban areas. Third, the political system itself was unrepresentative, and as such, was not responsive to rural needs and not accountable to the people.[34]

Under the dynamic leadership of Akhtar Hamid Khan, the Comilla approach made substantial progress in the field of rural development in spite of the above constraints. Therefore, immediately after the independence of Bangladesh, the Government launched an Integrated Rural Development Programme (IRDP) for the entire country based mainly on a modified version of the Comilla approach. However, the IRDP programme faced difficulties from the beginning due to structural constraints. The Planning Commission Evaluation Report on IRDP pointed out that:

> . . . the cooperative societies have turned into closed clubs of the *kulaks*. In particular, a village cooperative covers about one-fourth of the total farmers in the village. Membership is dominated by large and medium farmers and the small farmers are grossly under-represented. Leadership in the societies is also dominated by large farmers; medium farmers have some representation, but the small farmers are entirely unrepresented in the leadership. These leaders enjoy a greater share of benefits but their participation, as measured by contribution of shares, capital and savings, is relatively low. The leaders mostly fail to uphold the basic disciplines of the cooperative section.[35]

During 1974-79, various attempts were made to increase the coverage of the IRDP cooperatives in the village and to ensure representation of the small and landless farmers and other disadvantaged groups. From September 1975, a *Swanirvar* (self-reliance) movement was also launched to mobilize the people into viable rural organizations for local planning and development.

As a concept, *Swanirvar* (self-reliance) movements have a long history in this country.[36] The cooperative movement in this area started in 1904, but a systematic approach to *Swanirvar* movements is claimed to have started only since September 1975, when an effort was made to consolidate *ad hoc* and sporadic types of local responses made in different districts to face the post-flood situation of 1974. To impart flexibility into this programme, it was kept outside the normal government machinery and people and officers were asked to work cooperatively on their own. As a result, district administration undertook a number of mass mobilization programmes including small irrigation and drainage projects. It was

---

[34] Author's discussion with Akhtar Hamid Khan, 1980.

[35] Planning Commission, "Evaluation Report on IRDP" (Dacca, 1974).

[36] Shaikh Maqsood Ali, "Self-Reliance (Swanirvar) Movement in the 1980s — the Social Workers as Change Agents," *Administrative Science Review*, 9 (June, 1979): 77-108.

soon felt that the enthusiasm which might be generated from such programmes should be institutionalized. It was observed that there was no viable institution for people's participation in administration at the village level. The lowest tier of existing local government institutions, the Union Parishad, consisted of ten to fifteen villages. There was, therefore, the need to extend the existing local government institutions down to the village level. It was also felt that the village was not a homogeneous unit. People within a village were divided into different interest and functional groups. Hence, it was not always possible to organize all the villagers into one cooperative.

In fact, the functions of the Union Parishad or Village Parishad could be divided into two broad categories: the civic functions that should be the main responsibility of the central village organization, and the economic activities that should be handled by the various interest groups organized into different functional cooperatives, such as cooperatives for weavers, fishermen, and women. After prolonged discussion, the Gram Sarkar format finally emerged. On 30 April 1980, the President declared in a village named Zirbau at Savar in the district of Dacca, that all the 68,000 villages of Bangladesh should be organized into Gram Sarkars.[37] The task of accomplishing this was given to the Ministry of Local Government, Rural Development and Cooperatives. The Ministry claimed that the provision for organizing the Gram Sarkar was already made in the Union Parishad Ordinance. Therefore, they could make detailed rules for the organization of the Gram Sarkar under this Ordinance.

To a considerable extent, the macro-framework of Gram Sarkar, as well as the exact number and forms of interest group organizations to be formed in the village, has been kept flexible.[38] It is hoped that local situations will determine these details in the short-run. Over a period of time, a more concrete shape will gradually emerge. Within this constraint, a new kind of coordination mechanism for local development and planning is gradually emerging, because activities, such as canal digging and mass literacy at the village level, are also part of the President's mass mobilization programme. As such, these are linked with programmes at the district level through normal district administration, as well as through the District Development Coordinators. But Gram Sarkar has its own format for linking its development activities through the Union Parishad with the Thana administration. This linkage is evolving and varies from place to place according to local conditions, but by and large, the format of this development coordination may be described as follows:

1. When the Gram Sarkar has been formed within a village, it has a *Gram Pradhan* (head) and eleven members. These members represent various interest-*cum*-functional groups, such as farmers, weavers, fishermen, youths, and women. These members are also responsible for various port-

---

37 *The Dainik Bangla,* 1st May, 1980.

38 Shaikh Maqsood Ali, "The Sense and Sensibility of Gram Sarkar," *Administrative Science Review* 4 (December, 1979).

folios of development: agriculture, education, health, family planning, and social welfare. The different interest groups bring their problems to these respective members who, after due consultation and investigation, prepare projects for these interest-*cum*-functional groups and integrate these into a village development plan.

2. In order to be effective, the various interest and functional groups are organized into their own cooperatives so that they may produce viable projects for inclusion in the village plan.

3. The village plan may have three components — those projects which would be financed through local resources; those projects which cover more than one village and for which cooperation and resources may have to be mobilized at the Union Parishad level (like intervillage road construction and repairs); and those projects for which cooperation and resources have to be mobilized at Thana and higher levels (like tube-wells, power pumps, fertilizers, and insecticides).

4. The Union Parishad may collect village plans from all villages concerned and integrate these into a union plan. They may then arrange a date for discussion of this plan (and also the village plans) with the Thana officers concerned on a particular day of the month. Preferably, the Thana officers should all come together at a Union on a particular date to discuss the plans. This would give Union Parishad and Gram Sarkar members an idea of the extent of support that is likely to be available from the Thana administration for implementation of the village and the Union plans as well as allow introduction of necessary adjustments to these plans.

5. If a Thana has about fifteen Union Parishads under it, Thana officers may have to attend these Unions fifteen days a month (one day at each Union). For the remaining fifteen days of the month, they may stay at the Thana headquarters so that the villagers may contact them when necessary for technical input and assistance.[39]

This format is still flexible. In some places, Union Parishad members and village heads meet Thana officials at Thana headquarters. By now, Thana Training and Development Centres (TTDC) are available in most places for such meetings, discussions and coordination. However, when Thana officers are motivated, they also go to the Union Parishad offices and even to Gram Sarkar headquarters for such development coordination activities.

It is sometimes said that in spite of the Gram Sarkar format and the linkage model that is emerging within the Union Parishads and Thana administration, this system will not be able to work satisfactorily because of the existing power structure in rural areas. The ownership pattern of land in Bangladesh still remains highly skewed in favour of the rich farmers in spite of the Estate Acquisition and Tenancy Act of 1951, by which all intermediary rent receiving interests were

---

[39] Author's interviews with a number of Gram Pradhans (village headmen).

acquired by the State. At present, the top 10 per cent of the households in Bangladesh own about 46 per cent of all cultivable land, while the bottom 54 per cent of the households own only about 9 per cent of the land.[40] A large number of cultivators are, therefore, either landless or small farmers. They have to cultivate the land of the big farmers or absentee landowners on a sharecropping basis, under which they have to surrender about 50 per cent of their produce to the landowners even though the latter have not contributed any inputs for cultivating the land. This situation brings the landless and the poor under the control of the relatively better-off and, therefore, it is sometimes said that so long as this dependency situation continues, it would not be possible to organize the people in interest and functional cooperatives of their own. Even under the Gram Sarkar format, ultimately these organizations would also be dominated by the rural elites, as shown in the case of the Comilla and the IRDP cooperative.

The answer to this question may be as follows:

1. It is claimed that in some villages, the relatively well-to-do people gained Gram Sarker leadership in the beginning, but the leadership is gradually passing to the comparatively younger and active leaders because the system demands many development projects and activities which the traditional leaders are not in a position to deliver. Therefore, given some time, the Gram Sarkar format should be able to bring better leadership in the field of development activities.

2. The Government is actively considering the question of land reform, but in Bangladesh available land in relation to total population is so scarce [if the land is equally distributed, each man is only likely to get less than half of an acre (1 acre = 0.4 hectare)] that one must take caution in this field. The Government has already circulated an agrarian reform paper to the members of various political parties for consensus on this question.[41] The paper covers issues, such as landholdings, economic size of holdings, sharecropping system regulations, distribution of land to landless peasants, collection of land taxes, prevention of landholding fragmentation, unauthorized occupation of government land and elimination of middlemen in land use. It is hoped that some progressive legislations will be introduced soon.

3. There is a big programme to open at least one bank branch for every 300 families in rural areas. It is hoped that it should be possible to inject credit of about Tk3,000 million in rural areas through these banks. It is also hoped that about Tk2,000 to Tk2,500 million might be collected from the rural areas through the encouragement of small savings schemes. In order to ensure this mobilization of savings and the outflow of credit to the poor and needy, some banks like the Sonali Bank is training rural bank

---

[40] Bureau of Statistics, *Statistical Pocket Book of Bangladesh* (Dacca, 1979), p. 203.

[41] Government and opposition leaders discuss agrarian reforms. See *Bangladesh Times*, 10 Sept. 1980.

managers in total village development programme so that they may help organize the poor and advance loans for projects that would benefit them directly.[42]

4. Under the Swanirvar Gram Sarkar training programmes, there are special training courses for organizing the poor and the disadvantaged, and for preparing projects exclusively for them. It appears that where poor people have been organized, they did fairly well in mobilizing their own savings, in taking credit from the banks and in investing the money in viable projects. The recovery rate of these loans has been high and satisfactory. This, in turn, is encouraging commercial banks to go ahead with their rural credit schemes.[43]

5. Where the poor villagers have been organized, literacy rates have increased rapidly under them through adult literacy programmes and non-formal education. This has, in turn, reinforced their desire to organize.

6. Bangladesh villages have a significant number of educated youths today. It has been found that where these youths have been organized into their own organizations, they have also taken up the cases of the landless and the poor. These youths are organizing night schools, helping the poor to get loans and providing other inputs, helping them invest their labour and money in such economically viable projects as fish cultivation by re-excavating derelict ponds.

Thus, the Bangladesh village is changing in spite of the existing power structure. The Gram Sarkar format, the President's mass mobilization programme, the Divisional Development Boards, organization of Unions and villages into planning units, the posting of District Development Coordinators with the status of deputy ministers, as a link between the people and the sectoral ministries, and continuous efforts towards changing government servants into catalytic agents of change, are all helping in this process. The process may be accelerated through some structural changes in the near future (such as the Government's agrarian reform proposals). In this matrix, development coordination at multilevels has become crucial for this country. The Ministry of Planning has already identified a number of weaknesses in this coordination process. The traditional coordination mechanism with the Deputy Commissioner as the kingpin in the district has somewhat weakened, but its place is being slowly taken up by a new kind of consciousness and compulsion arising out of the people's active participation in the development process itself.

---

[42] M.M. Shahjahan, "Involvement of the Banking Sector in Rural Development in Bangladesh," *Bank Parikrama* (June 1980): 73-88.

[43] Ibid.

8

INSTITUTIONAL MACHINERY, COORDINATION AND DEVELOPMENT PERFORMANCE IN INDIA

T.N. CHATURVEDI

INTRODUCTION

THIS PAPER attempts to assess the institutional capability of India to perform the stated developmental tasks. The first section provides a brief assessment of India's development performance in general and regional development performance in particular. The second section deals with the actual functioning of the system, that is, the methods and procedures adopted for planning, budgeting and implementing developmental programmes. The third section describes the organization and functions of key coordinating agencies at the national level, pertinent to developmental planning and implementation processes, including monitoring and evaluation activities. The last section analyses the contribution of the institutional machinery in terms of its intra and interorganizational coordination performance.

The goals of India's development policy have been achieved with varying degrees of success. In agriculture, the methods of production have been modernized leading to commercialization of agriculture and increases both in production and productivity per hectare for some crops. The country has since attained self-sufficiency in foodgrains and has been able to build up considerable buffer stocks also. In the field of industry, there has been substantial increase in industrial capacity, especially in the production of capital goods. Infrastructure facilities in the areas of irrigation, transport, education, health, etc., also have increased to a considerable extent.

However, a close analysis of India's development performance over the past twenty-five years or so, reveals that the rate of economic growth has not always come up to the visualized expectations. While growth rates of about 5 per cent per annum were sought during the Five-Year Plans,[1] actual performance was uneven and lower than expected. Per capita income rate increases have also been very

---

[1] The Draft Sixth Plan (1978-83) envisages a growth rate of 4.7 per cent per annum.

slow. Looking at the twenty-four year period from 1954-55 to 1978-79, for example, per capita income at 1970-71 prices, increased by 42 per cent (from Rs500.7 to Rs712), compared to a 136 per cent increase in national income for the same period. Thus, the growth rate achieved on the economic front, has to a large extent been neutralized by an increase of about 2.4 per cent in the annual population growth rate.

The decline in the overall industrial output growth rate since the mid-sixties further widened the gap between the targets set in the Five-Year Plans and the actual achievement recorded for this sector. During the first, second and third Five-Year Plans, targeted growth rates for large-scale manufacturing were approximately 7, 10.5 and 10.25 per cent per annum, respectively, while the actual rates realized were around 6, 7.25 and 8 per cent for the corresponding Five-Year Plan periods.

With regards to the agricultural sector, the Economic Survey of 1976-77 states that:

> Despite the record level of production in 1975-76 the growth rate of agricultural production during the seventies so far has been lower as compared to the growth rate achieved during the sixties. This deceleration has occurred both in the rate of growth of acreage as well as yield. . . . Also the production of pulses continues to show a stagnant trend.[2]

Statewise indicators of development regarding the per capita net domestic product at current prices for 1976-77 show that only six states had per capita incomes higher than the national average of Rs1,080, namely, Gujarat (Rs1,341), Haryana (Rs1,472), Himachal Pradesh (Rs1,165. 1975-76 figure), Maharashtra (Rs1,489), Punjab (Rs1,812) and West Bengal (Rs1,143). Out of these states, Haryana, Punjab and Himachal Pradesh experienced considerable increases in the percentage of irrigated land area and higher agricultural production and productivity, whereas Gujarat, Maharashtra and West Bengal are industrially developed states.

The development of infrastructures in the different regions has also been varied. The leading agricultural and industrial states have higher literacy rates and better educational facilities than the backward regions. But even backward states fare well with regards to literacy, health facilities, roads, electricity and postal facilities, when compared with infrastructural development levels of the fifties. Considerable room for further development in matters of literacy, health and communication facilities still remains throughout these regions.

[2] Government of India, *Economic Survey 1976-77*, pp. 5-6.

PLANNING, BUDGETING AND IMPLEMENTATION PROCESS

The responsibility for the formulation and implementation of plans rests with various agencies in the context of the federal system and parliamentary form of government. The Planning Commission is primarily responsible for the formulation of the national plan, determination of priorities, allocation of resources therein, and the eventual phasing out of their involvement in operations. The Planning Commission, however, has no executive responsibility. It is only an advisory body which nonetheless exercises pervasive influence within the economic and social fields of development. The execution of development plan policies and programmes rests with the central ministries, state governments, local bodies and special agencies created for specific programmes and public sector undertakings. The right of adoption of proposed national plans lies with the Union Parliament, while that of state plans with the State Legislative Assemblies.

Planning Process: National Level

The first step in formulating a Five-Year Plan (the responsibility of the Planning Commission) is the preparation of an *approach document*. Initiated about three years prior to its final formulation, approach documents are prepared in consultation with the Union Cabinet. Preparations include an examination of the state of the economy, identification of social, economic and institutional weaknesses and an appraisal of economic growth rate trends. The approach document containing preliminary conclusions is then submitted to the Union Cabinet and National Development Council (NDC) for discussion. After reviewing the approach document, the cabinet and NDC suggest the growth rate to be achieved during the plan and designate objectives needing special emphasis.

A *Draft Memorandum* of the plan's physical contents is prepared during the second stage of medium-term planning. For this purpose, the Planning Commission undertakes broad studies in various sectors. These studies are conducted by working groups of specialists from the Commission itself and from the Union ministries concerned.[3] The working groups review the performance of the economy in their respective fields, assess the progress made towards achieving policy objectives as outlined in current and earlier plans and identify lacunae. The Commission also creates panels to advise on broad aspects of policy and implementation approaches to be followed in the sectoral plans. While the working groups are mostly composed of government officials, advisory panels include non-government experts. On the basis of studies conducted by these working groups and the advice of the panels, the Commission's Draft Memorandum emphasizes the specific features of the plan and its principal dimensions. Major issues requiring consideration at the highest policy level are raised, and shortcomings of earlier plans are taken into account as well.

---

[3] It is to be noted that the organization of the Planning Commission follows the functional government pattern of India.

After consideration by the Cabinet, the Draft Memorandum is submitted to the NDC for comments.[4] The details of the draft plan are worked out by the Commission, taking into account the comments and proposals of the NDC.[5] The document details the programme content envisioned for different sectors and spells out the main policy issues. It is circulated and discussed at various levels, namely, the central ministries, state governments, and organized interest groups such as chambers of commerce, industry, etc. After having circulated it to the central ministries and state governments, the document is finalized, submitted to the NDC for approval and published for public discussion.

Neither the perspective plan and the approach document, nor the initial Draft Memorandum are submitted to the Parliament. The Parliament only becomes involved with the development plan, once the draft has been published for public discussion. After general discussion for about two days in the House, the draft plan is discussed in detail by the various Parliamentary committees constituted for this purpose.[6]

While the draft plan is under public discussion, the commission and the union ministries concerned hold detailed joint discussions of individual state plans at the expert, administrative and political levels. Their objective is to examine the states' financial projections, prospects for raising additional resources and their outlays to various sectors. A final round of consultations with the chief ministers of states is held by the commission regarding the size and composition of their plans, the main priorities, targets and programmes to be implemented, and the specific obligations of the centre to provide financial assistance. Taking into account the broad agreements reached and the suggestions and comments from various other sources, a *revised memorandum* is submitted by the Commission to the Union Cabinet and the NDC. It details the main features of the plan, policy directions to be stressed and issues which may require further consideration. The conclusions reached by the NDC form the basis for drawing up the *final draft plan* which again is commented upon by the union ministries and state governments. After gaining cabinet and NDC approval, the *plan document* is placed before Parliament for adoption.[7]

[4] The NDC uses the committee system in considering the general approaches and policies connected with the plan. In 1954, the NDC constituted a standing committee from among its membership for this purpose. Since this committee has not been able to meet since 1963, the Council appoints *ad hoc* committees to report the details of certain specific matters such as price controls, savings, land reforms, etc., in order to arrive at informed decisions.

[5] The deputy chairman of the Commission confers with the main political shades of opinions represented in Parliament on some of the major issues in this process.

[6] A more detailed account of the nature of the discussion in the House is provided by V.D. Divekar, *Planning Process in Indian Polity* (Bombay: Popular Prakashan, 1978), pp. 51-103.

[7] There is no separate enactment giving statutory authority to the Five-Year Plan. It is only indirectly that the plan receives statutory sanction from the Parliament in the form of financing and bill appropriation made by the Government.

Planning at the State Level

Generally, the states start developing their Five-Year Plans after being told of national priorities, the tentative size of the national and state plans and other guidelines by the Planning Commission. If no definite indication is received, it is assumed that the previous level of central assistance will be maintained. The Planning Department determines the tentative size of the plan, after having worked out the internal resource potential in consultation with the Finance Department. It also works out the broad sectoral allocation according to the Commission's guidelines and the pattern of allocation and actual expenditure incurred during the previous plan period. These are communicated, in turn, to other state departments along with the Planning Department's own and the Planning Commission's guidelines. Working groups for each development sector or subsector are then set up. There is continuous dialogue at various administrative and political levels about plan priorities, special state problems, the quantum of resources to be raised, central assistance, etc. The working group on financial resources is also able to work out and determine during this time the states' quantum of resources and gain a firmer idea of resources available through central assistance. The overall size of the state plan and sectoral allocations are decided by the secretaries of finance and planning on the basis of these two criteria. Time permitting, these are communicated to the departments concerned. Otherwise, the sectoral outlays are adjusted when the sectoral plans are scrutinized by the Planning Department.

Working group reports are first approved by the government secretary concerned, who usually happens to be the group chairman, and the minister concerned. The chairman has the power to coopt any member to the group so as to have a meaningful discussion on programmes and proposals involving more than one department. Working group reports are then sent to the Planning Department for examination and scrutiny. Scrutiny is made of the size of the sectoral plan, its priorities, whether the programmes are spelt out in detail with target indications, etc., internal and intersectoral consistency, feasibility and any other special problems. In light of these comments, the planning secretary holds discussions with the department concerned and requests submission of revised proposals. Rulings of the planning minister are generally considered final in cases of disputes between departments. In a few instances, however, disputed cases have been carried to the chief minister. The plan proposals are placed before the state planning committee/board. According to their suggestions, proposals are consolidated sectorwise to the format suggested by the Planning Commission.

Budgeting

The Centre's annual budgetary process begins by about October every year when the Ministry of Finance requests the administrative ministries to submit revised annual estimates as well as budgetary estimates for the following year. In light of the previous planning exercise, the ministries arrive at the schemes to be included in the coming budget and work out their details. The expenditure is included in the budget under the head "plan outlay."[8]

After thoroughly scrutinizing individual schemes, the Plan Finance Division of the Ministry of Finance's Department of Expenditure includes them in requesting grants from the appropriate ministry which will be submitted later for Parliamentary approval. Once the budget has been approved by Parliament, the administrative ministries enjoy full sanctioning powers over expenditures on those items which have been closely scrutinized and accepted for incorporation in the budget by the Ministry of Finance. Administrative ministries for various reasons, however, do not find it practical to have the detailed scrutiny by the Finance Ministry into expenditure proposals completed during the pre-budgetary stage. Completion of pre-budgetary scrutiny is often delayed due to the additional details requested by the Finance Ministry which ministries complain are sometimes unnecessary. Pre-budgetary scrutiny streamlining continues to be a problem in the rationalization of budgetary and financial control procedures. This also affects the speedy introduction of the performance budget.

Both the physical and financial aspects must be provided in the budget and accounts formats for purposes of monitoring, control and review of programme/scheme progress and expenditure. Up till 1974, the Indian Government based its budget on organizational lines and objects of expenditure. It was, therefore, difficult to evaluate budgetary operations as well as fund allocation efficiency. These bases for the accounting format did not provide the information necessary for planning and budgetary decision-making. Upon recommendations of the Parliamentary Estimates Committee and the Administrative Reforms Commission, the Indian Government has been gradually introducing performance budgeting in all development departments.

As a first step, the budgetary and accounting formats have been revised in terms of programme/project activities and made consistent with the plan development heads so that there is a link between budget and plan. The present programme classification combines both economic and functional aspects. Secondly, maintenance of accounts, which traditionally had been under the auditor, is now under the control of the administrative ministries. It is, therefore, the responsibility of the departments concerned to keep their departmental accounts. Thirdly, a system of internal financial advisers has been introduced to enable the ministries to obtain financial advice from within their own organizations rather than from the Ministry of Finance.[9] The ambit of delegations has widened

---

[8] This is not synonymous with either investment expenditure or government's developmental outlay, as some non-plan expenditure also comes under the category of development expenditure. The nomenclature "plan expenditure" has very limited connotation in the Indian context. It means only the financial provision made in the annual budget towards schemes included in the annual plan. It is in fact difficult, if not impossible, to arrive at the total developmental expenditure figure incurred by the Government during any one particular year.

[9] Government of India, Ministry of Finance, Department of Expenditure, Office Memorandum on "Scheme of Integrated Financial Advisers" (New Delhi, 6 October 1975).

and they have complete authority within their respective fields.[10] The Ministry of Finance is concerned with pre-budget scrutiny, test checks and examination of accounting, other financial management procedures and information system management within the ministries.

District Planning

Some occasional planning has been attempted at the district level with the primary purpose of meeting certain limited objectives. The Intensive Agricultural District Programme (IADP) for instance, envisaged a time plan for the development of agricultural potential in selected districts. Planning for this was at the village level through preparation of individual farm plans with the assistance of the extension agency. Agricultural development planning at the district and block levels was done by the bureaucratic machinery as well. Despite the lack of comprehensive planning as such, the process helped establish certain linkages between extension, supplies, credit and marketing agencies, etc., and focus on the validity of district production plans.

These intensive agricultural development programmes also pointed out the inequities in public service utilization and "benefits accrued" by various classes. In an attempt to correct these inequities, entities such as the Small Farmers' Development Agencies (SFDA), the Drought Prone Areas Programmes (DPAP), etc., were created and corporate bodies have been given charge of programme implementation.

In 1969, the Planning Commission prepared certain guidelines for formulating district plans, in recognition of the need to examine specific problems, needs and aspirations of districts and blocks. Districts are the lowest territorial units where responsible department officers work out schemes and implement them on the basis of targets and schedules. The guidelines, therefore, assume that districts are closer to the people and better able to take into account local needs and resources. The district level is also considered most convenient for ensuring activity coordination and the bringing to bear local knowledge and experience on the choice of schemes. To ensure that the various conditions within a district are taken into account, it was suggested that the district be divided into subregions based on physiogeographical conditions and agricultural and industrial development patterns. A uniform format was not prescribed but a possible format was suggested due to the considerable variety found in district level planning and implementation machinery within different states, as well as variations in local institutional, self-government set up, i.e., Panchayati Raj.

Variation in the planning roles envisaged for Zilla Parishads (district level) in the Panchayati Raj Acts is considerable. The roles vary from block plan coordination and consolidation and preparation of entire district plans to those of plan, project, and scheme formulation advice common to two or more Panchayat Samities (block level).

---

[10] This extended power of delegation authorizes ministries to redelegate their powers to subordinate authorities except in such instances as creating posts, writing off losses, etc.

In December 1979, the Planning Commission issued guidelines on block level planning in accordance with the Dantwala working group's recommendations and other available sources of information on the subject. The guidelines delineate the scope and content of block level planning and the tasks and functions to be undertaken at that level. They also provide advice for strengthening administrative ties between block and district levels for carrying out block level planning. It has been suggested that benchmark surveys may be carried out in order to facilitate further progress evaluations, help generate information and identify existing gaps. Resource inventory is also essential for identifying potentialities which could best be exploited at the block level. States may consider earmarking about 10 per cent of the state plan budget for block plan outlays on the basis of population distribution among blocks. The other financial resources, including grants for centrally sponsored schemes and institutional credit, should also be taken into account in preparing block plans. The Planning Commission has asked the state governments and union territory administrations to react to these guidelines and to intimate the action taken upon these suggestions.

Implementation and Monitoring

Once plan programmes and schemes are formulated and funding provisions made for them in the annual budgets of the organizations concerned, implementation responsibility rests with the administering agencies. Union and state government field agencies draw detailed activities and time schedules for each programme and obtain technical and administrative sanction from their respective directorates and head offices.

In order to monitor the progress of development programmes and projects countrywide, a Monitoring Division was set up by the Planning Commission in the seventies.[11] The objective is to enable the Planning Commission and the Central Government to find out the shortfalls in implementation so that corrective action may be taken at the time of mid-term appraisal of the plan or even earlier. Even though the Division has responsibility of monitoring the progress of all sectoral plans, it has been doing so only for a limited number of sectors in view of its limited number of technical personnel. Monitoring reports are prepared on a sectoral basis, that is, including both Central and State Government's programmes and projects with respect to power, minor irrigation, agriculture and small-scale industries. Monitoring, however, is based on reports received by the administrative agencies at central and state levels. Financial monitoring is carried out, except in cases of construction projects which involve substantial expenditure amounts. In such cases, monitoring includes both expenditure and physical progress reports as well as timely identification of bottlenecks in implementation.

---

[11] The Division is headed by an adviser, who is assisted by a joint adviser, director, joint directors, senior research officers and other junior level technical and administrative staff. At present, some of the senior posts are vacant. There are only about eight senior technical personnel. The Sixth Five-Year Plan has allocated Rs100 million to strengthen the monitoring cells all over the country. At present, the Division is helping the central departments of health, education and urban development design a monitoring system.

Many central ministries have also created planning and monitoring cells for regularly reviewing their development programmes. Their organizational set up varies. For example, in the Ministry for Rural Reconstruction, a Directorate of Intelligence was set up during 1978-79 for the specific task of gathering information on rural development projects such as Small Farmers' Development Programme, Drought Prone Areas Programme, Integrated Rural Development, Antyodaya, etc.

At the state level, monitoring is conducted by the State Planning Department and the administering departments concerned. The former have separate monitoring cells in some states. But they do not have adequate technical manpower for conducting necessary analysis for monitoring the programmes.[12] Administering departments in many states do not have separate full-time monitoring cells. Monitoring cells are planned to be set up at block, district and state departments levels. The objective is to involve the implementing agencies in continuous and purposeful monitoring of programmes.

At the district level, the schemes are reviewed at district coordination committee meetings[13] by the collector/deputy commissioner and district development officers on a monthly and quarterly basis. The comments on the review are then sent to the state Department of Planning for review. At the block/taluka level, the block/taluka development officer reviews work progress in monthly meetings of all the functionaries.

Programme level progress reports on major activities highlighting the physical and financial progress are sent by the heads of task groups to the development commissioner.[14] The consolidated statement is prepared at the level of the development commissioner for the purpose of review at his level as well as for reporting to the administering and planning departments concerned.

COORDINATING AGENCIES

From the foregoing analysis of the planning processes it is evident that the Planning Commission plays a crucial role in the formulation and review of both national and state plans, even though it is only an advisory body which does not figure in the Constitution. Because of the nature of its tasks, it depends upon extensive consultations with many agencies as well as with the highest political and administrative central and state government heads. Due to wide variations in problems, interests and levels of regional development, the task of formulating a

---

[12] In the sixth plan, financial provision was made to assist the state governments in strengthening their monitoring cells. Seventy-five per cent of the expenditure incurred towards this purpose was regarded as a subsidy by the Central Government.

[13] The district coordination committee consists of heads of all the developmental departments and project officers of special schemes. The district functional heads send also separately periodical reports to their state functional heads.

[14] For example, under the command area programme, some of the tasks are: operation of irrigation system, water distribution, farm development activities, crop production, etc.

common plan of action is difficult. Directing and coordinating the entire national planning effort is the job of the deputy chairman of the commission.[15] When there are various political parties in power in different states and at the centre or when there is a government at the centre with differing viewpoints on development goals and strategy, the work of the deputy chairman tends to be more onerous, delicate and trying. Harmonizing divergent views on both the methods and content of planning is, therefore, an exacting task.

In order to lend authority and status to the Planning Commission in performing its tasks, the convention was adopted of having the Prime Minister serve as chairman of the Commission, and the finance and planning ministers as members. The deputy chairman and other members are also appointed by the union government. Through the instrumentality of the NDC, it has been made possible for the Commission to have direct access to and discussions with the highest political power centres in the country. The fact that the Commission has been able to function for the past thirty years and is carrying out the mission of planning at the district and block levels, testifies its acceptability by all levels of authority.

Another important agency in the process of planning and budgeting is the Ministry of Finance. The close working of the Planning Commission and the Ministry of Finance at all stages of resource estimation, priority areas identification and plan size calculations have been discussed in the earlier section of this paper. The Plan Finance Division of the Ministry of Finance works in close collaboration with the Planning Commission in formulating plans, programmes and schemes. The details and other particulars are also scrutinized by the same agency before including them in the budget. But in the case of public sector investments for either setting up of new enterprises or expanding existing ones, scrutinizing responsibility, approval, licensing, etc., rest with the Expenditure Finance Committee (EFC), the Public Investment Board (PIB), the Foreign Investment Board (FIB), the Licensing Committee (LC) and the Capital Goods Committee (CGC).

Generally, the ministry concerned prepares the feasibility study for the project by constituting a separate cell for this purpose. This is done by the ministry after consulting with the Planning Commission, the Ministry of Finance and the Cabinet. The secretary forwards the ministry's application for licence and other industrial approvals required for foreign collaboration, etc., to the Secretariat for Industrial Approvals (SIA) of the Department of Industrial Development. Institutional arrangements for issuing industrial approvals are the same for both public and private investments.

The detailed project report is prepared after obtaining clearance from the LC and FIB. Normally, only projects approved through a detailed project report are included in the budgetary demands of the administrative ministries. There are, however, instances where token provision is made in the budget on the basis of feasibility reports alone.

---

[15] "There is no corresponding minister in the cabinet assigned to coordinate and direct the process of plan implementation in the country." Divekar, *Planning Process in Indian Polity,* p. 10. At times, the deputy chairman of the Planning Commission, however, happens to be the planning minister himself (as at present), whereas at other times, there may be a separate minister of planning.

All proposals for the expansion of existing public services exceeding Rs10 million non-recurring and/or over Rs2 million recurring expenditures must be referred to the EFC. Recurrent items, however, need not be submitted. The EFC deals with all of the ministries' expenditure proposals, whereas the PIB handles public enterprises' proposals. The latter was set up in 1972 in an effort to avoid delays in decision-making due to protracted procedures and prolonged inter-ministerial meetings.

The PIB examines the broad contents of an investment proposal before the feasibility study is prepared and makes investment decisions on public investment proposals exceeding Rs10 million. The revision of cost estimates also have to be approved by the PIB.

The PIB is composed of the secretary, who serves as chairman and secretary, economic affairs secretary, planning commission secretary, industrial development secretary, secretary to the Prime Minister and secretary of the administrative ministry concerned. The director general of the Bureau of Public Enterprises is a permanent member. The PIB is assisted by the Plan Finance and Project Appraisal Wing of the Department of Expenditure. There is no such arrangement at the state level. All financial proposals are examined only by the Department of Finance.

At the state level, the Departments of Planning and Finance are the main coordinating agencies at the planning, budgeting and review stages. Coordination in the process of implementation is carried out by the chief secretary.[16] In some states he may be assisted by a development commissioner.

The chief secretary is secretary to the state council of ministers and to its various cabinet subcommittees. He prepares the agenda, processes all the cases and maintains records of their proceedings. He is consulted on all broad policy issues and represents other departments before the cabinet. The relationship between the chief minister and the chief secretary determines to a large extent the effectiveness of the latter.

As head of the state administrative machinery, the chief secretary is responsible for the effective coordination of different secretariat departments. He has to ensure that a certain degree of uniformity in policies is adopted in the different departments by the state government. He has the power to request any file from any department and upon examining it send it back to the secretary concerned for action, or else submit it directly to the minister-in-charge or to the chief minister. As adviser to the chief minister, he keeps tabs on urgent problems and bottlenecks in the implementation of government programmes and policies.

In order to assist the chief secretary, the system of state level coordination committees has been devised in some of the states. In Rajasthan, these are known as the planning and coordination committees. They review the progress of different schemes and problems faced in their implementation. There are also interdepartmental coordination committees for subjects such as (a) agricultural

---

[16] He derives his powers from the rules of business framed by the state government. He is also the head of the civil service in the state.

production, forestry cooperation and community development; (b) animal husbandry and dairy development; and (c) DPAP and Tribal Sub-Plan. The chief secretary, in many cases, is chairman of these committees. The finance and planning secretaries are ex-officio members of these committees in addition to the secretaries and heads of departments concerned. The planning or finance secretary acts as member secretary. Decisions taken by the committees are normally abided. All matters to be included in the agenda for discussion need to be sent to the committee secretary some ten to fifteen days prior to the meeting. Meetings also serve as forums for idea exchange, resolution of differences and discussion of other issues concerning government in general. Some of these official meetings held in districts resolve issues concerning certain regions. They are attended by all district collectors/deputy commissioners concerned, who also send administrative reports to the chief secretary on the implementation of public policies in their areas.

The chief secretary is also the head of certain departments, such as general administration, planning, etc., in some states. As head of the permanent civil service in the state, he keeps the services informed of changing state policy objectives and acts as friend and counsellor. He represents his state at the annual chief secretaries' conferences held at the Centre, as well as other important meetings or conferences having dealings with development. He also attends NDC and zonal councils meetings. He is consulted in all matters of interstate coordination.

The role of chief secretary as administrative coordinator is a crucial one in all states. His effectiveness depends upon his personality traits, such as his initiative, efficiency, capacity to inspire confidence in others and his relationships with the chief minister and the ministry in general. He is expected to provide leadership to the entire administrative machinery.

At the district level, the most important coordinating officer is the district collector/deputy commissioner. He has often been referred to as the "kingpin of district administration" not only because of the powers and responsibilities that have been conferred upon him by the statutes and rules framed under executive orders, but also because he has been the representative of the government at the district level, who maintains law and order, collects revenues, undertakes relief, etc., since British rule. With the introduction of planning, he has become the main coordinator of developmental activities at the district level, in addition to his traditional duties. As district development officer, in most states he functions as both vertical and horizontal coordinator. In this context, the district collector is charged with the responsibility[17] of effecting overall coordination with all district level officers.[18] In many states he is chairman of the district planning development

[17] The functions and responsibilities of district officers as collectors, district magistrates, returning officers, etc., are listed in S.R. Maheshwari, *Indian Administration*, Rev. ed. (New Delhi: Orient Longmans, 1979), pp. 465-69.

[18] With few exceptions, all state government departments are represented at the district level. Traditionally, developmental departments were not under direct control by the collector but rather through their own functional departmental heads. Consequently, district level officers turn to their heads for technical guidance rather than to the collector.

board, the planning cell and the recently instituted district development authority
as well. The district collector coordinates the various departmental tasks mainly
through:

1. district officers' meetings held monthly in many states;
2. a system of quarterly reporting made to the collector by the officers of the
   developmental departments; and
3. a system of tours and camps for supervision purposes.

The district collector provides a link between district and state administration
by submitting district reports to the chief secretary, attending collectors'
conferences, etc. Being in charge of revenue administration, law and order and
development administration at the district level, he supervises the work of all
functionaries from the district down to village levels. He is the officer who has an
overall awareness of the situation within the district essential for effectively performing the function of coordinator. The district collector provides intersectoral
and intergovernmental coordination at the local level. He discusses and resolves
implementation problems during monthly meetings of district officers.

This system of supervision allows the collector to meet the people and learn
about their problems, and thus, acquire first-hand knowledge of field situations.
Through his system of reporting, he is able to bring to the attention of state level
authorities problems of coordination which may necessitate solutions at higher
levels. Unfortunately, the collector is burdened with many diverse responsibilities
and meagre facilities. The collectors' functioning may be more effective in smaller
districts where he has less workload. The states of Maharashtra and Gujarat have
entrusted these developmental functions to the elected district Panchayat called
the "Zilla Parishad," and have established a separate chief executive officer with
equivalent rank as collector. The coordination role of the collector is considerably
diminished in cases where developmental functions are referred to Panchayati
Raj entities with the necessary funds. The collector nevertheless plays the general
role of coordinator in many states. When the Panchayati Raj was introduced, the
coordinating role of the collector had its ups and downs and there has been tension between these two bodies and various government functionaries during this
initial period. But a more positive perspective and mutual understanding so
necessary at this level have developed with time.

At present, cooperation necessary from the district officers has been good due
to the relationships which the collector has established with the state administration power centres. But their cooperation is dependent upon maintenance of
political relationship between district and state levels.

The taluka/block development officers (TDO/BDO) are charged with carrying
out horizontal coordination responsibilities and establishing relationships with
district administrators. Developmental department functionaries are under the
general supervision of the TDO/BDO, but under control of their respective
district level officers when it comes to programme administration and technical
guidance and must, therefore report their task performance to both authorities.
Block level functionaries, however, turn to their departmental district officers for

guidance and regard them as technical superiors to whom they should be responsible.

During fortnightly block level officers' meetings, the TDOs/BDOs discuss problems of horizontal and vertical coordination. Like its district level counterpart, the collector, he enjoys neither the authority nor the status necessary to secure his colleagues' cooperation. The TDO/BDO is also secretary of the Panchayat Samiti which is the block level elected body. These elected representatives also try to exercise effective control over block level officials through their connections at higher political levels. Thus, friction is more prevalent between these elected representatives and officials at this level. This problem inhibits the effective functioning of TDO/BDO coordination efforts at the block level.

Coordination of development programmes at the village level is the responsibility of the Village Level Worker (VLW) who is at the lowest administrative ranks. He is generally in charge of a group of villages and has the responsibility of providing a link between government and the people. He serves multipurpose functions such as overseeing agricultural production plans, extension work, seed and fertilizer supplies, credit, and dissemination of technological information to villagers. Since there is no chance for promotion, many VLWs tend to view their jobs as secondary. Studies reveal that job satisfaction among these functionaries is very low. Individuals who are so unmotivated can hardly be expected to motivate others towards adopting new and seemingly risky ventures. Knowledgeable villagers generally view him as less knowledgeable in such technical matters as dairying and agriculture. However, with the recent introduction of the Banor's training and visit system, considerable emphasis has been placed on the continuous training of the VLWs and their field of responsibility has also been limited to extension work only. These changes are likely to improve the role performance of the VLWs.

Thus, as one goes down the ladder of administration, the level, authority and status of the coordinating authority decreases vis-a-vis the functionaries whose work he is expected to coordinate. This leads one to conclude that coordination is more effective at the higher levels than at lower levels of administration.

SYNTHESIS

In India, despite policy pronouncements and efforts made by the government in that direction, there are certain factors which have led to regional and sectoral imbalances. One such factor is the uneven distribution of natural resources coupled with widely varying levels of socioeconomic infrastructure among the regions. For example, the development of physical infrastructural facilities in the areas of education, health, transport, banking and administration varied among the different states. Some areas were able to better utilize plan allocations than others due to certain inherent advantages they enjoyed at the time planning was initiated. This means that the initial development level of particular regions gave them cumulative advantage under the planning process.

The overall parameters of the federal and democratic character of India's polity and the mixed nature of its economy have to be kept in view in assessing the increase and direction of the country's economic development. It calls for decentralization of decision-making in plan formulation and resource allocation with respect to programme implementation. At the same time, the very attempt to have regional development within the framework of an overall national plan calls for centralized guidance and decision-making. Reconciliation has been sought between decentralized government decision-making and the centralized planning system through joint formulation of national and state plans by the Planning Commission and the states via various consultative bodies (such as committees, councils, working groups, panels, etc.) at political and administrative levels. These administrative devices, however, are helpful in extensive consultations. Decisions made by these groups are not always binding, and may be later modified by the various participants concerned. The chief ministers at the NDC, for example, may agree to raise the requisite resources or pursue a particular policy towards land reforms, etc., in accordance with the plans. But when they return to their states, they may find it difficult to live up to their agreements due to local political compulsions or administrative limitations. The centre only has financial persuasion over state governments in implementing national priorities. Its capacity to influence states through its policies, therefore, depends upon its resource position.

Intergovernmental relations in planning, budgeting and implementation thus have political as well as administrative constraints. But in spite of these constraints, the Planning Commission has been able to work through the operating governmental agencies at various levels towards some agreement on plan priorities and formulation of an integrated national plan. Above all, it has been able to develop its planning skills and is in the process of disseminating them to state and district levels crucial in regional development. The mechanism of coordination between the Centre and the States is by now well established.

The position is less satisfactory with regard to institutional capability at the regional level. Even though some states have already set up planning boards, many of them still lack competent planning mechanism. The composition of these boards varies from state to state. In some states, they only include representatives from the planning and finance departments and two or three from other important departments. In other states, these boards have more varied membership and include non-government experts as well. These boards, therefore, are not always adequately equipped with the required multidisciplinary expertise for effective planning and programme formulation.

It is always necessary in a federal polity to decentralize planning decisions with respect to specific activities, programmes and projects in the different levels, especially as the system of planning expands and gains momentum. Decentralization helps devise more realistic and purposeful plans that take into account local needs and potential while keeping within national guidelines, priorities and objectives. When planning responsibility is effectively decentralized, implementation will also improve due to increased commitment, involvement and accountability at lower levels in the process. Thus, the need for district and block level planning has been recognized since the sixties. The Administrative Reforms Commission, the Gadgil Committee on District Level Planning and the Dantwala Committee on Block Level Planning have also recommended strengthening planning capabilities at the local levels. Efforts made in this direction appear to be still inadequate compared with this task's urgency. This has been partly due to the absence of a clear cut demarcation of functions between the state and the districts as in the case of centre and states. There have been efforts in some states to demarcate the jurisdictions between state and district authorities. However, the main constraint has been the lack of planning skills, lack of data base required for planning and lack of financial resources. Planning capabilities need to be strengthened simultaneously at the district and block levels. Planning, especially at the local level, has to be realistically conceived, imaginatively and effectively pursued and consciously designed, keeping in view fundamental objectives and environmental constraints. Efforts at block level planning have to be seen as innovative experiments in democratic decentralization towards achievement of national development goals through people's participation and optimal use of their resources.

Before attempting district and block level planning, it is essential to identify locally conceived activities, programmes and projects that may be implemented by district and block level authorities. Some suggestions in this regard have already been made by the committees mentioned earlier. It is also necessary to disaggregate planning activities and resources so that these may be effectively entrusted to different government levels, and sufficient thought has to be given to this basic necessity. Some activities could be taken up by two or three states at the regional level, but it would be better to entrust them to regional boards or to River Valley authorities if they happen to be irrigation or power projects. This device is used to some extent,[19] but a more systematic adoption of multilevel planning concepts requires, as a first step, disaggregation of planning activities and resources.

It is agreed by all concerned that the capabilities at the state and district levels of government need to be augmented for detailed programming of projects. The major lacunae in the planning process is the programming aspect. In case of big investment projects, especially in construction, care is taken to disaggregate the task into a number of work packages, fix responsibilities and assign and integrate requisite resources at a later stage. However, the same is not always true of a number of other programmes and schemes undertaken by federal and state governments. Detailed physical planning is not always done by the concerned agencies. This is particularly true of programmes where public participation or cooperation is also one of the necessary ingredients. In absence of detailed work and time schedules, fixing responsibilities for implementing tasks, and taking

---

[19] Four regional councils have been set up under the Parliamentary status after reorganization of the states. Apart from these councils, there are also councils for backward or special problem regions such as the Northeastern Hill Regions. There are also Regional Boards, like the Telangana Regional Board, where a particular region within a state needs special attention. The functioning of these bodies, however, varies and some of them have not been too active.

action in cases of non-implementation, become difficult. In such situations, money may get spent without achieving full results. Unless detailed programming for the task is undertaken, coordination, monitoring and evaluation are apt to become ritualistic. Strengthening the monitoring system on the basis of detailed programming helps to generate requisite data for effective evaluation purposes. The importance of detailed planning and programming is even more relevant at the field agency level where it enables officers to withstand local pressures.

The close relationships maintained between the Planning Commission and Finance Ministry at the federal level, and between the Planning and Finance Departments at the state level, help to effectively coordinate the annual plan and budget, crucial in the operationalization of Five-Year Plans. These agencies deploy a number of devices such as issuance of circular letters, office memoranda and guidelines to implementing ministries and departments, in bringing about plan-budget linkages. These documents, generally deal with national priorities, special problems, procedures to be adopted for preparation of budget estimates and presentation of information on capital projects, schemes, etc. Making plans and budgets also reflect national policies and priorities.

The uniformity brought about by accounting reforms in plan classification structure, budget and accounts documents, helps in the preparation of estimates and in the evolution of programmes at a later stage. The present classificatory structure is a combination of economic, functional, programme, activity and input classifications. Format revision, however, is only the first step in making internal management tools out of plan budget documents. The physical data that has to go into budget and accounts presentations need to be improved. It requires working out norms and yardsticks for each task to be executed. In the absence of data, the budgetary and accounts structure will be unable to generate the required information for further planning and evaluation of present development programmes. Working out these norms and guidelines also requires involvement of people concerned with programme implementation.

Reforms brought about in the delegation of financial and administrative powers of implementing ministries and departments are another important step towards improving their capabilities in timely programme implementation. The delegations effected have so far been from the Ministry of Finance to administering ministries. Should they have to percolate down to the field levels, each ministry and department has to review the powers and responsibilities at each level and accordingly redelegate the necessary powers. Some ministries and departments have taken steps in this direction. Progress has not been uniform and needs closer scrutiny and more adequate appraisal.

Separation of accounts from audit and introduction of the Integrated Financial Advisers is another important step taken to integrate the finance function with the other functions of implementing agencies. It is hoped that this will inculcate financial prudence in administrative agencies, help in arriving at realistic budgetary estimation and provide agencies with regular and reliable flow of information. There is some extent of improvement in the timely sanction of funds. Steps need to be taken towards designing a management information system through improvement of accounting and budgetary systems and procedures.

Interagency meetings designed to estimate resource mobilization potential of different government levels help to dovetail fiscal and financial policies into plan and budget documents. The Planning Commission helps formulate the budget by making sectoral allocations known prior to the detailed formulation of state and district plans. The physical targets spelt out for each sector are the basis for estimating financial targets of the ministry and department concerned. However, the position at the regional level is not so clear. In the absence of financial resources of their own and the indication of the quantum of resources available for the district from state government, the district planning authority feels constrained to formulate a meaningful plan. In some states, steps have recently been taken to allocate specific resources to district planning bodies.

The coordinating role of the District Collector needs further strengthening through formation of smaller districts or providing a competent and experienced officer to assist in his traditional functions. Since the system of revenue collection and maintenance of revenue records has been systematized, this job may be carried out by a junior class-one officer. Overall coordination of developmental departments and traditional ones remains to be the Collector's task. Alternatively, developmental functions may be entrusted to elected local government institutions supported by adequate administrative capabilities and financial delegation. Their success, however, would depend on the way the political process facilitates the emergence of local leadership in all states, as has been the case in Maharashtra and Gujarat. Many Panchayati Raj commissions and committees have, however, recommended the Maharashtra pattern of Panchayati Raj for the rest of India.[20]

At the block level also, there is need to strengthen the BDO's coordinating role. Traditional organizational structures were found inadequate for effective implementation of development programmes and delivery of public services required in planning. To overcome this, the unity of command in organizations that are based on project approach has been superimposed upon the functional pattern. The emerging organizational structural matrix has not adequately strengthened institutional capability either, especially the coordinating capability of the BDO. This is partly due to the fact that departmental officers still look up to their respective departmental heads for technical guidance. The BDO is also not always able to provide leadership to the rest of his officers, as he has no task leadership role. The BDO's administrative control is also limited, unlike his counterpart, the Collector, who traditionally has also been government representative at the district level, enjoys higher status as a member of All India

[20] L.N. Bongirwar (Chairman), *Report of the Evaluation Committee on Panchayati Raj* (Bombay: Government of Maharashtra, 1971); G.L. Vyas (Chairman), *Report of the High Power Committee on Panchayati Raj* (Jaipur: Government of Rajasthan, 1973); Sadiq Ali (Chairman), *Report of the Study Team on Panchayati Raj* (Jaipur: Government of Rajasthan, 1964); Ram Murti (Chairman), *Report of the U.P. Study Team on Panchayati Raj* (Lucknow: Government of Uttar Pradesh, 1965); Zinabhai Darji (Chairman), *Report of the High Power Committee on Panchayati Raj* (Gandhinagar: Government of Gujarat, 1973); and C. Narasimham (Chairman), *The High Power Committee on Panchayati Raj in Andhra Pradesh* (Hyderabad: Government of Andhra Pradesh, 1972).

Services and maintains connections at top administrative echelons. One way of improving the coordinating role of BDOs would be to do away with the functional organization pattern at the block level and place all block level officers under BDO's authority. There is also a need to improve the means of promoting block level departmental officers and VLWs, as their morale and motivation are adversely affected due to the lack of promotional opportunities. The importance of improving the situation is being increasingly realized.

People's participation in the development process is an ingredient essential for the successful implementation of programmes. For a variety of reasons the experience so far has been varied and not always encouraging in all of the states. The Panchayati Raj has succeeded in bringing the people's felt needs to the administration. The extension agency has also succeeded in making people adopt improved agricultural practices and inputs, particularly in Special Programme Areas. The issue to be considered in the dynamics of change is how far the bureaucratic machinery could be an adequate instrument to mobilize people towards developmental programmes. But more direct and effective involvement of people and their institutional arrangements and modalities require radical measures for eradicating feudal vestiges in village economies as well as administrative orientation and approach towards the weaker sections of society.

It can thus, be seen that there have been conscious efforts over the years towards improvement of institutional capability for development performance. Continuous efforts are still necessary, however, for adapting the system to changing circumstances. The specific direction which these efforts are to take, however, will not effectively crystalize unless systematic and further research is undertaken in a number of identified areas. In order to design programmes suitable for particular areas and target groups and to institutionalize appropriate arrangements to achieve developmental goals promptly and efficiently, it is necessary to analyse special characteristics and area problems through multi-disciplinary research. It is a matter of gratification that there is national consensus about the operationalization of the concept of redistributive growth and balanced regional development. The people and the government are aware of the exacting implications of this process and this awareness is making increasing impact on the policies and programmes as are now emerging for the future.

9

INSTITUTION BUILDING FOR REGIONAL DEVELOPMENT IN SRI LANKA

K.P.G.M. PERERA AND P.N.M. FERNANDO

OVERVIEW OF REGIONAL DEVELOPMENT PERFORMANCE

Introduction

SRI LANKA, one of the smaller countries of South Asia, is an island of 65,000 square kilometres with a population of fourteen million. The mainstay of the economy is plantation and domestic agriculture with smaller urban and industrial sectors. The noteworthy geographical features of Sri Lanka are a higher elevation area within the centre of the country and the division of the country into two clearly marked climatic zones — a wet zone in the central and southwestern part and a dry zone in the northern and eastern three-fifths of the country.

Sri Lanka is an ancient land with a well-developed agricultural civilization dating back to pre-Christian times. During this early period, major settlements and developed areas were located within the dry zone where the early inhabitants built an elaborate agricultural irrigation system. The wet zone, with its dense tropical and equatorial forests remained inaccessible and unpopulated. With foreign invasions over the centuries and the weakening of early indigenous civilizations through internal dissension and the incidence of malaria, however, human settlements shifted progressively southwards. During the advent of the Portuguese in 1505, the main concentration of population was in the wet zone. By that time the dry zone had reverted to jungle with only a few scattered village settlements.

Following 300 years of Portuguese and Dutch rule over the maritime provinces of Sri Lanka, the British established their rule in 1815 over the whole country, including the Kandyan Kingdom. After the British had consolidated their occupation, the major economic developments in Sri Lanka were the opening up of plantations, particularly in the hill country, and the development of supportive infrastructure. The dry zone suffered further neglect. The food producing sector of the economy continued to be neglected so that the inability of local food production to meet the country's needs is a persistent problem even today. This problem was aggravated by a phenomenal population growth during the last few decades.

Review of National Development Strategies

Sri Lanka obtained its formal political independence from Britain in 1948, but that year really signifies the culmination of a progressive transfer of power to the local people within a smooth political process. In 1931, universal suffrage was adopted in Sri Lanka. Sri Lankan ministers were appointed, though they had restricted powers. This change brought about a new political dimension. The British government's interests were mainly concentrated on development of the plantation sector which was owned mostly by British interests, whereas the Sri Lankan ministers were keenly interested in pursuing policies and programmes that would more directly benefit the local people whom they represented. Thus, particularly after 1931, the progressive transfer of power to local ministers on the one hand, and a larger component of governmental policies benefiting local people on the other, could be observed.

The national development strategy adopted by Sri Lanka during the post-independence period focused mainly on: (a) massive agricultural investments; (b) development of transport, banking, agricultural credit, agricultural extension and other services; (c) improvement of education and health services; and (d) the provision of direct assistance in food production by subsidy schemes and consumer assistance by launching free commodity and food distribution schemes.

One of the main objectives was to increase production, particularly of food, in order to achieve self-sufficiency. This was a goal the realization of which still eludes the country. In the 1970s, rapid population growth (which started in the 1940s and continued into 1950s) began to have its most serious impact on the unemployment situation, particularly of young and educated people entering the labour force. Thus, income and employment generating activities became the major concern of government policy-makers.

Sri Lanka is a classic example of a dual agricultural economy with plantation agriculture (with its capitalistic commercial organization, high levels of management and productivity) vigorously developed, alongside a domestic agriculture sector mainly operated by local peasant farmers with low levels of inputs, management and productivity. One of the main, overall economic development strategies for increasing income and self-sufficiency in food, was the modernization of the domestic agricultural sector. Successive governments have undertaken a wide range of interconnected activities in an attempt to achieve this important objective of modernizing domestic agriculture. These include such activities as intensive plant breeding programmes, particularly rice; improvement of physical infrastructural facilities such as irrigation, developing agricultural roads and input supplies; providing subsidies on inputs such as fertilizer and machinery; launching guaranteed price programmes, agricultural credit, agricultural insurance and other services; effecting legal and institutional changes for strengthening tenurial rights, regulating rents on agricultural land, and strengthening local level organizations for participatory decision-making on agricultural development programmes and projects.

National Strategy and Regional Policies

Sri Lanka, like its South Asian neighbours, spent a great deal of effort in the preparation of macroeconomic plans. An equal degree of conscious effort, however, was not made for following through with the implementation of these plans. This also could be attributed to frequent political changes of government, as well as to fluctuations in external economic and commercial conditions to which Sri Lanka is particularly vulnerable.

The Post-War Development Proposal (1946) was the first attempt to put together a series of investment proposals, as a rudimentary plan for national economic activities. This was followed by the Six-Year Plan of Development (1947-48 to 1952-53) and by the Six-Year Programme of Investment (1954-55 to 1959-60). The Planning Secretariat set up in 1953, was the first formal planning agency in the country with adequate status, staff and resources to discharge the planning tasks. The result of these efforts was a comprehensive planning document, the Ten-Year Plan of 1959-69. The first of its kind, it clearly laid out a picture of the status, prospects and strategy for developing the economy and its different sectors. However, this plan was not implemented because of political changes at the time. Instead a more restricted plan was adopted, the Three-Year Short-Term Implementation Programme of 1962, with more limited objectives, in contrast to the broad spectrum of development measures envisaged in the original Ten-Year Plan. During 1965-70, several sectoral programmes were also prepared, of which the Agricultural Development Proposals were the best known. After 1970, there was a shift again to formal planning and the Five-Year Plan of 1972-76 and sector programmes were prepared.

Though efforts were made to draw up formal plans, none of these were seriously implemented. Therefore, the government's annual budget became the main instrument of investment decision-making, and affected government policies which involved financial implications. But without the guidance of a longer duration plan, the annual budget became more of a shorter term financial exercise subject. to immediate concerns and priorities. The plan documents (referred to above), budgets, government policy statements, election manifestos, etc., are the sources for determining the policies, objectives and strategies, as well as the actual measures taken by the government.

The focus in this section is on the regional development policies adopted. Current concepts of regional rural development usually emphasize two distinct aspects: (a) development of backward regions and interregional balance (geographically balanced development); and (b) concern with the welfare of disadvantaged groups, the poor, popular participation, basic needs, income distribution, etc. Sri Lanka's economic and social policies over the last three decades have generally represented a balance between these two major concerns.

The opening up of the desolate dry zone (reverted to jungle and plagued by malaria) for intensified human settlement was a major development with regard to the first aspect. The reconstruction of irrigation facilities which had deteriorated over the centuries was also affected. The government's enormous efforts in opening up the dry zone by eradicating malaria and by irrigation development and settlement of landless farmers in new agricultural communities continue with even greater vigour.

With regard to the other aspect, the government's role in alleviating poverty, by providing education and health services, food subsidies and food rations, and other distributional measures has ensured a greater measure of average welfare than many countries at similar income levels.

Overall Evaluation of Development Performance

The overall performance with respect to each of the major efforts/strategies may be measured in two complementary ways. The first method would be to assess general performance over a selected period, with reference to the situation at the beginning of the selected period. The second method would be to assess the performance against the goals set in the national plans and the annual budget. Since many of the national plans were not implemented with vigour, it would be more meaningful to view overall performance within the Sri Lankan context. However, it is also interesting to compare targets and achievements with the Five-Year Plan of 1972-76. This surfaces the unpredictable planning exercise hazards in a world where external events could completely nullify the assumptions upon which plans are based.

Production

If GNP is taken as an overall production index, this indicator not only remained at a low level, but also grew at a modest rate between 1970 and 1977. When considering the population growth rate over this period, however, per capita incomes were stagnant and showed a decline in some years. Yet during 1978 and 1979, economic growth was remarkable, particularly in contrast to the preceding years. This has been explained "largely as a spontaneous reaction of a long depressed economy and to its liberalization by the new economic policies initiated in 1977."[1]

The overall growth of the agricultural sector over the last ten years is not impressive as reflected in the following statistics relating to the agricultural, forestry and fishing sectors, according to constant (1970) factor cost prices shown in Table 9-1. This sector has continued to maintain its relative position. On the

---

[1] Central Bank of Ceylon, *Review of the Economy* (Colombo, 1978), p. 1.

other hand, population grew steadily from 12.5 million in 1970 to 14.5 million in 1979. It may be concluded that the net result was to keep up with population growth with only incremental growth being achieved in this sector over the period up to 1977.

Table 9-1. Agricultural Product at Constant (1970) Factor Cost Prices

	1970	1976	1977	1978
Amount (Rs. Mn.)	3,732	3,894	4,299	4,532
Percentage of GNP	28.8	25.4	26.9	26.2

Employment

The Five-Year Plan reported an unemployment figure of 550,000 or a rate of over 12 per cent, out of a work force of 4.5 million.[2] The labour force had grown to 5.6 million by 1978, representing 39 per cent of the population. With regards to unemployment, the Consumer Finance and Socioeconomic Survey of 1978 indicates a figure of about 900,000. But these figures are probably lower at present due to increased economic activity, as reflected in: (a) the 8.2 and 6.5 per cent GNP growth rates for 1978 and 1979, respectively; (b) the expansion of government and other public sector employment; and (c) the migration of skilled and semiskilled workers to the Middle East during the last few years. Under the liberal and open economic policies for creating more employment, are the government's strategies for accelerating major development projects such as the Mahaweli Project, the Urban Development Investment Promotion Zone and private sector incentives for rapid expansion. However, the basic problem of middle-level educated young people aspiring to organized sector jobs has not yet been solved, and remains to be a difficult one.

Policy Relevance and Intersectoral Consistency

Successive governments following three decades of independence, were committed to the country's rapid economic development, while at the same time maintaining free welfare services in health, education and direct food assistance for the lower income groups.

The period 1970-77 was one of near stagnation or slow growth, partly due to unfavourable external economic circumstances, an unfavourable investment climate and adverse climatic conditions for agriculture. The agricultural sector

---

[2] As revealed in the census data, the figure was 839,000 for 1971; and 1,000,000 according to the Consumer Finance Survey of 1972.

fared poorly, showing an average growth rate of 1.7 per cent over this period. Investment, savings and capital formation, all indicated downward trends up to 1974, but an upward trend since then. In terms of overall income growth, the performance of the economy has been far below expectations. The structural weaknesses of the economy were most evident, particularly its vulnerability to exogenous forces such as external economic or climatic factors.

Even though overall growth performance has been poor (now showing signs of recovery), the social gains in attaining higher levels of welfare, as measured by income distribution, food consumption, medical and educational services, higher life expectancy, lower mortality rates for infants and children, have been significant. These gains are the result of continued policies followed by successive governments in spite of per capita GNP being less than US$200.

Apart from the provision for education and health services at state expense, the provision for free or subsidized food is almost a tradition in Sri Lanka since the Second World War. With the supply of a minimum quantity of essential food items, food rationing at fixed, lower than market prices, is one of the methods by which the real incomes of poorer groups have been maintained. Thus, monetary earned income does not reflect real income enjoyed due to such resource transfers. Presently, a Food Stamp Scheme (a system of encashable coupons), has replaced the earlier ration book scheme.

Thus, in an extremely difficult development situation, with very low incomes aggravated by unprecedented population increases and an economy subject to uncertain external economic factors, the government has chosen a development path aimed at maintaining a balance between overall growth and equitable distribution. This is a difficult path, and achievement of success is subject to a number of variables. This should clearly be taken into consideration when measuring development performance. This effort is also being made while maintaining a democratic framework for political development. People's aspirations continuously rise, whereas oil imports and international inflation add a new complicating factor in the country's development process.

Government development programmes have generally considered the necessary intersectoral linkages. This is evidenced by the major resource development projects in irrigation, where social necessities such as schools, health, marketing facilities, extension and credit, as well as irrigation and other physical infrastructure are planned into one integrated package.

One major objective of the government has been the modernization of the traditional domestic agricultural sector. This has been attempted by providing a complete package, comprising legal and institutional bases, organizations, provisions for research and extension facilities, credit, marketing and insurance, etc. Nevertheless, there are deficiencies in the overall functioning of the agencies responsible for integrating development in particular areas of the country. But in general this package, supported by appropriate incentives and subsidies, constitutes the overall approach that has been adopted.

Some instances of development inconsistencies are:

1. The increase in unemployment reflected not only in low outputs, but also

in the high capital intensive demands of development. Between 1963 and 1971, employment growth was 38 per cent of the increase in output, while employment growth in the manufacturing sector was only 17 per cent of the increase in output. This indicates that even though unemployment is a pressing and urgent problem, the capital intensity of industrial production has nevertheless increased. This may further indicate inappropriate technology in the context of Sri Lanka's factor endowment, particularly the labour surplus situation.

2. The failure of medical services to balance curative and preventive measure on the one hand at par with the provision for family planning services on the other, despite the government's declared policy for pursuing both objectives.

3. The educational services which do not provide a system for meeting the demands of the economy and for training people with the required skills and more particularly the attitudes, to match job opportunities. The objectives of education during colonial times were to provide general education and training for government jobs. This remained unchanged when education was expanded to reach a much larger segment of the population. As a result, the educational system produced excessive numbers of high school educated people whose training induced them to eschew manual or skilled work in preference of comfortable middle level or even lower level government jobs.

4. The growth of import substitution industries since the early 1960s. Government policy actively supported their establishment and growth with a view towards saving foreign exchange (by increasing the value added domestically), increasing employment and eventually laying the foundations for a viable industrial sector. However, the industries established effected only a marginal foreign exchange saving, being heavily based on imported raw materials and components with a minimum of local materials. The capital intensive technology adopted could only provide employment to marginal numbers within the labour force. On the other hand, lack of any quality control resulted in the production of inferior products at monopolistically high prices, over which no control was exercised.

Income Distribution

One of the major achievements of development performance in Sri Lanka was the improvement of income distribution patterns. This is especially noteworthy in periods of modest GNP growth, as illustrated by Table 9-2. The clear drop of percentage income at the highest decile and the gains at the lower deciles is significant, though a strong reversal of this trend is indicated by the surveys carried out in 1978.

Table 9-2. Income Distribution in Sri Lanka

Decile	Percentage Share of Income			Percentage increase in income between 1963-73
	1953	1963	1973	
1	1.90	1.50	2.79	243.22
2	3.30	3.95	4.38	204.63
3	4.10	4.00	5.60	158.34
4	5.20	5.21	6.52	130.94
5	6.40	6.27	7.45	119.26
6	6.90	7.54	8.75	114.15
7	8.30	9.00	9.91	103.19
8	10.10	11.22	11.65	91.61
9	13.20	15.54	14.92	77.17
10	40.60	36.77	28.03	40.67

SOURCES: Central Bank of Ceylon, **Consumer Finance Surveys**, 1953, 1963 and 1973.

An analytical report suggests other noteworthy features in this regard as follows:[3]

1. The estate sector spending unit has on the average 2.41 income receivers as against 1.26 in the urban and rural sectors.
2. Food expenditure as a percentage of total expenditures amounted to 55 per cent, indicating the low levels of overall income.
3. Marginally adequate food intake is observed at household incomes of Rs201-400 (1973). Even so, estate and urban sectors are above adequacy level, whereas the rural sector is marginally below adequacy level.
4. Absolute poverty is negligible in the estates, and low in the overall urban areas. However, about 19 per cent of the households suffer absolute poverty. Most of the households in absolute poverty are in the rural sector.
5. About 1.68 per cent of the estate households (0.54 per cent of the estate population), 6.45 per cent of the urban sector households (3.68 per cent of the urban sector population), 26.06 per cent of the rural sector households (17.62 per cent of the rural sector population) suffer from absolute poverty.
6. Widespread poverty among rural districts is also obvious with 26.89 per cent of the rural sector households below the nutritional norm.
7. The highest geographical concentrations of rural poverty are in districts with high percentages of estates, reflecting the depressed condition of villages within such areas, where much of the agricultural land area is not available for domestic agriculture.

[3] Marga Institute, *Analytical Description of Poverty in Sri Lanka* (Colombo, 1978).

8. Basic needs appear to be satisfied in households with income levels of Rs400-800 and a per capita basis of Rs94 every two months. It is noteworthy that as much as 78 per cent of the disadvantaged group is from the rural sector.

People's Participation in Political and Developmental Processes

Sri Lanka has a highly literate and politically conscious population. Universal suffrage was introduced in 1931, and representative democratic institutions have developed especially since the last few decades of British rule. The political maturity of the country and the strong commitment to democratic rule is evidenced by frequent changes of government at general elections based on a political party system. The political parties themselves have organized an elaborate system with district and local branch organizations. One noteworthy feature of the election system is the very high percentage of voters exercising their suffrage rights. The majority of voters attend political rallies and meetings and everyone has a feeling of involvement in the outcome of the elections. A high degree of participation in the political process may be observed. Aside from general elections, equally keen participation is evident in local elections.

One cannot expect, however, the same participation in developmental processes due to the nature of developmental decision-making and administration. On the other hand, it is impractical to separate the developmental and political decision-making processes. The major aspects of the government's development role are effected through economic policies, projects and their administration. If people are in a position to influence their choice so that their preferences and needs are served, then popular participation assumes some meaning. In the case of Sri Lanka, one may observe that the major choices have been made in favour of policies and activities favouring the large majority of the people rather than the richer minority of urban enclaves. In fact, income distribution and the high levels of achievement according to social indicators bear this out.

At the same time, an increasing trend towards decentralization which has been strengthening decision-making at the district level may be observed. This has been accompanied by the growing power and influence of the local Members of Parliament. The pressure that people exert on Members of Parliament has enabled government activities to be more responsive to the needs of the people and local areas.

OVERVIEW OF INSTITUTIONAL MACHINERY

With independence in 1948, Sri Lanka inherited a British style administrative system. Except for minor functionaries filling the lower levels, public officers were drawn from the English educated elite. The administration was insulated from the influence of political processes and affiliations during the early years of independence. Outside the control of politically appointed ministers, all recruitments, disciplinary control and promotions were handled within the administration and by the Public Services Commission. The members of the public service could not engage in any political activities (except the right to vote at elections), nor could they be members of political organizations or parties. The concept of an impartial and politically neutral administration was intended to ensure that it could serve any elected government loyally.

Major changes in the administrative system that have occurred during the intervening years are:

1. Greater degree of political involvement in the administration.
2. Greater political control of administration.
3. The growth of technical departments vis-a-vis the "regular administration."
4. The growth of government corporations and other statutory bodies.
5. The enlargement of avenues of entry to government service for a wider population.

A major administrative reform was the abolition of the Ceylon Civil Service and the creation of a more broad-based Ceylon (Sri Lanka) Administrative Service in 1963. The Ceylon Civil Service was an institution directly inherited from British colonial rule. The highest administrative positions were earmarked for members of this service and were mostly held by Englishmen. After independence, the Civil Service continued to exist in the same fashion, under similar rules of select recruitment by competitive examination, and a few others in service were allowed promotion into this exclusive grade. The lower echelons of administrative cadres had to be content with the second best positions. In 1963, all administrative grades were amalgamated into one service, including the exclusive and elite Civil Service, thus providing opportunities for administrative officers to aspire to higher offices as well as enable larger numbers to join this service.

There are three distinct levels of administration in Sri Lanka, i.e., the national, district and divisional levels. A fourth level, that of the village, may be more appropriately considered part and parcel of the divisional (local) level itself, due to its operational linkages with the divisional level.

The national level administrative machinery consists of the ministry organizations. Each ministry has a chief executive officer or secretary (some large ministries have additional secretaries) who are assisted by a handful of top management officers. The secretary is responsible for advising his minister on policy matters and for directing the affairs of his ministry through the heads of departments and other agencies under the ministry. There are at present about 100 government departments and another 100 corporations and statutory bodies undertaking various administrative, commercial, service, and judicial functions. Most government department heads are designated either as Commissioners or Directors.

The district level is next in importance within the general administrative framework. Although the British regarded provinces as immediate subnational administrative units, the proliferation of government departments and expansion of government activities brought into prominence the provincial subdivisions or districts. The trend for districts to supplant the prominence of provinces became official policy with the Administrative Districts Act of 1955. Today, there are twenty-four Administrative Districts in Sri Lanka, varying in size from about 1,300 to 7,200 square kilometres. District population densities range from 40 to 1,300 inhabitants per square kilometre. The various districts exhibit considerable differences in climate, vegetation and distribution of resources. Within each district today, there is a Government Agent (GA) who is Head of the *Kachcheri* (the traditional District Head Office) as well as being the District Minister's Secretary. The expansion of departments and their activities during the pre-independence era and immediately thereafter, caused the GAs to lose their coordinating supervision over some departments, especially technical ones, at the district level. Many statutes nevertheless, confer necessary powers upon the GAs for the performance of certain legal and regulatory functions. The need to coordinate other development and service functions has also required that several important department branch offices operate under the GA's administrative control.

In addition, the GA is expected to coordinate most or all of the agencies under the District Agricultural Committee (DAC) and/or District Coordinating Committee (DCC). The former is provided for under the Irrigation Ordinance (1945), and the latter under the Manual of Procedure (1953). The Agricultural Plan Implementation Programme initiated by the Food Drive of 1966, was handled by an official subcommittee of the DAC headed by the GA. The DCC also seeks to prepare or approve the annual development programme. There are a number of government departments and agencies, such as the Departments of Agriculture, Agrarian Services, and Cooperative Development, working outside the *Kachcheri* complex. In many instances, the investment programmes of these agencies were submitted by them to their central departments and ministries for consideration without integration with other district level programmes. But coordination has improved from about 1974, particularly with the introduction of the Decentralized Budget (DCB) Scheme whereby limited capital expenditure allocations were granted to districts to undertake local capital investment projects. Some departments outside the *Kachcheri* also receive DCB allocations from the *Kachcheri,* and consequently, are subject to its horizontal coordination. For purposes of the Agricultural Development Programme, the GA has also been appointed deputy head of the key Departments of Agriculture, Agrarian Services, Cooperative Development and Marketing in order to facilitate coordination.

Most government departments having regional field operations, accept the district as the subnational unit of operations and have established district offices. Despite the countervailing tendency of the local level electorate as an emergent unit supported by Decentralized Budget (DCB) funds being allocated electorate-wise (with individual Members of Parliament asserting an increasingly decisive role), the district is considered a desirable intermediate level at which development efforts should be integrated, with the District Ministers and GA/District Secretary playing key coordinating roles. With the intended establishment of District Development Councils, the district concept would gather additional momentum. This level has also assumed significance due to the appointment of twenty-four District Ministers for facilitating democratic political participation, as well as coordination and implementation of development programmes.

The role of local government authorities in development administration within the districts (and at the national level too) is somewhat limited, compared to government departments and government sponsored corporations. There are four types of local authorities in Sri Lanka, i.e., Municipalities, Urban Councils, Town Councils, and Village Councils. The first three are confined to developed urban localities covering small areas of operation. The services of local authorities centre round the provision of civic amenities. Town Councils and Village Councils are dependent largely on government for their recurrent expenditure. Due to their limited administrative capacity, these agencies are guided by Local Government Department officials. Local government institutions in Sri Lanka are elected bodies. According to statutory provisions, however, the Minister of Local Government is empowered to dissolve any council for reasons of mismanagement. Many local bodies in Sri Lanka were dissolved since 1972 and came under the management of appointed administrative officers. Elected councils have again been formed in the municipalities and urban councils after the elections of 1979. In accordance with an amended Act of Parliament, a system of proportional representation has also been adopted.

The subregional or local level is called the "divisional level" in Sri Lanka. This is perhaps the most operationally significant unit within the development management framework. The Divisional Revenue Officer (DRO) at the sub-district level and the Village Headman *(Grama Sevaka)* at the village level were under the traditional provincial/district administration. The DRO, designated Assistant Government Agent (AGA) in 1972-73, as the GA's representative at that level had long been a multifunctionary officer and chief coordinator of various government functions at that level. The DRO/AGA division assumed special significance as "planning" units with the Agriculture Programme in the 1960s and with the DCB in the 1970s.

The AGA and the development departments have village level officers too. The AGA has a multifunctionary *Grama Sevaka* officer in charge of a cluster of villages attending mostly to specific regulatory functions and reporting on many other matters channelled through the AGA. In the same area, the Cultivation Officer operates under the Divisional Office of Agrarian Services, attending to agricultural development administrative functions. Similarly, the Agricultural Extension Worker (KVS) works under the Agricultural Instructor in charge of a larger area. There are other personnel such as midwives, Public Health Inspectors, Coconut Development Officers and Cooperative Inspectors operating at units lower than the AGA division. Some of the functional departments represented at the District *Kachcheri* have officers connected with the AGA to assist him in relevant fields, such as the Rural Development Officer (RDO), Supervisor Land Development Ordinance or Colonization Officer (SLDO/CO) with a village level overseer to assist, the Statistical Investigator, Divisional Development Officer (DDO), Sports Officer, Social Service Officer, etc.

COORDINATION IN THE PROCESS OF PLANNING, BUDGETING AND IMPLEMENTATION MANAGEMENT

Coordination of planning, budgeting and implementation management for regional development in Sri Lanka takes place at the central, regional, and sub-regional levels. At the central level, the coordinating agencies are the Cabinet, the Development Secretaries Committee, the Ministry of Finance and Planning, the Ministry of Plan Implementation and the sectoral ministries and departments. At the regional level, the District Ministry is responsible for these functions. At the subregional level, the coordination of regional development is the responsibility of the divisional Assistant Government Agent.

An important consideration in the formulation of the plan framework is the election manifesto put out by the political party in power at the last general elections. This manifesto spells out in broad outline the various socioeconomic objectives that the party desires to achieve during its term of office should it form a government. When it has subsequently been voted to power, the government initiates action to prepare development programmes to achieve the objectives spelt out in the election manifesto. Different ministries in charge of various functions are expected to prepare development plans and programmes according to available resources. In this regard, the Ministry of Finance and Planning plays the key role in finding ways and means of obtaining the necessary resources for these sectoral development plans and programmes and in determining allocations among them. The ministry and departmental officials prepare concrete plans for approval in principle by the Cabinet of Ministers. These plans are coordinated and further processed at the central level by the Development Secretaries Committee and the Ministry of Finance and Planning.

Identification of Sectoral Programmes and Projects

The identification of sectoral programmes and projects for plan formulation constitute both a top-down as well as a bottom-up process. The initiative in identification of sectoral programmes and projects operates at three levels:

1. Subregional level — local capital expenditure projects are identified for financing under the DCB. These projects are mainly of an infrastructural nature and are identified by the Members of Parliament of the area, people's organizations at the local level, as well as field officers from the different departments of government working at this level.
2. Projects are identified at the district level by the District Minister and other district level officials for inclusion in the annual plan and the budget. Funding is sought either through the DCB or the functional ministries' budgets at the central level responsible for such work activities.
3. At the central level, functional departments and ministries identify and formulate programmes and projects of interregional or national importance, as well as process and evaluate bottom-up programmes and project

proposals. The Development Secretaries Committee and the Ministry of Finance and Planning function as an interagency coordinative body processing sectoral programmes and projects so identified.

Integration of Intersectoral Programmes and Projects

The National Planning Division of the Ministry of Finance and Planning with the Budget Division of the same Ministry, undertakes the intersectoral integration exercise based on a rolling plan concept. The medium term plan to which the annual plan is fitted, covers a period of five years, with one year added for each lapsed year. The macrolevel plan framework provides details of inputs and outputs of the sectoral targets for the ensuing year. The overall resource availability is also revised each year. This information is used by the sectoral ministries as a guideline for admission of new projects to the capital budget which is the main component of the development programme included in the annual budget.

In the light of the implementation capacity, the National Planning Division examines the proposals received from each sector during the previous year, and draws conclusions as to the sector's performance capacity.[4] The annual public sector performance report by the Ministry of Plan Implementation also provides data for this examination. The determination of sectoral resource allocation levels takes these factors into account. Determination of sectoral priorities is largely left to the line ministries which frame their proposals in line with national policies and annual plan priorities.

Budget Formulation

The Budget Division of the Ministry of Finance and Planning plays the key role in preparing the annual budget.[5] The instructional guidelines for preparation of budget estimates are circulated to all secretaries of ministries, heads of departments and chairmen of corporations before March of each year. The heads of departments and statutory bodies submit their estimates of capital and recurrent expenditures to their ministries, according to programmes and projects. Upon receipt of annual budget proposals from all departments and corporations, the secretary to each ministry arranges for discussions with their heads of departments/corporations in order to finalize the budget proposals of the ministry.

Finalized budget proposals are submitted to the Treasury annually in May by the secretary to each ministry, along with a copy to the National Planning Division. Budget Division officials evaluate and review these programmes and estimates. Disputes are settled first at the official level and then at the ministerial level after a series of budget conferences, while unresolved problems are conferred with the President. Once these programmes and expenditure estimates are

4 See Government of Sri Lanka, *Estimates of Revenue and Expenditure* (Colombo, 1980), v. 2, p. 786.

5 Ibid., p. 782.

finalized by the Treasury, revenue estimates are computed in detail and the budget is prepared.

Implementation Management

The review and implementation control of the annual budget plan is carried out by the Progress Control Division of the Ministry of Plan Implementation. Such monitoring is done with the assistance of the sectoral ministries and departments on a quarterly basis. The Ministry of Finance and Planning periodically reviews the national plan's implementation progress in consultation with the Ministry of Plan Implementation. There is also a mid-year implementation performance review, when new project proposals are examined for inclusion in the forthcoming year's plan. The following evaluation reports are utilized in evaluating implementation management at the end of the plan period:

1. Review reports from each ministry.
2. Performance reports from the Ministry of Plan Implementation.
3. Information on the progress control conferences available through the National Planning Division.
4. Capital and recurrent expenditure estimates.

The Materials and Manpower Resources Division of the Ministry of Finance and Planning, monitors the availability of supplies, equipment and manpower for implementing sectoral programmes and projects according to the time schedules within the annual plan. Information on logistical problems of main development programmes and projects within the annual plan is collected and processed by that Division from project locations and worksites. On the basis of information supplied by the Division and the Ministry of Plan Implementation (in addition to periodic reports from the sectoral ministries concerned), adjustments are made in the annual plan programme implementation schedules by the National Planning Division in consultation with the various sectoral implementation ministries and agencies.

The sectoral ministries on the other hand operate a more detailed evaluation system on the implementation of the annual plan and budget. For example, in the operation of the annual Agricultural Implementation Programme, the Ministry of Agricultural Development and Research receives monthly reports from the GAs on regional agricultural programme performance in contrast with plan targets. The Minister of Agriculture is briefed regularly on the progress made and problems are taken up for solution at the interministerial or cabinet levels. The progress of the agricultural programmes of the districts are also reviewed at ministry level monthly meetings chaired by the Additional Secretary of Development. Heads of departments and corporations concerned with the agricultural sector, participate at these meetings. A monthly progress review bulletin indicating both the targets and achievements is prepared monthly by the ministry and circulated among those involved in the implementation programme.

The ministries, departments and the GAs are required to submit monthly statements to the Treasury of the committed expenditure and actual expenditures
incurred. At the Treasury level, these statements are compared with the monthly
estimates for each organization in order to control expenditure. Internal audit
systems have been introduced by each organization to carry out audits of accounts
at central, regional and subregional levels. In addition, the Auditor-General
carries out independent auditing functions with his staff at central, regional and
subregional levels. In the past, auditing was done at the end of the project period,
but now a management auditing system has been introduced and a running audit
of programmes and projects is effected. The main focus of the Auditor-General's
investigations is to evaluate development performance of operating agencies with
regard to annual programme budgets.

Coordination at the National Level

The President is vested with the main executive powers of the State, and his
office is the highest coordinating agency in the government, as he has executive
control over other ministers of the cabinet.[6] The President is also the Minister for
Plan Implementation. Two important functions performed by the Ministry of
Plan Implementation are regional development and the monitoring of annual
plan implementation. The Regional Development Division of this Ministry is
concerned with coordinated regional planning, Decentralized Budgeting, and the
implementation of Integrated Rural Development Programmes. On the other
hand, the Progress Control Division of this Ministry monitors the implementation of the annual plan, clears implementation bottlenecks and provides an
evaluation of implementation performance to the planning and budgeting agencies. The Ministry of Plan Implementation Secretary is a member of the Development Secretaries Committee, and is therefore, an important channel for
highlighting concerns in regional development and the progress of annual plan
implementation with the sectoral ministries.

The methods of coordination with regard to regional development planning,
budgeting and implementation management adopted by the President, are mainly
by discussion and settlement with the sectoral ministries concerned. Presidential
orders are issued specifying functional areas as well as providing authoritative
guidelines for coordination in solving regional development problems. The
Ministry of Plan Implementation ensures coordination by adopting several
mechanisms. It exchanges information on the status of annual plan implementation at the regional and national levels, and it also resolves differences of views
with sectoral agencies on implementation process problems. On occasion, when
negotiations fail, authoritative guidelines are obtained by this Ministry from the
President. This Ministry has also institutionalized the process of holding progress

---

[6] *Constitution of the Democratic Socialist Republic of Sri Lanka.*

review and evaluation meetings at the National Operations Room in order to settle coordination problems in annual plan implementation by effecting speedy, on-the-spot solutions.

The Cabinet

The Cabinet of Ministers constitutes the second most important coordinating agency at the national level. All programmes and projects for regional development, together with the annual investment plan, the national and decentralized budget are examined and approved by the Cabinet. The coordination of sectoral ministries is effected at Cabinet meetings. Problems in implementation management are discussed and settlements are negotiated by the ministers concerned. On occasions, Cabinet subcommittees comprised of the relevant Cabinet ministers concerned may be appointed to examine a problem in detail and effect necessary solutions.

Development Secretaries Committee

The Development Secretaries Committee comprises the highest body of government officials. Its chairman is the Secretary to the Cabinet, and the Director of National Planning of the Ministry of Finance and Planning is Secretary of the Committee. These two appointments ensure a greater degree of coordination with national development strategy and the policy intentions of the Cabinet, and the effective formulation of national development plans. As the secretaries of the main sectoral ministries are members of this Committee, the composition of its membership facilitates its job virtually as a Planning Commission on the one hand, and as the apex body of officials for monitoring plan implementation on the other.

Medium and annual plans are considered by this Committee and its sectoral subcommittees. Effective coordination among sectors is facilitated, as sectoral ministries are represented in this Committee. As in the case of other national level coordinative bodies, this Committee adopts different coordination methods. Weekly discussions among representatives of ministries provide useful exchange of information. All capital development programmes and projects and their justification needs to be submitted to this Committee for approval. This provides an avenue for information exchange as well as a forum for settling intersectoral difference through negotiations. The Committee also issues directives on matters of intersectoral disputes, and sets up subcommittees consisting of officials from several ministries to examine and settle complex technical problems of intersectoral coordination.

Ministry of Finance and Planning

Both national planning and national budgeting are functions discharged by the Ministry of Finance and Planning,[7] which has enabled effective national plan and budget coordination. The Secretary to this Ministry also functions as the convenor of the Development Secretaries Committee. The Director of National Planning who serves this Ministry, is Secretary to the Development Secretaries Committee as well. This overlapping membership has assisted in providing a well coordinated transmission belt between the highest official body and the planning and budgeting functions. All capital projects must be evaluated and recommended by this Ministry before the Development Secretaries Committee makes a decision. Preparation of the annual plan which involves sectoral coordination of programmes and projects on the one hand, and regional development on the other, is also effected by this Ministry.

This planning cycle is closely linked with the national budgeting exercise, as the Budget Division is also represented in the planning committees and services the Development Secretaries Committee as well. This Ministry coordinates implementation performance directly in the field of financial management. It also coordinates the availability of materials and manpower to enable speedy implementation of strategic programmes and projects. The mechanisms for coordination adopted by this Ministry vary. The Ministry is the important focal point for exchange of information with regard to national programmes and projects. It holds a series of round table conference with sectoral ministries, departments and GAs on financial allocations required by them through the annual budget. The Ministry has also regulatory power over disbursement of public monies.

Coordination at the Regional Level

The administrative district is under the overall supervision of the District Minister appointed by the President, under Article 45 of the Constitution; the district has a chief executive who is a Member of Parliament and a politician of the government parliamentary group. The District Ministry is expected to coordinate all development activities within the district by:

1. Formulating district development plans.
2. Preparing the district budget.
3. Monitoring and evaluating the implementation of the plan.
4. Identifying bottlenecks in implementation in the government sectors and effecting corrective actions.
5. Directly supervising interdepartmental activities.

---

[7] See Government of Sri Lanka, *Estimates of Revenue and Expenditure.*

The GA is the Secretary to the District Minister and is the chief administrative officer within the district. The District Minister heads the District Coordinating Committee encompassing all the district department heads and public corporations.[8] This Committee holds meetings monthly, or whenever necessary. The District Minister exercises supervisory control over the use of resources allocated by the DCB to the district. Development proposals are discussed by the District Coordinating Committee and programmes for district development formulated.

In the agricultural planning sphere at the regional level, the District Agricultural Committee meets once a month under the chairmanship of the District Minister or the GA.[9] The membership of the District Agricultural Committee is confined to the departmental and statutory bodies dealing with agriculture, animal husbandry and the farmers. It comprises the district heads of the agencies performing agriculture, agrarian services, animal production and health, irrigation, cooperative development, paddy marketing board, and banking.

Coordination of plan formulation and implementation management is accomplished through the District Coordinating Committee and the District Agricultural Committee. The coordination methods and techniques used are: (a) exchange of information; (b) instructions by means of circulars; (c) negotiations; and (d) mutual adjustments. Occasionally coordination effected through these Committees is inadequate. As such, standing subcommittees are set up to perform special tasks on a continuing basis.

As the political executive head within each region, the District Minister provides political leadership in the coordinating process for regional development. He has ready access to the President, who is the Minister in charge of regional development functions. Periodic meetings of all district ministers are held by the President in order to discuss individual coordination problems within the main developmental programmes, as well as issues of interregional coordination. The District Minister also has frequent discussions with individual sectoral ministers and their ministry officials to settle resource allocation problems as well as to solve work problems relating to such sectoral ministries operating at the district and subdistrict levels. By these means coordination is facilitated through formal and informal discussions.

Coordination at the Local or Subregional level

The divisional level coordinating agencies for subregional development planning and implementation management are the AGAs,[10] the Members of Parliament (MPs, who represent the people of the electorate) and the divisional

---

[8] See Government of Sri Lanka, *The Establishments Code,* v. 1, Chapter 38, Section 7.

[9] See *The Irrigation Ordinance,* No. 32, (1946).

[10] Divisional Revenue Officers were upgraded to posts of Divisional AGAs since 1975.

committees. The Divisional Coordinating Committee membership is comprised of the officers from the various departments and corporations who serve at the divisional and subdivisional levels.[11] They meet at least once a month under the chairmanship of the MP or the AGA.

As at the district level, the coordination process at the divisional level is facilitated by the functioning of the Divisional Agricultural Committee in formulating the Agricultural Implementation Programme. This Committee which is chaired by the MP or the AGA, plays an important role. It consists of all divisional level officers of government departments and statutory bodies connected with the implementation of the Agricultural Programme. At the subdivisional or village level, coordination is accomplished through village level officers representing various departments and corporations, such as the Cultivation Officers and Cooperative Inspectors.

The methods of coordination used may be identified as: (a) consultation, (b) circulars, and (c) directives received from higher levels. In the operation of the coordinating system at the village level, mention must be made of the political factor. The MP of the area plays an important role in the formulation of programmes and projects (especially under the DCB), and also helps to coordinate activities both at the divisional and village levels.

Over the years, an increase may be observed in the power and influence of the MPs within divisional and subdivisional administrative and social processes. The extent of such power and influence in many instances exceeds specific statutory or legal authority vested in an MP. The MP acts as an intermediary between different interest groups and functional bodies operating at the local level, in their transactions with governmental processes at the subregional, regional and central levels. In his role as MP, he performs an important brokerage function in the selection of DCB or nationally financed development projects in different functional sectors within each local area. He has frequent consultations and informal meetings with officials of sectoral departments functioning at the divisional and subdivisional levels. In this task, he also reconciles conflicting interests of different functional agencies in the process of plan implementation.

The divisional AGAs perform a similar coordinative role at the divisional or subdivisional levels as does the GA at the regional level. By virtue of his position, the AGA functions as chairman of the Divisional Coordinating Committee and the Divisional Agricultural Committee. However, by virtue of power and influence at the subregional level, the Member of Parliament chairs these meetings whenever he is present. The relationship of the divisional AGA with the MP is therefore an important factor in the successful coordination of plan preparation, budgeting, and implementation management.

[11] See Government of Sri Lanka, *The Establishments Code,* v. 1, Chapter 38, Section 8.

Multilevel Coordination

The clustering of coordination roles and tasks performed with relation to regional development crystallize along five vertical levels, as follows:

1. Supra-political level — the President and the Cabinet.
2. Supra-administrative level — the Development Secretaries Committee, the Ministry of Finance and Planning, and the Ministry of Plan Implementation.
3. Central administration level — sectoral ministries, departments and corporations.
4. Regional administration level — the District Ministry and district officers of departments and corporations.
5. Subregional administration level — the divisional AGA's office and sub-offices of departments and corporations at the divisional level.

A schematic illustration of the coordinative processes at these five levels is found in Figure 9-1.

The main function of the Budget Division is the preparation of the Budget Estimates of both capital and recurrent government expenditures.

EVALUATION OF COORDINATION FUNCTIONS

In this section, a critical examination will be made of the key aspects of coordination which relate to regional development performance. As an overall evaluation, it is observed that institutional coordination in the past has not functioned as the principal determinant of regional development — though several influencing relationships could be identified. Regional development performance is directly related to the successive government's policies providing for the basic needs of the people, and in particular the development of the rural areas and the Dry Zone. In this effort, resource availability for regional development is an important factor, due to the vulnerability of the economy to international trade conditions as well as to prevailing climatic conditions for agricultural production. Different governments have all operated within a democratic framework with all its possibilities and constraints. This feature has a direct bearing on the processes and pace of regional development.

The contribution of regional development coordination is greater with regard to indicators of policy relevance and impact, but less so with respect to inter-sectoral consistency or performance efficiency. The bulk of investment expenditures and development programmes since independence have been channelled towards regional development. As such, a high degree of policy relevance may be observed. Similarly, due to state welfare policies providing for the basic needs of rural people and the development of backward areas, the Physical Quality of Life Index has resulted in a high score of 83.[12] This is higher than most other Asian countries, even though per capita GNP levels in Sri Lanka may be lower.

206

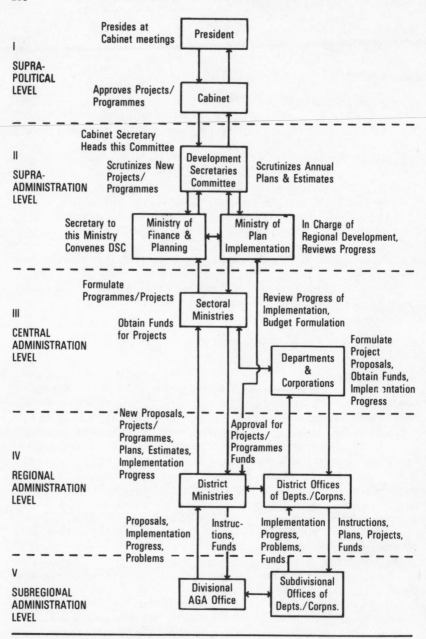

Figure 9-1. Multilevel Coordination

On the other hand, deficiencies are identifiable with regard to intersectoral consistency and the complementarity of sectoral investments by area at specific points in time. However, over a longer time frame there have been attempts to rectify such inconsistencies. In this respect, the process of regional development indicates imbalances at any particular period with forces which operate over a longer time period to smooth such imbalances.[13] Due to this factor, deficiencies could be observed in optimizing performance efficiency in the regional development process.

The role of the institutional machinery in coordinating the identification and integration of sectoral programmes for regional development reveals many shortcomings. At present, there is no annual plan for overall district development within each region. Besides the absence of such an overall plan, the two most important annual programmes that are undertaken (namely, the Agricultural Implementation Programme and the DCB Programme), also reveal deficiencies. The Agricultural Programme is to some extent an aggregation of targets of different agencies operating in the agricultural sector. The matching of these targets in terms of area considerations is weak. The weakness of the institutional machinery and planning expertise for overall agricultural planning at the regional and local levels has partly contributed to this situation. The multiplicity of agencies (including public corporations and statutory boards) which function within the agricultural development sector has also complicated prevailing coordination problems.

With regard to the DCB, identification of capital investments for projects is not carried out in a planned manner to secure intersectoral complementarity. A high proportion of capital expenditure under this budget has not reinforced the agricultural programme or other directly productive activities, as investments have been concentrated in the social and economic overhead sectors. Priorities are mainly determined by MPs who prefer conspicuous construction projects. Construction programmes undertaken also exceed the implementation capacity available at the regional level. The present rate of implementation has been lower than what has been programmed annually.

There are practical difficulties in Sri Lanka in identifying and integrating sectoral programmes for securing synchronized complementarity. A considerable degree of regional development has already taken place in the country. As such, any programme of development undertaken annually is intended to fill up investment gaps in the present development situation. Annual development plans based on such an orientation and need, tend to be disjointed as they primarily emphasize "project gaps in development." Similarly, a mechanistic requirement for overall comprehensiveness may overlook the importance of integrating projects

---

12 J.W. Sewell, et. al., *The United States and World Development* (New York: Praeger, 1977).

13 Readers may be reminded of the theory of "unbalanced development" by A.O. Hirschman.

to serve *the real needs* of the local people. Integration of projects in this sense may be required rather from the judgemental standpoint and perception of the rural beneficiaries emerging from an active democratic process. Also, a greater degree of technocratic comprehensiveness introduced through regional development programmes and projects require a greater degree of governmental intervention and resource deployment. This process might dampen popular initiative and the need for local communities to be self-reliant in their own development, and may thus be counterproductive.

With regard to coordination and linkages of multilevel planning and budgeting, present performance on the whole is satisfactory. This is partly due to the integration of both planning and finance functions with one central ministry. The close interaction which has resulted between these two processes, as well as the integrative role played by the Development Secretaries Committee has contributed to this situation, though in actual day-to-day operations, some practical difficulties have emerged, such as the need for additional funds due to cost escalations and inflation, disrupting the planned cost structure of capital projects.

The institutional machinery for coordination at the central level reflects varying deficiencies. Currently, the Presidential Secretariat is a comparatively small establishment which may not facilitate the coordination of all development policy at the regional level. This function is being performed by the Cabinet with the assistance of the Development Secretaries Committee. The task of coordinating the process of planning, budgeting and implementation management on a systematic and continuous basis may perhaps require a more permanently staffed organizational arrangement. This need is even more pronounced, as the activities of over thirty central ministries and twenty-four district ministries need to be synthesized and coordinated.

The separation of the plan implementation function from the machinery of regional development has also created problems of coordinating regional planning with implementation management. The allocation of functions and work to different ministries has not kept in view the requirements for coordination within each sector of the economy. The fragmentation of socioeconomic sectors for purposes of planning and implementation management into numerous subsectors has created its own coordination problems. The responsibility for coordinating the plan and implementation management of different ministries operating within the same socioeconomic sector is somewhat diffused. This has resulted in many instances of duplication and overlapping of efforts.

Within each ministry there are also instances of poor coordination especially in the implementation management of programmes undertaken for regional development by ministry departments with corporate bodies under the same ministry. Staffing patterns and organizational arrangements of public corporations discharging regional development functions have not been adequately designed to ensure coordination practices. Occasional changes in the allocation of departments and other agencies to different ministries have tended to disrupt the process of institutionalizing a system of coordination. Staff transfers within these organizations (especially from the Combined Services) militate against the crystallization of settled interpersonal arrangements for coordination.

Operational weakness may be observed in the integration of operational plans and budgets of sectoral ministries at the centre with the annual developmental programmes at the district level. Coordination between central sectoral ministries and departments is inadequate with respect to their annual project plans and finances for implementation with the district ministries. In some instances, the coordinating agencies at the regional and local levels are unaware of the nature of development projects and expenditures that sectoral ministries and their departments or corporations are intending to mobilize and utilize at the regional and local levels during the year.

Several problems and deficiencies may be observed in the standardization of procedures and methods, as well as responsibilities and functions for implementation management coordination among different horizontal and vertical agencies. The need for technical specialization in different sectors of development, as well as the compulsion to accelerate the development process has created a proliferation of over thirty sectoral ministries at the centre with over 150 departmental agencies as well as public corporations. The task of coordinating this number of specialized agencies has indeed been a difficult one, in both vertical and horizontal dimensions. With regard to vertical relationships between the central and regional levels, the main problem that needs resolution is the dual control and supervision of staff and programmes at the district level by the sectoral ministries at the centre, and the District Minister and GA in the region. At present, the extent of authority and specific coordination functions of sectoral ministry programmes by the District Minister have not been specified. This factor weakens vertical coordination and creates similar horizontal coordination problems, both at regional and local levels.

Though on the whole, the process of regional development coordination has been distinctly strengthened by the establishment of district ministries, several problems remain to be resolved. Although the authority and status of district ministers functioning at the regional and local levels have not been questioned by the public sector personnel, this may not be the case with the relationship of district MPs with their district minister concerned. The identification of projects for financing under the DCB is a function mainly performed by individual MPs, and the district minister generally plays a marginal role. The district ministry, therefore, does not have adequate resource allocation powers. Similarly, the investments of central ministries at the district level are not within the financial control of the district ministry. There is reluctance on the part of central ministries to allocate resources as well as to delegate financial authority to the district ministry with regard to projects undertaken by such ministries at the regional and local levels. This reflects the need to stabilize the relationships between centre and region in terms of authority, status and resource allocation powers.

Regarding the location of the coordinating agencies within the hierarchical structure and its accessibility to political decision-making, several features may be identified. Prior to the setting up of district political authorities and subsequently district ministries, district GAs had considerable difficulties in discharging coordination functions. However, the present arrangements have improved this situation. District Ministers have become accountable to the President and therefore are able to influence decision-making at the highest level. Similarly, they also have access to sectoral Cabinet ministers at the centre. For settlement and reconciliation of implementation problems, these communication and access links have proven useful.

Demarcation of authority and responsibility between the central ministers and District Ministers has not been specified. No reference to the institution of district ministers is observed in the Constitution. They are appointed under Section 45 of the Constitution. In terms of Presidential decisions they discharge coordinating as well as agency functions at the district level. Within the framework of a unitary state, it has been found necessary to prevent central ministers from having authority and jurisdiction over subjects and functions identical to those of District Ministers. The Constitution only provides for the delegation of power and authority to deputy ministers from central ministers. Because this factor militates against the delegation of powers, the government is considering modifications.

Within the internal bureaucratic structure of the regional and local level coordinating agencies, two types of coordinating units exist, the committee system and formal bureaucratic organizational arrangements. District and divisional level committees have not been effective organizational forms for planning and budgeting. The committees themselves are rather unwieldy due to large membership. Both the District Agricultural Committee and District Development Committee are not vested with resource allocative powers and have, therefore, been more useful only in handling problems of implementation management. Subcommittees of these committees have shown better performance in discharging planning and budgeting functions. In some districts, discussions on the DCB are held separately, whereas in other regions these discussions are included in the deliberations of District Coordinating Committee meetings. No standardized practice prevails.

It is clear that the district ministry's permanent bureaucratic arrangements were grafted on the earlier *Kachcheri* system. The structure created has accommodated prevailing patterns more than create an agency designed to perform specific coordinating roles. Similarly, the organization's internal structure under the GA has not been redesigned to perform the tasks and functions of regional level development coordination.

In many instances, the functions of the *Kachcheri's* Planning Unit is limited, and its linkage to other sectoral ministries' district agencies is weak. In the relationship of the Planning Unit to the work performed by the District Agricultural Committee and District Development Committee, different arrangements are practised from district to district. Regional and local level coordinating officers (i.e., the GA and the AGA) perform multiple functions. In addition to coordination, they are also responsible for discharging several line management activities as part of the responsibilities of their office. This has reduced to a considerable extent the time available to them for concentrating on coordination work. This is especially evident at the divisional AGA level, as these officers have major responsibilities in social welfare programmes and other regulatory activities, which interfere with their available time for discharging coordinating work.

The leadership factor is an important contributing influence to coordination.

Convergence of the authority of office with the authority of knowledge has secured the best results, by synthesizing political and administrative elements. The best results in coordination have been achieved in instances of complementary and harmonious role combinations between the district minister and the GA at the regional level, as well as between the MP and the divisional AGA at the local level. This factor is, therefore, one of the most important determinants for the success of coordination. This factor, in turn, also determines to a substantial extent the degree of harmony and complementary inter-supportive relationships that prevail among different sectoral organizations at the regional and local levels.

On the other hand, the extent of standing and acceptability, especially of the district minister and the GA as perceived by others, is an important consideration. The majority of the district ministers holding office at present have entered Parliament for the first time and have to still build up a viable political base within their own political party. As such, they may not readily earn the recognition of the senior MPs who occupy portfolios of the Cabinet ministries at the central level. Similarly, many district GAs are comparatively junior members of the Sri Lanka Administrative Service. Thus, they have problems of being accepted by senior staff from technical departments functioning at the district level, and senior administrative personnel manning ministries and departments at the centre.

With regard to the technical and professional competence of the coordinating agencies' staff, a reduction of such skill-availability may be observed as one moves from the central ministries and departments to the administration at the regional and local levels. Coordination of development at the regional and local levels not only requires adequate technical and professional competence, but also the ability to lead multidisciplinary teams. The institutional arrangements at the district ministry as well as the divisional AGA office do not facilitate this requirement. Technical competence in spatial and physical planning is particularly lacking at the regional and subregional levels. Similarly, the planning staff at these levels have yet to develop skills and abilities in integrating the programmes and projects from different sectors. Partly due to these reasons, programme and project planning of different sectoral and functional agencies concerned lacks adequate consideration for coordinating linkages in intersectoral interaction.

There is room for improvement in the present conditions of communication flows and the diffusion of information. Programme and project implementation needs to be supported by more intensive inspection of projects in the field. Similarly, more relevant types of information need to be collected and processed for facilitating the preparation of comprehensive regional development plans. A greater degree of information sharing among different sectoral agencies vis-a-vis the coordinating agencies at the regional and local levels, seems to operate in regions further removed from Colombo compared with districts closer to Colombo. In the latter case, a greater degree of communication operates between the centre and the region than within the region as in the former case.

Within a longer period of time, however, an improvement in coordinating functions and practices for regional development may be distinctly seen after 1973. Prior to this year, the GAs and their assistants were the principal coordinating agencies. However, such administrative coordination through public officials alone is seen as inadequate. With greater political intervention strengthening the coordinating mechanism since 1973 (by the establishment of district political authorities and of district ministries), an improvement in the coordinative process is evident. Thus, the combination of political and administrative elements has distinctly improved coordination practices, in contrast to purely administrative arrangements for coordination which prevailed in the past. The strategy of enhancing the coordination function by introducing a greater element of political steering into this process has been successful.

Close examination of coordination styles indicates variations. It cannot be stated that one coordination style is dominant, either with reference to "integration, compromise, domination," or with respect to "standardization, planning and mutual adjustment." The particular coordination methods used are relative to the personalities of the actors concerned, and to the situational context. As such, a mix of these coordinating styles may be identified according to different problems and situations encountered.

It may be generally stated that integration of related functions within the same agency facilitates coordination. At the central level, inclusion of the planning and budgeting function within the same agency illustrates this condition. Also, combination of authority of knowledge with that of office, strengthens coordination performance. Coordination is more successful in instances where the mutual interests and advantages accruing to the agencies concerned are pronounced. In such cases, each agency assists the other in facilitating achievement of their own programmes and goals. The interdependence of different agencies in the task of coordination is also facilitated if the cause of these agencies' problems is common to one another, and also, in instances where they have to share resources or utilize the same institutional arrangements for implementation.

Some of the coordination processes described in the foregoing section have been distinctly improved in regions under the District Integrated Rural Development (IRD) Programme. Of the twenty-four districts, eight are covered under this programme at the moment — Kurunegala, Matara, Hambantota, Nuwara Eliya, Puttalam, Matale, Mannar and Vavuniya. All these regions constitute rural districts, where no high investment projects are taking place. The broad objectives of this programme are to bring about an increased income, employment and general living standards for the rural population. For this purpose a mixed approach is practised, involving resource development of underdeveloped areas and integrated rural development strategies. The projects are intended to fulfil local needs as well as to optimize the use of local resources for development.

In the districts where this programme is under way, several of the deficiencies outlined in the earlier paragraphs have been minimized to some extent. Procedures for integrating sectoral programmes, as well as for relating such programmes to physical and spatial conditions, are being effected. Multilevel planning and budgeting have also been facilitated by bringing central and sectoral ministries and departments directly as actors in regional planning and implementation.

A greater degree of horizontal and vertical coordination has also been ensured.

ᵢ ᵤₑ institutional machinery has been strengthened by funding the districts directly with resources to be used for such IRD projects. Special project directors with more technically competent office staff have been set up to discharge the functions of regional planning, budgeting and implementation management in coordination within the eight districts already under the IRD programme. These levels of coordination performance are an improvement over the coordination patterns that generally prevail within the other sixteen administrative regions of the country.

CONCLUSION

With regard to institutional factors of organizational design, several important elements may be identified. There have been no systematic or continuous effort at administrative reform in the public sector. The system has evolved over time with adjustments being made to meet specific crises as well as situational exigencies. The broad patterns of central ministries with their secretariat, the numerous centrally-controlled transferable cadres of personnel and the *Kachcheri* system of regional administration were inherited from the British period. These features still play an important role in shaping the administrative machinery. Some of these institutional forms and practices are not well suited to discharge development functions at an accelerated pace required to meet national priorities and problems.

Similarly, the number of sectoral ministries has increased with time to over thirty ministries at present. The proliferation of subsectoral ministries has not been compensated by equally powerful and necessary integrating and coordinating mechanisms at all levels within the administration. Such coordinating institutions that are available at present, require more powerful integrating devices to offset problems of intrasectoral fragmentation. Side by side with the proliferation of ministries, is the increase in number of public corporations and statutory boards which have been vested with development functions in the fields of agriculture, industry and services. Many of these agencies prefer to operate independently according to their corporate status. A significant problem has therefore emerged, not only to coordinate the work of different corporations with one another, but also to synthesize their activities with other departmental government agencies. The diffusion of responsibility with the resultant proliferation of ministries and corporate bodies, has weakened accountability and responsibility for overall results in regional development. This emphasizes a greater need for coordination to be strengthened.

A tendency for centralization is generally evident with regard to the institutional framework and its authority patterns. The capital city of Colombo, together with its head offices of ministries and departments, exercises central control and resource allocation powers. Experiments in delegation of authority to regional and local levels have not been adequate or sufficiently effective. Most of the more experienced and senior staff in public service prefer to serve in organizations at the centre. This has emphasized hierarchical control of the centre over activities at the regional level. Central ministries and departments are generally unwilling to vest the district ministries and the GAs with authority to supervise and control their staff at district and local levels. This has resulted in dual staff responsibility, accountable to both centre and regional authorities. This salient line hierarchy in administrative action also militates against development of intersectoral teams horizontally at the district and local levels for better coordination.

In examining the question of authority, it is observed that there is no statutory definition of the district minister's functions nor his relationship to the authority of the GA, or between the MP and the divisional AGA. As there is no constitutional or statutory definition of their political authority, different relationships prevail in different regions. Generally, the role of political steering performed by the politicians has led to conditions of de-bureaucratization of the administrative system. In this context, the administrative machinery and its programmes tend to be moulded and operated to fulfil political priorities and needs. On the other hand, the bureaucracy has tended to bureaucratize local government and other village level people's organizations. These organizations operate as extension arms of central administration and its regional suboffices. The reciprocal tendency to depend on the central government has in turn weakened the element of self-reliance in the people's agencies.

In behavioural terms, public sector personnel are more comfortable in coordination tasks on the basis of authoritative directions from a common superior officer. This tendency places reliance on hierarchy and weakens willingness for lateral coordination among different officers of similar hierarchical levels when discharging common interagency projects. This is partly due to greater security afforded when implementing directions received from hierarchical supervisors in comparison to the need for individual or group responsibility in lateral coordination among peers. This problem is aggravated in situations of coordination among personnel belonging to different administrative, technical and professional grades and services. For instance, technical officers may be less prone to coordinate their work with administrative personnel and vice versa due to rivalry and competition within these different services.

Friendship, social relations and interpersonal contacts are also important factors among the public sector personnel in the coordination task. To some extent, interservice rivalries are minimized due to friendly relations prevailing among staff officers working in different sectors at the regional and local levels. It is also observed that many of the departments at the regional and local levels are manned by staff from the central Combined Services such as the Sri Lanka Administrative Service, Sri Lanka Government Accountants Service, General Clerical Service, etc. In-service loyalties and familiarity of personnel pertinent to each such service is a strong integrating force, facilitating the coordination of different sectoral agencies and between the central and regional levels of administration.

Mutual role relationships among different sectoral agencies are diffused by the proliferation of sectoral agencies and operating departments/corporations. This is partly due to overlapping functions and tasks expected to be performed by these agencies. Though governmental policies have deemphasized the preparation of macro-plans in favour of specific project planning, it has not spelled out the basic objectives and missions of different agencies. Similarly, responsibilities of different agencies on a common project being unspecified, have resulted in the diffusion of responsibility and appreciation of the individual and common roles of such agencies.

With regard to technology, the extent of managerial skills available in the public sector does not adequately match the requirements of the programmes and projects undertaken for development. Apart from managerial ability, the evaluation of administrative feasibility and capability for undertaking and implementing complex programmes and projects for regional and local development is also not adequately done. Personnel at the regional level need to be trained in methods of programme planning as well as macro-planning of individual projects. In this task skills in spatial and physical planning required in regional development work, need improvement.

In the paragraphs that follow, an evaluation will be made of the noninstitutional or external factors that block coordination in regional development. Apart from coalition arrangements for the sharing of executive power, the allocation of authority and functions to Cabinet ministers has tended to fragment functionally interrelated work activities, even within single sectors. Overlapping functions are also performed by different sectoral ministries. In addition, as already mentioned, the ambit of authority and responsibility of the district minister for development at the regional and local level, and his relations with the central ministries are undefined as yet. The resolution of these issues can facilitate the achievement of a higher degree of coordination. Due to the prevalence of a highly articulate electorate, which has changed each government at the end of its term of office, politicians must respond to and be sensitive to public opinion for their survival. The operation of an open political democracy of this nature with the pressures and interactions of different interest groups which it generates, imposes strains upon the government's coordination machinery. The political system also applies pressure on the administration in its decision-making which, in turn, has resulted in the de-bureaucratization of the administration.

With regard to the policy framework, the selection of programmes and projects for regional and local development reveals certain inconsistencies. This is partly due to the project approach in planning adopted, which tends to emphasize single projects, but not their forward and backward linkages within an intersectoral context. The project approach to planning is further complicated by sudden changes and differences in political priorities of the various MPs. Politicians at the local level sometimes lack relevant information and are also misled by more articulate and powerful interest groups at the local level when selecting projects in their electorates. Also at the central level, the synthesizing of policies and approaches of related sectoral ministries is difficult to achieve when framing policies within a specific economic sector.

Some of the key elements which relate to the coordination function with regard to the local power structure must be referred to. Local power groups usually expect Government agencies to discharge development work for their benefit.

This has generated a pattern of paternalism by the Government. Articulate local groups influence the decisions of MPs and district ministers on matters of parochial interest, and usually not on development priorities for comprehensive regional development. In this process, less vociferous or powerful interest group in less developed areas within the regions may be overlooked. As MPs of the governing party are given priority in resource allocation, local power group demands in electorates not represented by MPs of the governing party tend to be neglected.

With a view to mobilizing popular participation, as well as facilitating articulation of local community felt needs, the Government has established a variety of people's organizations at the village level. These organizations vary from local government bodies to people's agencies discharging specific functional activities (such as village cooperatives) or more general-purpose functions (such as rural development societies). The scope of local government functions and authority is limited to the provision of basic civic amenities and performance of other functions on an agency basis. As the bulk of the funding for these bodies is provided by the central government, the degree of central control of their operations is also high.

There has been no government policy continuity on the role and operations of people's organizations, and frequent changes of political emphasis are evident. For instance, different governments have placed different emphasis and priority on rural development societies. The policy at present is to form a society for each village. The nature of these people's bodies is general purpose, but not all government agencies make use of their capabilities. Similarly, in the agricultural sector, people's organizations have been merged into multipurpose societies and these, in turn, have been transformed into primary societies with village branches. Also, Cultivation Committees, which have served the farmer, have thereafter been operationally abandoned and their apex bodies, the Agricultural Productivity Committees, are now being transformed into Agrarian Service Centres. Frequent changes in the institutional machinery of people's organizations have prevented the development of an institution building process to facilitate rural level planning and implementation. It has also been observed that local power groups "capture" office in many of these local bodies, and thereafter, tend to operate these agencies in their own self-interest. In such situations, the unrepresentative character of village agencies interferes with their effective functioning.

Regarding the cultural aspect as one of the environmental factors, the nature of the value system is important. Buddhism is the religion practised by the majority of the people. This religion with its message of tolerance and nonmaterialistic value-orientation, has moulded the attitudes of the people. In general, public sector personnel manifest a high tolerance level for not causing discomfort to others, even in situations of managerial disorganization or laxity. A high achievement orientation is also generally absent, partly due to nonmaterialistic cultural values. Motivation to work with a sense of urgency and commitment has not been generated by the prevalent cultural system. Sympathy is extended even to public officers who are lax or inefficient in performing their duties. Rarely are such types discontinued from government service. This factor is further reinforced by a system of disciplinary procedures which are cumbersome and do not easily enable the public sector to get rid of its poor performers.

Similarly, social ties, family and kinship relationships, locality affiliations and friendships are important in the social milieu. Subordinate staff may cooperate with their superiors due more to personal and informal bonds rather than as a requirement of public office (based on a Weberian model of bureaucracy). In this context, coordination is facilitated by personal friendships, informal relationships and social familiarity with the staff of the coordinating agencies concerned. In many instances, if any specific job or work in a government office requires execution by a client, the intervention of another employee from the same office who is known personally to the client (or who has been contacted through an intermediary personally known to the staff of that agency), would usually facilitate expediting such work. This factor places constraints on the nature and extent of coordination that could be effected among different government agencies. In turn, some of these cultural factors tend to limit the attention of individual public sector personnel to performing their work within the bounds of their own departmental activities.

There are also several constraints regarding resources which affect coordination. Due to unfavourable conditions in the balance of payments and deficit financing in the government budget, adequate public funds may not be available to undertake comprehensive and integrated development programmes in all regions of the country. As such, investments on different projects need to be undertaken, as and when finances are available, which may interfere with the imperatives of balanced rural development. Similarly, scarcity of financial resources entails a greater degree of central control which may not provide adequate arrangements for delegation and flexibility in budget operations at the regional level. There is also a reluctance for allocating large sums of money from the budgets of central ministries for use by the districts on a decentralized basis. On the other hand, there is a scarcity of skills in management as well as project and regional planning expertise within the regions. Available skills constitute a scarce resource which is not utilized to its optimum.

10

REGIONALIZING FOR ADMINISTRATION AND DEVELOPMENT: THE PHILIPPINE EXPERIENCE

ARMAND V. FABELLA

INTRODUCTION

THE PHILIPPINE experience at regionalization has been basically oriented towards attaining a two-fold objective: (a) the achievement of administrative decentralization through the process of deconcentrating governmental authority and functions from the central offices to the regions, and (b) the acceleration of regional development by turning the regions into focal points from where planning and development activities are to be undertaken.

This paper is intended to review various facets of the regionalization process experienced in the Philippines, with particular focus on the rationale, structures, administrative and coordinative arrangements and other related features which have characterized such efforts. This paper will also review the efforts undertaken to operationalize this regionalization concept, to assess the effectiveness of the regionalization strategies adopted, and to identify and evaluate the problems and issues arising from these efforts.

REGIONALIZATION: OBJECTIVES AND RATIONALE

A major objective of regionalization is administrative decentralization. There are several reasons for this, the most basic one having to do with the very purpose of government. A large percentage of the populace looks to government primarily for the quantity and effectiveness of services it is able to deliver. Services, therefore, are considered to be more effective when there is greater personal contact between government personnel and the general public it serves. Rather than transact business from central offices in the Metro Manila area, people throughout the country, especially those in rural areas, prefer to take their problems to readily available local officials who have decision-making authority in handling their problems on the government's behalf.

By effecting administrative decentralization through regionalization, action on many matters is facilitated through their handling at the regional and subregional levels without having to refer them to the central offices in Metro Manila. This is especially true of routine and ordinary operational matters that are already adequately covered by established policies and standards. The past practice of referring most matters to the central offices for resolution and action is unnecessary and only serves to unduly extend bureaucratic red tape. This procedure is also undesirable because it is both inconvenient and expensive for the public clientele.

The purposes of regionalizing the government, through administrative decentralization, are indicated in the report of the Commission on Reorganization, thus:

> By standardizing field service areas where the boundaries and regional centers are common to all departments (now ministries) and agencies, the goal of bringing public services as close as possible to the people and in an effective manner will be achieved. This will rectify the present diversity in the regionalization of government departments and agencies. Such diversity has brought about many problems which may be summarized, as follows: (a) transactions with the government have to be taken up by citizens who need the services of field offices, particularly those of regional offices, in many different places at increased cost in terms of time, money, and effort; (b) varying regional compositions, boundaries, and centers for the different bureaus of a department entail more appropriations for personal services, maintenance and other expenses, and capital equipment than standardized regionalization; and (c) field offices encounter difficulties in taking concerted action on related programs because varying regional boundaries and centers impose impediments to effective communication and operations.[1]

A second major objective of regionalization is the identification of the region as a major unit for purposes of planning and development. With regard to this, it has been the government's declared policy that

> the socioeconomic development of the various regions shall be promoted by undertaking regional planning and development within the context of aggregative planning at the national level and specific planning and programming at the local level.[2]

There are good reasons for putting emphasis on the region as the focal point for development planning. The national development plan, for instance, would not be as meaningful unless it is indicative of the major individual programmes and projects to be undertaken. When it comes to programme and project planning, often it is enough to express this in general terms, such as the establishment of a certain number of hospitals within the next five years. To be effective, project

---

[1] Commission on Reorganization, "Summary Justifications and Supporting Tables" in *Reorganization of the Executive Branch of the National Government* (Manila, 1972) v. 2, p. 59.

[2] Integrated Reorganization Plan [as adopted under Presidential Decree No. 1], Section 1, Article 1 (Declaration of Policy), Chapter 1, Part 7 (Regional Planning and Development) (Manila, 1972).

planning must be oriented towards projects in specific areas. The determination of specific projects within regions may be undertaken according to actual local conditions rather than in more abstract national terms, resulting in decidedly more rational and effective regional level planning.

Moreover, taking into consideration the economic aspects of regionalization, regional development has been identified as one of the major objectives of the government's development effort. As the Five-Year Philippine Development Plan, 1978-82 states, one of the country's major development goals is the "increased development of lagging regions, especially the rural areas." This is a response to the existing situation wherein some regions of the country are well-developed (e.g., Metro Manila, Central Luzon, Southern Tagalog), while others remain relatively underdeveloped (e.g., the Cagayan Valley, Bicol Region, Eastern Visayas and major portions of Mindanao).

While regionalization is an objective of development efforts, it is also a strategy utilized to reduce disparities between regions, to enable lagging regions to catch up with more developed ones and ultimately to provide balanced economic and social progress within the country. The Philippine Government has adopted this strategy to express development goals in specific spatial terms. For instance, development is translated in terms of the numbers of irrigation dams, school houses, health centres, and length of highways and farm-to-market roads to be built throughout the country over a time period. Programmes become more meaningful when their locations and beneficiaries are identified, and their links to the overall goals are defined. The land, area for spatial dimension, serves as the focal point in the development process.

OVERVIEW OF THE REGIONALIZATION EFFORT

In the Philippines, the concept of administrative decentralization is not new. The concept of dividing the country into several administrative regions in order to provide greater uniformity and standardization in the decentralization of government functions was first envisioned in the government reorganization of 1955-56, specifically in Reorganization Plan No. 53-A submitted by the Government Survey and Reorganization Commission (GSRC). This plan divided the country into eight administrative regions. The regional areas recommended by GSRC Plan No. 53-A were based on factors of provincial contiguity and geographical features, transportation and communication facilities, cultural and language groupings and population and area. In 1968, another major government reorganization was authorized under Republic Act No. 5435, which created the Commission on Reorganization to spearhead the effort. The Commission's major accomplishment was the Integrated Reorganization Plan (IRP) which was adopted on 24 September 1972 into law under Presidential Decree No. 1. Among other things, the plan provided for the division of the country into eleven (later increased to thirteen by subsequent amendatory laws) administrative regions.

A distinct mode for regional development evolved during the 1960s was the creation of development authorities at the regional and subregional levels.

Among these were the Mindanao Development Authority, the Bicol Development Company, the Central Luzon-Cagayan Valley Authority, the Laguna Lake Development Authority and a host of provincial development authorities which up to now have not been actually activated due to funding constraints. These structures are corporate entities mandated to engage in viable self-sustaining projects to help develop the regions. Under the IRP, the role of regional development authorities as major complementary efforts in regional development is recognized and recommended for institutionalization in every region where adequate funding is available. The regional development authority is envisioned to be the implementing arm for many of the regional development council's individual projects.

The adoption of the "Integrated Area Development" approach, a variant of the regional development authority, as an innovative pattern in regional development gained momentum in the 1970s. Under this scheme, a particular area, usually a subregional one, is earmarked for intensive development efforts on a multisectoral basis involving the coordinated participation of various sectoral agencies. At present, a number of integrated area development programmes are operational, such as the Bicol River Basin Programme, the Mindoro Integrated Development Programme, the Cagayan Integrated Agricultural Development Programme, and the Leyte-Samar Development Programme. It is envisioned under the Five-Year Philippine Development Plan that this development model will be continued as a strategy for accelerating regional development.

Special regional administrative models have recently evolved with the establishment of the Metro Manila Commission as well as the Autonomous Regions in Mindanao (in regions IX and XII) stipulated by Presidential Decrees Nos. 824 and 1618, respectively. A more detailed discussion of the dimensions and features of each of the above-cited pattern and model for regional development is given below.

PRESENT REGIONALIZATION PATTERN

The existing pattern for the delineation of the country into thirteen administrative regions, each with a common regional centre, is prescribed under the, IRP, as amended.

Regional boundaries were determined primarily on the basis of the "river basin" approach, taking into account economic and sociological aspects of the regional areas surrounding the river basin. The following set of criteria and factors were considered in dividing the country into viable areas for development: (a) physical characteristics or geographical features such as mountain ranges, river basins, plains, bodies of water, etc.; (b) transportation and communication facilities; (c) cultural and ethnic factors; (d) land area and population; and (e) planning, administrative and political factors. Another basic consideration was the political element, since aside from being technically feasible, any rational regionalization scheme must also be politically acceptable. Thus, regional delineation does not cut across existing local government jurisdictional areas;

instead, the regional boundaries prescribed respect and are congruent with the local government's geographical boundaries. Because of political considerations, the originally proposed ten regional districts (recommended by a technical group created to study and propose the proper regional subdivision of the country) were further subdivided to include another regional area, totalling eleven regions. This regional pattern was eventually incorporated in the Integrated Reorganization Plan. Later, however, they were increased to the present thirteen regional areas through various legislative amendments.

Selection of regional area centres on the other hand, was based on the following factors: (a) accessibility to the centre from all provinces within the region; (b) presence of developed facilities such as buildings, power, water, etc.; and (c) potential for economic, administrative and political growth. As was the case in the determination of regional areas, strong political pressures were manifested in some particular instances, such as in the choice of a regional centre for Region V (Bicol Region), located between the cities of Legaspi and Naga.

With the establishment of standard regional areas, the Integrated Reorganization Plan prescribed that the various ministries (formerly referred to as departments) and national government agencies establish regional offices where necessary, especially where there are strong outreach programmes or extensive field operations. The various regional area offices are seen as extensions of the ministries and agencies having functional jurisdiction and assuming responsibility for the implementation of sectoral programmes and projects within the region.

Two organizational models are provided for the establishment of regional offices: (a) ministry-wide regionalization and (b) bureau-wide regionalization. In the first model, the regional offices are placed under the office of the minister to which they directly report, while the staff consists of the central office bureaus whose responsibility is to develop policies, standards and guidelines and to provide only technical and functional supervision over the regional offices. In the second model, the regional offices are bureau extensions within the ministry. They are under the bureaus and not the minister to whom they directly report. Thus, the bureaus retain their line functions with direct supervision and control responsibilities over their respective regional networks. In the Philippine context, ministry-wide regionalization is preferred because this model provides better ministry field operations integration and coordination at the regional and sub-regional levels. Hence, bureau-wide regionalization is acceptable only when the functions of ministry field operations are clearly heterogeneous.

Institutionalized administrative decentralization through the establishment of regional offices, however, would be useless unless accompanied by a liberal delegation of authority on administrative and substantive matters to the regional offices. Thus, Presidential Letter of Instructions No. 448 issued on 18 August 1976 directed that a minimum standard set of administrative authorities be delegated to the regional offices which encompass some power relative to: (a) appointing authority over certain levels of regional personnel; (b) approval of personnel actions such as transfers, leave of absence, travel orders, and other related matters; (c) disbursement of fund approvals; (d) formulation and submission of regional budget estimates, including the administration of the regional office budget; and (e) requisition and procurement of supplies and materials up to a prescribed amount. With respect to authority over operational and substantive matters, it was also enjoined that substantial powers be delegated to the regional offices by the ministry or agency heads within two years after their establishment.

INTEGRATED AREA DEVELOPMENT APPROACH

As mentioned earlier, adoption of the integrated area development approach is an innovative strategy for accelerating regional development. This approach is in pursuance of the declared government policy (contained in Presidential Decree No. 1378, dated 17 May 1978) "to promote and support the improvement, growth and development of the countryside through integrated area development consistent with the principle of self-help and self-reliance." The overall coordinative mechanism for implementing this approach is provided by the National Council on Integrated Area Development (NACIAD) which replaced the former Cabinet Coordinating Committee on Integrated Rural Development Projects. The Council is incorporated within the framework of the National Economic and Development Authority (NEDA), the government's central planning agency, with the President as Chairman and selected cabinet officials as members. The powers and functions of the NACIAD are to: (a) institutionalize the implementing mechanism for integrated area development through formal planning, monitoring and budgetary controls; (b) formulate an integrated framework plan to guide the development of depressed areas; (c) rationalize rural people's participation in development planning and implementation via their local governments; (d) initiate small-scale, high-impact integrated projects utilizing existing indigenous resources; and (e) mobilize efficiently multisectoral resources and properly channel these into integrated rural development projects.

A basic feature of the integrated area development concept is that the cabinet coordinator has the responsibility of overseeing the implementation of a particular area development programme or project undertaken within the NACIAD. Invariably, the cabinet coordinator is selected from the region where the programme or project is being implemented. This technique assures attainment of political and high-level administrative leadership necessary to secure effective coordination of efforts from various agencies involved in the programme or project.

For a better understanding of the operational arrangements established for the implementation of integrated area development programme, particularly with regard to the coordinative processes involved, it would be useful to examine the Bicol River Basin Development Programme administrative framework as forerunner and prototype of such area development programmes. At the top of the organizational hierarchy is the designated cabinet coordinator who, among others, is responsible for coordinating the planning and implementation of the programme. As the coordinating authority, the cabinet coordinator is vested with the power to review the programme's consolidated plans, budgets and work programmes as well as to approve requests for budget releases by the implementing ministries and agencies for projects to be undertaken. There is also a programme office, headed by a programme director, which serves as coordinating centre for interagency planning and management of Bicol River Basin projects. A Programme Coordination Committee consisting of representatives from the implementing agencies (usually the regional directors) and chaired by the Programme Director further facilitates the coordination process for day-to-day operations. Thus, coordination is a built-in facet of programme structure operations, both at the national and regional levels.

Because of the apparently successful experience with the integrated area development approach, it is envisioned that this mode of operation will be given further impetus and wider application in regional development. To quote from the Five-Year Philippine Development Plan (1978-82) document:

> Development programs suitable to the integrated area development approach, both regional and subregional, will be identified and implemented. . . . Additional specific areas, especially the depressed ones, will be identified for integrated area development similar to the Bicol River Basin Program and the Mindoro Development Program. Administrative capability for the coordinated implementation of integrated rural area development programs based on the interagency approach will be strengthened.

SPECIAL MODES FOR REGIONAL ADMINISTRATION

The Philippine experience in regionalization has seen the evolution of special modes for regional administration oriented towards further strengthening the coordinative process in regional development. These are the Metro Manila Commission (for the National Capital Region) and the Autonomous Regions established in two Mindanao regions (IX and XII).

Metro Manila Commission: A Model for Metropolitan Development

By virtue of Presidential Decree No. 824 dated 7 November 1975, the Metro Manila Commission was instituted to provide central governance over four cities (including the capital city of Manila) and thirteen municipalities located within a contiguous geographical area designated as Metropolitan Manila. The area constitutes one of the standard regional subdivisions of the country. Originally known as Region No. 4, it came to be known as the National Capital Region pursuant to a subsequent Presidential Decree. Because Metro Manila is a highly urbanized region, it was felt that the integration of common services was essential in attaining maximum effectiveness in the provision of such services. Hence, the establishment of the Metro Manila Commission has been described as "an attempt at the institutional integration of existing local units with a general purpose governmental machinery at a higher tier."[3]

The Commission is comprised of a Chairman or Governor; a Vice-Chairman or Vice-Governor; and three Commissioners, one for planning, another for finance, and the third for operations. The Governor and Vice-Governor are also the Commission's General Manager and Assistant General Manager, respectively. The Commission is mandated to act as the central government to establish and administer programmes and provide common and essential services to the Metro Manila area. Local government units on the other hand, are directed to implement the integration of common public services pertinent to their respective jurisdictions.

The novel experiment of instituting a Commission type of governance for Metro Manila may be perceived as successful, inasmuch as it has achieved effective integration and coordination of local government unit operations, particularly with respect to essential services. It may not be exactly correct, however, to attribute the apparent success of this unique venture completely to its inherent soundness as an organizational model. It is certain that the imposing quality of political leadership provided by the Metro Manila Governor, who currently is the First Lady, has been a major factor in attaining this success. There is good reason to doubt whether the same degree of success could have been attained had some other personality, other than the First Lady, been the governor. Thus, the Metro Manila Commission experience clearly indicates that the personality factor is a strong influence of determinant in the degree of effectiveness that may be attained in the coordinative process.

Autonomous Regions

The institution of a special regional administrative system in the two Autonomous Regions of Mindanao (IX and XII) has been effected pursuant to a law enacted by the national assembly and implemented under Presidential Decree No. 1618 dated 25 July 1979. This system, already veering towards some form of regional government, represents just about the most advanced type of administrative model for regional administration that has to date been adopted in the Philippines.

Under this system, a Regional Assembly and a Regional Executive Council are constituted within each Autonomous Region. The Assembly consists of members elected at large by the region's qualified voters, is tasked with the function of enacting regional laws and ordinances, and in effect, is the Autonomous Region's legislative arm. The Executive Council, on the other hand, is a five-man body comprised of a chairman and four members, is tasked with the function of implementing the policies, programmes and legislation enacted by the Assembly, and in effect, is the region's executive unit.

---

[3] Raul P. de Guzman, "Proliferation of Regional Government Bodies and the Duplication of Functions at the Regional Level" [Memorandum submitted to the Presidential Commission on Reorganization, Manila, 25 September 1978].

The Autonomous Regions are given relatively extensive powers. The Regional Assembly, for instance, may exercise taxing authority through legislative imposition of taxes, fees and charges. The Regional Executive Council, on the other hand, is given some degree of coordinative authority over the regional offices with respect to regional development project implementation, as well as ample delegated supervisory and regulatory powers over local government units. With regards to regional planning, coordination is attained by designating the Regional Executive Council Chairman as ex-officio chairman of the Regional Development Council, and by providing that the Regional Development Plan formulated by the Council be submitted for adoption by the Regional Assembly before being submitted to the national government for assessment by the NEDA and incorporation in the national development plan.

It is still too early to assess the effectiveness of the regional administrative model established in the Autonomous Regions. Should this model prove to be successful, this prototype could serve as the blueprint for its institutionalization in other administrative regions on a nationwide basis.

REGIONALIZATION OF THE PLANNING FUNCTION: THE CONCEPT OF THE REGIONAL DEVELOPMENT COUNCIL

A new dimension in the planning process has been added (pursuant to the Integrated Reorganization Plan), which has also been established under the Plan within each region, through the institution of regional planning within the framework of the Regional Development Council. Before discussing the various facets of plan formulation at the regional level, however, it may be helpful to examine how the planning function is undertaken at the national level.

Planning at the National Level: Linkages between Budgeting and Implementation

At the core of the planning function is the National Economic and Development Authority (NEDA), the central planning agency of the national government. The NEDA Board is chaired by the President himself and includes cabinet members whose ministries are directly or principally involved in economic development, such as the Ministers of Finance, Budget, Public Works, Public Highways, Agriculture, Industry, and others. It was felt that this arrangement in the composition of the NEDA would provide a positive bridge between plan formulation and execution since the main executive officials responsible for implementation are involved in plan formulation.

Horizontal linkages with the ministries responsible for sectoral plan formulation are provided by instituting planning services within the various ministries, while vertical linkages with the regions are provided by the establishment of the Regional Development Councils, a feature which later on will be discussed in more detail. Linkage between planning and budgeting is effected through the establishment of the Development Budget Coordination Committee, tied with the NEDA but chaired by the Minister of the Budget, which is intended to bridge the gap between plan formulation and translation of the plan into annual fiscal programmes. The national planning process generally involves the evaluation and integration of sectoral plan inputs submitted by the various ministries, which is then translated into a five-year plan document (which includes a ten-year projection and a long-term perspective plan) and officially approved by the President.

A plus factor in the NEDA's planning function competence is the professionalism of its technical staff due to the relatively higher salary levels that are allowed for its personnel. A sampling survey conducted by the NEDA of the planning services in selected ministries, however, indicated that the orientation of the actual functions of these services was not quite proper and that the quality of their personnel component was not exactly to the degree desirable for such a critical function. A much more serious concern with regards to the increasing attention given by the budget ministry to long-term budgeting, is the possibility of divergence arising between the NEDA development plan and the fiscal plan. At this early stage, a coordinative mechanism needs to be established to prevent this problem.

Planning at the Regional Level

A Regional Development Council (RDC) has been established in each region as the unit responsible for the coordination of regional planning processes and the formulation of a comprehensive regional development plan. Just recently, under Presidential Executive Order No. 589, the planning role of the RDC has been further strengthened. The RDC is mandated under this order to prepare and adopt a Regional Development Investment Programme (RDIP), as the implementing programme of the regional development plan, through the identification and development of programmes and projects designed to substantiate the objectives and strategies of accelerating regional development.

Organizationally, the RDC is considered to be an extension of the NEDA, with the NEDA regional office serving as the Council's technical staff and the NEDA regional director as ex-officio vice-chairman of the Council. The RDC is comprised of regional directors of national line ministries and agencies and provincial governors and city mayors within the region. The President designates the chairman from among the elective members (except in the Autonomous Regions where the Regional Executive Council Chairman is ex-officio chairman).

To further strengthen the operational viability of the RDC, the President issued Letter of Instructions No. 542 (as supplemented by Letter of Instructions No. 542-A), prescribing the powers and functions of the RDC chairman which shall be exercised for and on behalf of the Council, as follows:

1. Direct the formulation of an integrated regional development plan to include plans of national government agencies, regional development bodies and local governments within the regions.

2. Coordinate the implementation of development programmes and projects within the region and establish a monitoring system.
3. Recommend to the NEDA and the Ministry of the Budget a system of priorities in allocating budgetary resources according to the regional plan for national government programmes and projects within the region.
4. Administer the share of the region from the Regional Development Fund provided under the National Budget decree, and such other funds as may be provided by the national government and/or local governments for regional projects.
5. Coordinate local planning activities within the region to ensure consistency between local and regional development plans.
6. Call on any agency, government instrument, private entity or organization within the region for cooperation and assistance in the performance of the council's functions.
7. Course through the NEDA Director-General all regional plans, programmes, reports and other developmental matters for submission to the NEDA Board and the President.

Linkage between regional planning and budgeting is provided for under Letter of Instructions No. 447 dated 12 August 1976, which institutes a system for regional budgeting. Among other responsibilities, it provides that: (a) regional offices develop their respective regional budgets in conformity with priorities established by the RDCs; (b) the budget ministry shall furnish information to the RDC chairman on fund releases to regional offices; and (c) the NEDA Director-General concur in the promulgation of rules and regulations to implement the system of regional budgeting. But a much more stronger fiat to link budgeting with regional planning is the provision in Executive Order No. 589 which provides that the RDIP prepared by the RDC shall serve as the basis for public sector resource allocation within the regions.

COORDINATIVE MECHANISMS AT THE REGIONAL LEVEL

Coordination of the implementation of the various regional offices' programmes and projects at the regional level has been a problem area in regional management. To appreciate this, however, an overview of the coordinative mechanisms at the national level would be helpful.

At the national level, coordination among the ministries is initially effected through the cabinet and the NEDA Board at the top policy level. A Cabinet Standing Committee had been constituted to facilitate the resolution of ministry problems. At the operational level, coordination among ministries is usually done through a host of interagency arrangements which serve as a forum for synchronizing ministry actions that are taken separately. In some instances, purely coordinative bodies, such as the Commission on Population and the National Nutrition Council, are created to provide coordinative direction to pertinent operations of agencies concerned.

At the regional level, the RDC Chairman is the most appropriate regional official to provide the necessary leadership for effective coordination of the implementing activities of regional units, agencies and local governments. In fact, he has the authority to do so under Letter of Instructions 542 and 542-A previously mentioned. In actual practice, however, it appears that he lacks due recognition and stature necessary to carry out his command. At the most, therefore, his coordination function is merely a persuasive one. Of course, the degree of his effectiveness in this regard varies according to how closely associated he is with the Presidency.

Other techniques have been used to realize more effective coordination of implementation activities at the regional level. One of this was the institution of a Presidential Regional Officer for Development (PROD), as well as a Presidential Regional Action Officer (PRAO) in each region. The PRODs were made responsible for monitoring the progress of the implementation of critical priority development projects within the region, as well as for taking measures to alleviate bottlenecks and resolve problems that could cause delays in implementation. The PRAOs, on the other hand, were tasked with the responsibility of coordinating the efforts of agencies in the region with respect to increased food production. In all cases, those designated as PRODs and PRAOs were part-time officials, such as regional directors, army officers, provincial governors and city mayors. Initially, the PRODs and PRAOs were actively involved in carrying out their respective functions, but this involvement gradually tapered off to the point that these positions were formally abolished under Presidential Decree No. 955 dated 8 July 1976. These were replaced by Regional Presidential Assistant (RPA) positions within each region (except Metro Manila). These act as personal representatives of the President within their respective regions. Up until now, however, the RPAs have not been named; thus, the PRODs and the PRAOs continue to function with diminished intensity, albeit only somewhat perfunctorily.

Another technique used, was the creation of a Regional Commissioner within each of the two regions in Mindanao (Regions IX and XII), with ample powers for achieving development planning and implementation coordination within the region. For this purpose, among others, he was given the following powers and functions:

1. Serve as Chairman of the Regional Development Council. As such, he has primary responsibility in directing the formulation of a development plan for the region.
2. Monitor the implementation of development programmes in the region. He shall anticipate and where necessary step in to resolve any bottlenecks that may arise in the planning or implementation of development programmes in the region. He is vested with presidential authority to call upon any agency of the national or local government, to undertake actions deemed necessary to attain the development objectives of the region.
3. Monitor the performance of local government officials. For this purpose, he shall coordinate with the Ministry of Local Government and Com-

munity Development in conducting periodic audits on the performances of local government officials.

In terms of effectiveness, the coordinative process at the regional level was thus strengthened, but then much of this may probably be attributed to the personal leadership quality of the Regional Commissioner, especially in Region IX where the commanding officer of the Southern Command was Regional Commissioner. With the establishment of the Autonomous Regions, the offices of the Regional Commissioners were abolished and their functions assumed by the Regional Executive Council.

CONCLUDING STATEMENT: FURTHER AREAS OF CONCERN

Administrative reform measures are indicated for certain areas of concern towards further strengthening the system for coordination of planning and implementation, particularly at the regional level. These are, among others:

1. With the establishment of additional ministries and increased specialization in governmental functions, it has become exceedingly difficult for individual ministries to operate and act on matters without first touching base with other ministries involved. Thus, the coordinative process has become much more difficult. It is necessary, therefore, to strengthen and further refine the interagency approach as an effective medium for intraministry coordination.
2. Delegation of substantive authority to the regional offices is necessary in order to facilitate more effective interaction among the various regional offices. A weak regional office with limited powers in terms of delegated authority cannot be an effective partner in the regional development process. ·
3. At the subregional level, particularly at the level of the municipality and the barangay (the lowest political unit), no single authority is given the responsibility of coordinating the national government's outreach programmes carried out by the subregional units of national government entities' personnel. At this level, coordination with local government units is also more critical. The municipal mayor, a political person, may possibly be tapped as the medium for effecting this desired coordination.

PART THREE

CONCLUDING OVERVIEW

11

COORDINATION, PLAN IMPLEMENTATION AND INSTITUTIONAL REFORM: SEARCH FOR NEW APPROACHES

G. SHABBIR CHEEMA

THERE IS a significant variation in the regional development performance of the selected Asian countries in particular with regards to increases in growth, employment opportunities, social welfare and infrastructural facilities. As past experiences in Bangladesh and Malaysia show, this could be attributed to their respective resource bases. Yet, an analysis of development planning and implementation in most of the selected countries points to several similarities: The accomplishment of equity-oriented targets have proven to be extremely difficult, resulting in further widening the gap between the various social groups as well as between the rural and urban areas; intersectoral consistency and complementarity in governmental activities have faltered, especially in the implementation stage; the utilization of efficiency criteria in resource allocation and investment decisions has proven to be increasingly difficult; a large percentage of the populace is still below the national poverty line; and the lack of meaningful participation by the people in the development process continues to be a nagging problem. It can be contended that the effectiveness of government agencies as well as nongovernmental organizations in performing their tasks is perhaps the most critical factor in accelerating a country's development pace. More specifically, appropriate institutional support structures are a prerequisite in ensuring intersectoral consistency, policy relevance and efficiency in governmental intervention in the economy.

The purpose of this chapter, therefore, is to assess the effectiveness of the institutional machinery of the selected Asian developing countries in articulating and implementing regional development programmes and policies. Though the main emphasis is on the performance of the coordination functions within the interrelated processes of planning, budgeting and implementation management, other institutional dimensions, such as decentralization, local constituency organization, planning and budgeting linkages, monitoring and evaluation are also analysed. Based on the different countries' experiences discussed in this volume as well as on other published and unpublished materials, an attempt is made to describe the structures and processes of coordination in the selected

Asian countries, analyse the coordination agencies' effectiveness and examine the contextual factors which impede coordination and plan implementation. This is followed by identifying the key issues in strengthening institutional support structures for promoting regional development. Given the limitations of the comparative data, the complexity of the phenomenon, and the peculiarities of each country, the statements in the following sections should be considered tentative.

STRUCTURES OF COORDINATION

In the developing countries, several structures and agencies have been created to coordinate and integrate the governments' developmental actions. Some of these are bureaucratic organizations while others are both administrative and political decision-making entities. The authority and status of these entities are statutorily defined or *ad hoc* and informal in nature. Some are entrusted with the sole task of coordinating a set of activities and others undertake operational responsibilities as well. These structures also exist at multilevels and perform horizontal and/or vertical coordination functions. In most cases they deal with either the processes of planning, budgeting or implementation management.

The key bodies that coordinate the processes of plan formulation at the national level, are the Economic Planning Unit (EPU) and the National Developmer Planning Committee (NDPC) in Malaysia; the Planning Commission and the Cabinet Division in Bangladesh; the Planning Commission and the National Development Council (NDC) in India; the Ministry of Finance and Planning in Sri Lanka; the National Economic and Social Development Board (NESDB) in Thailand; and the National Economic and Development Authority (NEDA) in the Philippines. At the regional and subregional levels, the task of coordinating the process of plan formulation is undertaken by the regional planning units, the branches of the national planning bodies, the line departments, and the statutory bodies. In India, for example, Planning Boards and Planning Departments at the state level, and Planning Departments at the district level, have this primary responsibility. In Malaysia, the State Planning Unit and State Development Planning Committee at the state level, and the District Development Committee at the district level, perform the coordination functions. Similarly, in Sri Lanka and Thailand, these functions have partially been delegated to the District Planning Departments and the Provincial Development Planning Committee, respectively. In the Philippines, the Regional Development Council (RDC) coordinates all planning activities of sectoral departments and local planning boards within the region. Below the district level in India, Malaysia and Sri Lanka, and the provincial level in Thailand, the planning functions are only marginally decentralized.

The key bodies for coordinating the implementation management process at the national level include the Implementation and Coordination Unit (ICU) and the Executive Committee of the National Action Council (NAC) in Malaysia; the ministries, the interministerial committees and the Cabinet in India; the

Development Secretaries Committee and the Ministry of Plan Implementation in Sri Lanka; the ministries, the Prime Minister's Office and the interministerial and interdepartmental committees in Thailand; and the Cabinet Division and the Bureau of Project Implementation in the Ministry of Planning in Bangladesh. In actual practice, however, the concerned ministry or department in most cases undertakes the responsibility of horizontally coordinating its activities. Though there exist specific bodies for implementation coordination at the regional and subregional levels, such as the District Coordinating Committee and the District Agriculture Committee in Sri Lanka and the District Action Committee in Malaysia, a key coordinator at the regional and subregional levels has been identified in each of the selected countries for integrating the manifold governmental activities. These key coordinators include the Chief Secretary, the District Officer, and the Block Development Officer at the state, district, and block levels, respectively in India; the Commissioner, the Deputy Commissioner, and the Circle Officer (Development) at the divisional, district, and Thana levels, respectively, in Bangladesh; the State Secretary, the State Development Officer and the District Officer in Malaysia; the Governor and the District Officer in Thailand; and the District Minister, the Government Agent and the Assistant Government Agent in Sri Lanka.

Though there exist mechanisms for coordination in planning and implementation at each level, it is within the lower levels of the administrative hierarchy that development projects are actually implemented. These are the district and thana levels in Bangladesh; the district and block levels in India; the district and *mukim* levels in Malaysia; the district and divisional levels in Sri Lanka; the provincial and district levels in Thailand, and provincial and municipal levels in the Philippines. At these levels, usually five types of agencies and organizations exist: (a) field offices of the national ministries and departments, (b) branches of the state and provincial departments, (c) branches of statutory bodies, (d) units of regulatory administration, and (e) local government units.

The above coordinating structures in the processes of planning and implementation correspond to the administrative and political subdivisions of the countries. In addition, several coordinating bodies have recently emerged which frequently cross political and administrative boundaries. These include corporate-type organizations created for the development of resource-rich, frontier regions, such as the Pahang Tenggara Development Authority in Malaysia; organizations for the development of economically depressed regions, such as the Drought Prone Areas Programme in India; organizations dealing with one sector in a specified area, such as the Muda Agricultural Development Authority in Malaysia; bodies for the coordination of interregional plans, such as the Joint Planning Board for the Development of the Southeast Resource Regions in India; and agencies for coordinating intersectoral planning and implementation superimposed above the provincial level, such as the Regional Development Council in the Philippines. The proliferation of the above types of organizations has been prompted by the fact that the government agencies and departments at the multilevels are frequently characterized by rigid procedures and red tape, and are not conducive to handling complex tasks in development management.[1] These organizations are given operational flexibility within the administrative system in order to enable them to initiate administrative innovations.

Coordination Processes

It could be assumed that the regional development coordination processes consist of the following five steps:

1. The formulation of an overall planning framework.
2. The identification of sectoral programmes and projects.
3. The integration of intersectoral programmes.
4. Budget formulation.
5. Implementation management, including monitoring and evaluation.

Among the selected countries, there are many similarities with regards to the formulation of an overall planning framework. This initiative is undertaken by the planning body which, based on the political leaderships' broader guidelines incorporated in the governments' policy statements, more concretely delineates national objectives and priorities and attempts to operationalize these according to the availability of human and nonhuman resources. In actual practice, planning is considered to be a technical task which should be performed by specialists. The extent of the involvement of political institutions in this process naturally depends on the characteristics of the national political system. In Malaysia, for example, planning and policy formulation are undertaken by the EPU and the NDPC, in consultation with the National Economic Council (NEC) and the Cabinet. The views of the various interest groups and political parties which are predominantly communal are channelled through among others the Parliament, the NEC and the Cabinet. At the state and district levels, similar patterns exist. The people's representatives are included in both the State Development Committee and the District Development Committee.

In Sri Lanka, a critical factor in plan framework formulation is the election manifesto of the political party in power. Some ministers attempt to ensure that development programmes and plans prepared by the Ministry of Finance and Planning reflect party priorities. The views of various interest groups, such as businessmen, trade unions and youth groups must be taken into consideration in the formulation of sectoral programmes. On the basis of this often conflicting aggregation of manifold interests, the plans and programmes are coordinated by the Development Secretaries' Committee and the Ministry of Finance and Planning at the national level, and the District Coordinating Committee, the District Minister and the Government Agent at the regional level.

---

[1] For a discussion on the reasons for the emergence of public enterprises in the Asian countries, see, among others: A.S.H.K. Sadique, "Coordination and Control of Public Enterprises: An Overview of the Asian Situation" in *Public Enterprises in Asia: Studies on Coordination and Control* (Kuala Lumpur: Asian Centre for Development Administration, 1976), pp. 3-76.

Identification of sectoral programmes and projects is the responsibility of the line ministries and departments, though programmes involving more than one sector are delineated according to the recommendations of interministerial or interdepartmental committees which usually function on an *ad hoc* basis. The role of these committees has assumed greater significance due to the proliferation of government agencies and public enterprises within such key sectors as agriculture. The level at which a project is identified depends upon its size. Identification of large-scale projects is the responsibility of the national bodies, while small-scale projects are usually proposed by the units of field administration and local authorities. In most cases, the process of project identification is essentially top-down, with inadequate mechanisms for eliciting popular involvement.

In India, for example, projects may be identified by the national ministries and departments, the public enterprises, the state government departments, the field offices of ministries and departments and the Panchayati Raj institutions.

Similarly, small projects of an infrastructural nature in Sri Lanka are identified at the divisional level by Parliament members from the area, the people's organization and the different departments' field offices. Some of these projects are included in the Decentralized Budget, while others are proposed as part of the central ministries' annual plans. At the district level, projects are identified for funding by the District Minister, the Government Agent and other government functionaries, either through the Decentralized Budget or the central ministries' budgets. The initial step in identifying development projects at the national level is undertaken by the respective ministries and departments.[2] Like in the cases of India and Sri Lanka, mechanisms exist at each governmental and administrative level in Malaysia for proposing development projects. In practice, however, the process of project identification is top-down since the lower levels of government do not have adequate financial resources and planning capacities resulting in predominant positions of the central ministries and departments. Furthermore, most of the development projects in the country are sectorally based rather than based on the aggregation of functions and spatial location.[3] Though projects are identified by agencies at each level in Thailand, line ministries and departments play the most predominant role, and the process of project identification is essentially top-down.

In each of the selected countries, mechanisms exist for horizontal and vertical integration of intersectoral programmes and projects. Vertical integration is the responsibility of key agencies at each level, while horizontal integration is undertaken primarily at the national level. There are three types of inevitable conflict in this process, i.e., interdepartmental, interlevel and interjurisdictional. This makes the integration of intersectoral programmes in the planning process a very complex and difficult task to accomplish. This is particularly true at the regional and subregional levels. The intensity of conflicts in the processes of integrating

2 Perera and Fernando, chapter 9 of this volume.

3 Mat, chapter 5 of this volume.

intersectoral projects depends upon the administrative system's characteristics and the country's territorial subdivisions.

In Thailand, for example, the NESDB is expected to be the development integration focus after the line departments have identified projects and financial support requirements and manpower increases have been examined by the Bureau of the Budget and the Civil Service Commission. At the provincial level, however, the NESDB is responsible for only a portion of the provincial development programmes. Even though the line agencies agree on policy guidelines during interagency coordinating meetings, in actual practice they fail to provide concrete proposals for the harmonization of their activities.[4] This is a factor which obstructs the country's intersectoral integration. In Sri Lanka, integration of intersectoral programmes is undertaken by both the National Planning Division and Budget Division of the Ministry of Finance and Planning. Proposals received from various sectoral ministries are examined according to their implementability and the sector's performance capacity.[5]

Budgeting is the most vital instrument for coordinating the government's developmental actions.[6] To a considerable extent, the accomplishment of stated targets depends on the extent to which planning and budgeting are interlinked and on the financial allocations made available to the operating agencies that are actually spent prior to the due date. In most developing countries, nevertheless, linkages between the planning and budgeting processes seem to be weak in practice; performance measures utilized in budgeting are not rigorous; information and monitoring within the budgeting system are inadequate; and systematic use of analytical techniques is rather limited.[7] Furthermore, despite the existence of procedures and specific structures, constant delays in the release of budgetary allocations continue to happen. Even when funds are made available on time, procedural rigidity at the regional and local levels obstructs the implementing agencies' capacity to actually spend them.

In India, for example, the Ministry of Finance requests the administrative ministries to submit their budgetary estimates which are scrutinized by the Plan Finance Division of the Ministry of Finance. The administrative ministries, however, complain about scrutiny of expenditure proposals during the pre-budgetary stage by the Ministry of Finance. With revision of the budgetary and accounting formats in terms of project activities, and programme classification based on both economic and functional aspects, the link between plan and budget has been strengthened.[8]

---

[4] Noranitipadungkarn, chapter 6 of this volume.

[5] Perera and Fernando, chapter 9 of this volume.

[6] For an excellent discussion of planning and budgeting in developing countries, see Naomi Caiden and Aaron Wildavsky, *Planning and Budgeting in Poor Countries* (New York: John Wiley, 1974).

[7] Abdul Kadir Prawiraatmadja and Doh Joon-Chien, eds., "Findings and Recommendations" in *Integrated Approach to Budgeting* (Kuala Lumpur: Asian Centre for Development Administration, 1976), 1: 1-28.

[8] Chaturvedi, chapter 8 of this volume.

Before 1977, the planning and budgeting functions were performed by two separate ministries in Sri Lanka. The Ministry of Finance and Planning was established due to the difficulty in creating linkages between the planning and budgeting processes. The current practice of formulating the budget is for the Budget Division of the Ministry of Finance and Planning to send the guidelines to the ministries, departments and corporations. Based on discussions with all departments and corporations, the secretary of each ministry finalizes budget proposals and submits them to the treasury. These proposals are evaluated by officials from the Budget Division.

Differences are resolved through discussions at the departmental and ministerial levels and may even be taken up with the President.[9] In the Philippines, several mechanisms exist for linking planning and budgeting. The NEDA, which is chaired by the President and includes various cabinet members, is the highest body for accomplishing this purpose. The Development Budget Coordination Committee, which is attached to the NEDA and is chaired by the Minister of the Budget is responsible for translating plans into annual fiscal programmes.[10]

In Malaysia, the budget consists of operating and development expenditures. While the operating expenditure is budgeted annually, the development expenditure is based on approved five-year plans. The EPU elicits proposals from ministries, state governments and statutory bodies, and compiles these every five years upon approval from the NDPC. A list of the approved projects is sent to the agencies concerned. The Budget Division examines the annual financial requirements of those projects which have been approved under the five-year plan. The annual budgeting process is almost the same as that in Sri Lanka. Despite the existence of formal procedures for linking planning and budgeting in Malaysia, there are complaints that the development targets of the national planning body (EPU) are overly ambitious in some cases; that the allocation of Treasury funds is both inadequate and slow; that manpower requirements are not adequately taken into consideration; and that implementation agencies are unable "to fully spend their monetary allocations according to projected schedules and amounts."[11]

In Thailand, budget requests are prepared by various departments upon compiling requests from their respective divisions, and regional, provincial and district field offices. The committee responsible for determining budget expenditure ceilings for various ministries includes representatives from the NESDB, the Bank of Thailand, and the Ministry of Finance. Yet, there are several barriers towards operationally linking planning and budgeting. Though the NESDB is empowered to approve all projects that are to be financed, its decisions in reality could be overruled by the cabinet. The Budget Bureau has to separately scrutinize

[9] Perera and Fernando, chapter 9 of this volume.

[10] Fabella, chapter 10 of this volume.

[11] Mat, chapter 5 of this volume.

budgetary requests for each department since very few integrated projects are formulated. Additional personnel must be requested several years in advance. In such cases, the Budget Bureau may not have sufficient resources for the acquisition of additional positions. The procedures involved in making money available to provinces are such that there is "little guarantee that it will get there in time to meet their needs."[12] For example, funds to the provinces might in some cases not be made available before the rainy season, resulting in programme implementation delays. In the case of new schemes for provincial planning and new village development, however, the central committee directly allocates funds to provinces without going through the line departments.[13]

Implementation of development programmes takes place through the field offices of national ministries and departments, statutory bodies and the state government. In Bangladesh, for example, national ministries and departments have their branch offices at the divisional, district and, in most cases, the thana levels. Overall responsibility for the coordination of developmental activities has been delegated to generalist administrators at each of these levels. In India, the same pattern exists at the divisional, district and block levels. In Malaysia, the state and district levels are utilized for the implementation of development programmes. The state development officer serves as a link between the federal and state governments. The district officer, a generalist administrator, is responsible for overall supervision and coordination of the activities of each department within the district. In Thailand, the governor at the provincial level is expected to coordinate the implementation management processes.

During the colonial period, generalist administrators at the local level, such as the district officer in India and Malaysia, played the most vital role in maintaining law and order, collecting revenue and providing social welfare and infrastructural services. Due to an expansion of governmental activities after independence, representatives from the various technical departments appeared at the regional and subregional levels. The traditional role of generalist administrators in coordinating implementation management processes has been considerably weakened due to many factors, such as the desire of local political leaders to assert their power as representatives of the people; the increased competition from the technical departments; the expanded role of public enterprises; and greater degree of control by the central government.[14]

Due to the rapid expansion of governmental activities and the subsequent proliferation of governmental agencies at the regional and subregional levels, there are several problem areas which have emerged in the processes of coordinating the implementation of development programmes. First, officials in the

---

[12] Noranitipadungkarn, chapter 6 of this volume.

[13] Ibid.

[14] More specifically, for a discussion of the Malaysian situation, see G. Shabbir Cheema, "Changing Patterns of Administration in the Field: The Malaysian Case," *International Review of Administrative Sciences* 45 (1979): 64-8.

sectoral agencies are responsible to their head offices at the national and state levels, and their transfer, salary and promotion depend upon favourable reports from their departmental superiors. Obviously, their primary responsibility is to their own departments at the national and/or state levels. More often than not, the generalist administrator finds it difficult to undertake his functions as coordinator in the implementation management process since he lacks adequate authority to ensure integration and consistency in governmental activities at the grass roots.

Secondly, professionals from sectoral ministries, such as agriculture, education and health, could be reluctant to work under the guidance of the generalist administrator who in some cases may be less qualified or junior in their length of service. Indeed, the generalist administrator in several countries, such as India, Malaysia and Sri Lanka, belongs to an elite civil service cadre having more promotion opportunities and occupying more policymaking positions vis-a-vis the professional. Mutual suspicion affects the performance of coordination functions.

Thirdly, the decentralization of authority has been accomplished through administrative deconcentration rather than through the devolution of political authority. This has strengthened the position of individual brokers who foster patron-client relations with local officials by monopolizing government services due to the weak organizational channels for accessibility to these. The local level coordinator, therefore, has to balance conflicting interests in situations in which interpersonal relations could play a more important role than do formal procedures. Finally, there usually is a lack of effective communication among agencies in the implementation process. This results in the misunderstanding of each other's roles, and in the intensification of interagency conflicts. These factors impede the effective performance of horizontal and vertical coordination functions.

Recognizing the significance of coordination in the processes of implementation management, developing countries have been attempting to strengthen the authority and the role of coordinators at key intermediate levels. Several approaches have been utilized with regards to these objectives. One approach implies that the task of implementation management coordination be assigned to an elected politician, as has been the case in Sri Lanka. Another is to let the generalist administrator undertake this responsibility in consultation with the field level functionaries of government departments. This is the actual practice in most developing countries. A third approach entails that this task be assigned to a government functionary who, in turn, is responsible to the peoples' elected representatives. This practice has been followed in some states in India, such as Maharashtra. There are advantages as well as disadvantages in politicizing the role of the local coordinator. While a politician is in a better position to elicit popular involvement in development programme implementation and facilitate access to government facilities, the complexity of development management requires skills which he might lack. Furthermore, party or factional interests of the political coordinator could hinder rational utilization of local resources. Yet, it is widely recognized that interaction between politicians and government functionaries in performing the coordination task needs to be institutionalized so that both the politician and the generalist administrator are aware of each other's role.

Despite country variations, there are two factors which seem to negatively affect the role of the local coordinator in harmonizing government's developmental actions at the district and subdistrict levels in the selected Asian countries. First, there is inadequate decentralization of financial authority in most cases. As the case of Thailand shows, a major portion of developmental expenditure is directly channelled through the line departments. Centralized controls and schematic budgets further weaken the position of the local coordinator. Second, nongovernmental and constituency organizations are weak in the selected countries. These organizations thus, are unable to provide (a) information about their needs and priorities, and (b) necessary support for and understanding of the programmes and projects being articulated or implemented. In the absence of institutionalized channels for seeking information about people's preferences and for eliciting their support, the local coordinator is forced to respond to political pressures and interventions from the influential local political elite. This negates his desire to ensure consistency and complementarity in government actions.

Analysis of the Asian experience with regards to the coordination of planning, budgeting and implementation management points to several conclusions. First, in each country there exists adequate procedures and structures for facilitating coordination between different agencies. Second, the coordination procedures are more clearly defined and more widely practised at the national level than at the regional and subregional levels. Third, coordination as an end product is impeded not by the lack of adequate statutory provisions, but by the difficulty of putting these into practice. Fourth, the processes of coordination are predominantly top-down, based on centralized controls. Fifth, interagency coordination is more effective than that between people's organizations and coordinating bodies. Sixth, operationally, the weakest points in the whole process are the linkages between planning and budgeting that ensure intersectoral consistency.

EFFECTIVENESS OF KEY COORDINATING AGENCIES

Coordination in the processes of planning, budgeting and implementation management takes place at multilevels of government and administration. Therefore, in each country there exist several agencies which perform coordinative functions within a sector, among agencies belonging to more than one sector, and between coordinating bodies. This makes the evaluation of the system's level of coordination performance functions extremely complex. In each developing country, however, key coordinating agencies exist which are assigned the most critical role of harmonizing governmental activities and programmes. To a certain extent, it could be assumed that the success of these agencies in performing their tasks depends upon their authority, status and location within the administrative system, the leadership quality and professional competence of key actors within these agencies, their internal bureaucratic structure and their communication with other organizations. The extent to which one of these agencies is able to effectively perform its assigned tasks in a country would be indicative of the coordination effectiveness within the government's development machinery.

In Malaysia, the responsibilities of the Implementation and Coordination Unit (ICU) include monitoring and evaluating the implementation of the government's economic and social policies, and coordination of the ministries' and government departments' programmes. It serves as secretariat of the National Action Council (NAC). While the implementing agencies and departments brief the NAC Working Committee on planned development programme implementation, the ICU prepares its own evaluation reports for presentation to the Committee. In addition, it is empowered to monitor the decisions made by the NAC during the various implementating agencies' briefings. The ICU coordinates development programme implementation by utilizing several other procedures and techniques. One of these is a computer data-based monitoring and evaluation system which contains fund figures allocated to each ministry and state, the implementation progress of each project and reasons for delays. Other mechanisms are: participation in interministerial committees which are responsible for planning, budgeting and implementation management; direct intervention by the ICU staff in the implementation processes at the state or district level; and control over a portion of resources for social and community development programmes at the village level.[15]

The strengths of the ICU in performing its tasks are that it is strategically located within the administrative system; it has adequate authority and status for performing its tasks which are reinforced by its access to political decision-makers; it can influence developmental activities at the state and the district levels through the state development officer; its role is well understood by the implementing agencies; its key actors have the adequate professional qualifications; it has direct control over the allocation of a portion of resources for community development projects at the village level; and it has a massive data base through which impediments to project implementation may be identified. Yet, effective performance of the ICU's coordination functions is partly constrained by two factors. First, the ICU's Director-General is lower in the administrative hierarchy than the ministries' secretary-general. Second, despite successes in the coordination of infrastructural and economic development programmes, the ICU is relatively weak in coordinating and monitoring those projects dealing with "social restructuring" and participation of Malays in commercial activities.[16]

The National Economic and Social Development Board (NESDB) in Thailand is expected to play the most critical role in coordinating the preparation and

---

[15] Mat, chapter 5 of this volume.

[16] Ibid.

implementation of development programmes and projects and in integrating the government's developmental actions. It has been given formal authority in order to enable it to accomplish its assigned tasks. For example, line offices are required to submit their development projects to the Office of the Board for review before sending these to the Budget Bureau for financial allocations. The NESDB is represented in the Budget Scrutinizing Committee, and has adequate access to political decision-makers at the national level. Yet, its effectiveness in coordinating development programmes depends upon the extent to which the other relevant agencies, such as the Budget Bureau and Civil Service Commission, cooperate with it; the degree of support it receives from the line ministries and departments which are responsible for actual implementation; and the extent of support it actually receives from the Cabinet. Among the internal weaknesses of the NESDB are that some of its divisions pursue their own strategies and lack team work, and that many of its staff members lack experience.[17]

In India, the Planning Commission and the Ministry of Finance play the most vital role in development coordination. With the Prime Minister as chairman and the Finance and Planning ministers as ex-officio members, the Commission has adequate authority and status to harmonize the governmental development activities at the national and regional levels. Through the National Development Council, in which the chief ministers are presented, the Commission has access to political decision-makers at the subnational level. The Ministry of Finance and the Planning Commission work closely in estimating resources, identifying priorities and fixing the size of the plan. As in the case of Thailand, however, the effectiveness of the Planning Commission and the Ministry of Finance depends more upon the degree of cooperation received from the state and district government levels as well as the implementing departments and ministries.[18] The complexity of the federal structure, under which the two opposing political parties might control the national and the state government, respectively, makes the task of ensuring consistency in the government's development programmes extremely difficult, if not impossible.

In the Philippines, the Regional Development Council (RDC) is perceived as the most crucial unit for coordinating development activities at the regional level. The RDC consists of regional directors of the national line ministries and government agencies and provincial governors and city mayors of the area. The regional office of the National Economic and Development Authority (NEDA) serves as the Council's technical staff. The Council chairman is expected to provide leadership in harmonizing government activities at the regional level. With regards to this and in accordance with Letter of Instructions No. 447, the budget ministry is expected to provide information to the RDC chairman about funds to be released to the regional offices. Another statutory provision provides

[17] Noranitipadungkarn, chapter 6 of this volume.

[18] Chaturvedi, chapter 8 of this volume.

that regional public sector resource allocations shall be made on the basis of the Regional Development Investment Programme (RDIP) which is prepared by the RDC. In actual practice, however, the Council chairman appears to lack due recognition and stature that are necessary for him to be obeyed.[19] His effectiveness though, would generally depend upon his capacity to persuade those involved in development planning and implementation at the regional level as well as his links with the Presidency.

In Sri Lanka, the District Minister and the Government Agent have been assigned the role of coordinating the government's development actions through the District Coordinating Committee. In 1973, the government introduced the District Political Authorities (DPA) recognizing the negative implications of the colonial pattern of administrative coordination at the regional level which gave generalist administrators a predominant position. This was followed by decentralized budgetary allocations for local level development projects. The Government Agent was instructed to consult the DPA and to follow his guidelines with regards to decentralized budgets and agricultural development programmes. In 1977, the DPA system was reorganized. District Ministers were appointed and were given the clearly defined role of coordinating development programmes. Their position was made constitutional and the Government Agent was expected to serve as secretary to the District Minister. Such an institutional coordination mechanism has facilitated the harmonization of administrative and political roles, both of which are necessary in meaningful coordination.[20] Indeed, the District Minister has to depend upon the Government Agent due to the latter's experience, while the Government Agent has to seek the approval of the District Minister for the programme to be politically acceptable. This has created an interdependency between the administrator and the politician.[21] In the process of the institutionalization of this, excessive political interventions are of course inevitable. Recently, the government decided to introduce Development Councils consisting of Parliament members from the district and other elected members. The extent to which the new changes in institutional arrangements for coordination would lead to more effective integration of government activities at the district level, however, remains to be seen.

THE ENVIRONMENTAL CONTEXT

The effective performance of coordination functions and indeed, successful plan implementation, necessitate collaborative efforts on the part of organizations involved in planning, budgeting and implementation management. In

---

[19] Fabella, chapter 10 of this volume.

[20] Perera and Fernando, chapter 9 of this volume.

[21] Ibid.

addition to formal procedures, whether an agency is able to accomplish coordination as an end-product is influenced by the environmental framework within which interactions among organizations take place. As the experiences of countries, such as Thailand have shown, mere granting of formal authority to a coordinating agency and specification of rules and procedures do not necessarily imply that coordination actually takes place. Similarly, the professional competence of the coordinator, the location of the agency within the administrative system and the availability of adequate information are necessary but not sufficient, conditions for achieving harmonization, consistency and integration in the government's developmental activities. This is particularly true in programme implementation.

Any attempt to suggest prescriptions with regards to the institutional reform should, therefore, be preceded by an identification of the contextual factors which impede coordination, especially within programme implementation. Some of the factors are political styles, local power structures, sociocultural traditions, resource constraints, organizational designs and authority patterns, personnel structures and behaviour and territorial subdivisions.

The experiences of developing countries discussed in this volume show that coordination as a process has administrative as well as political dimensions. As such, the characteristics of the political system, and subsequently the emerging political styles, have a significant bearing upon the mechanisms utilized in harmonizing government activities, on the one hand, and successful programme implementation, on the other.[22]

For example, whether to assign the task of local coordination to a politician or an administrator depends upon the peculiarities of a country's political process. In Sri Lanka, which is relatively more politicized, this task has been given to an elected representative of the people. On the contrary, the role of the generalist administrator in coordinating the government's development activities at the district level in Malaysia has been recognized since the decision-making process is such that it accords a predominant position to the bureaucracy at the national and regional level. Indeed, in the multiethnic Malaysian society, the administrators are involved in policy formation and programme implementation as well as in the management of communal conflict.[23] In Bangladesh and India, several attempts have been made to further define the role of the local administrator and the politician in the processes of planning and implementation. In the past, coordination processes at the grass roots in Bangladesh have reflected political styles and priorities at the national level.[24]

---

[22] For a general discussion of the political considerations in development process, see Norman Uphoff, "Political Considerations in Human Development" in Peter T. Knight, ed., *Implementing Programmes of Human Development* (World Bank staff working paper no. 403) (Washington, D.C.: World Bank, 1980).

[23] Milton J. Esman, *Administration and Development in Malaysia* (Ithaca: Cornell University Press, 1972).

[24] Ali, chapter 7 of this volume.

Most developing countries are characterized by inegalitarian patterns of landownership and a high degree of landlessness in the rural areas resulting in the emergence of dependency relationships. Unless such an environment changes, the coordinating agencies remain inaccessible to the vast majority, negating the main purpose for which they were created and further widening existing economic disparities within the rural communities. The patterns of local power structures in most developing countries are such that these impede the articulation and communication of the rural poor's interests to the local coordinator; lead to the monopoly of most government facilities in rural areas by large- and medium-size farmers; and obstruct most efforts involving programme beneficiaries in the implementation processes.[25] Furthermore, despite the existence of formal procedures, the local political elite who have strong linkages with higher level political and administrative decision-makers are able to bypass the formal channels for coordinating the programme identification and implementation processes at the grass roots. Indeed, in local power structure situations which are highly inegalitarian, the local coordinator's role in balancing conflicting interests is an extremely difficult, if not impossible, task. The gap between statutory provisions dealing with coordination and their actual practice in developing countries could, thus, be attributed in varying degrees, to local power structure constraints.

Sociocultural traditions are another constraint on effective programme coordination and implementation.[26] Traditional deference to authority and the reluctance to openly disagree with superiors lead to situations in which individual initiative is negatively affected. Thus, coordination takes the form of domination through centralized controls rather than through mutual adjustments, and there is a lack of spirit of interagency task interdependency. The dilemma of developing countries is that while the indigenous institutions through which collective actions could have been facilitated, have been weakened due to urbanization and industrialization, the attitudes and behavioural patterns of Western societies have not emerged. Even when formal procedures are delineated, for example, for the decentralization of decision-making, senior officials are reluctant to actually delegate authority or, in some cases, local coordinators might be reluctant to fully utilize their enhanced position. Traditionally, they might be expected to merely follow the guidelines of their superiors in harmonizing government activities. The lack of a meaningful dialogue between coordinating agencies at the subregional level and the people could, in part, be attributed to the status orientation of government officials. It could also be due to the cultural attributes of the people. In the case of Thailand, Noranitipadungkarn has succinctly put it: "Thais prefer to work independently and to avoid confrontation

---

[25] For an analysis of local power structure in the processes of rural development, see Keith R. Emerich, "The Functions and Uses of Rural Power in Asian Rural Processes," Inayatullah, ed., *Rural Organizations and Rural Development: Some Asian Experiences* (Kuala Lumpur: Asian and Pacific Development Administration Centre, 1978), pp. 431-70.

[26] Rondinelli and Ingle, chapter 4 of this volume.

with one another, for fear of mutual encroachment and criticism of each other's affairs."[27]

Resource constraints and the lack of adequate communication facilities also negatively affect the coordination processes. In countries with large geographical areas and heterogeneous pupulation, coordinating local priorities with those of the nation becomes an uphill task. With limited funds available and the large number of claims on public resources, it is almost impossible for the local coordinator to ensure consistency even in projects implemented at the village level. Indeed, there is in most developing countries such a great demand for services such as rural electrification, schools, water supply, etc., that given the limited resources, it would be unrealistic to expect that the local coordinator thoroughly examine the complementarity of projects before these are actually implemented. Similarly, where adequate communication facilities are unavailable, interaction between local coordinating agencies and people's organizations is minimal.

Organizational designs and authority patterns in most developing countries are characterized by a high degree of centralization, which is the "enemy" of local coordination.[28] Though in several countries attempts have been made towards administrative deconcentration and political authority devolution, such attempts have faltered in the implementation stage.[29] In India, for example, Panchayati Raj institutions were introduced in 1957 to accomplish "democratic decentralization." Yet, as the Mehta Committee reported, towards the end of 1970s, with the exception of a few states such as Maharashtra and Gujarat, the financial base of Panchayati Raj institutions was weak and these were playing only a marginal role in governmental efforts towards rural transformation. In Malaysia, ministry and department officials at the national level continue to play predominant roles even in detailed programme operations. Local governments are responsible primarily for providing civic amenities rather than for functioning as agencies for articulating and communicating people's aspirations as a catalyst for development. In developing countries, the lack of adequate decentralization of authority to lower governmental and administrative units has led to several consequences: The local coordinator finds it extremely difficult to coordinate government ministry and department activities at the grass roots; excessive bureaucratic procedures dealing with programme supervision have emerged; professional competence and technical capabilities at the national level are developing at a much higher rate than at the regional and subregional levels; interaction between people's organizations and local coordinating agencies is minimal; bureaucratic responsiveness and citizen participation are negatively affected; the cost for the delivery of public services has, in some cases, increased;

---

[27] Noranitipadungkarn, chapter 6 of this volume.

[28] Esman, chapter 1 of this volume.

[29] Rondinelli and Ingle, chapter 4 of this volume.

and the spatial integration of projects at the stage of implementation has proven to be difficult.

Personnel structures and practices in most developing countries are characterized by unequal promotion opportunities to the various civil service cadres, political intervention and favouritism in recruitment and promotion, red tape, misuse of trained staff due to frequent transfers, rigid personnel regulations, policy inadequacies for personnel development and a high degree of compartmentalization. In some countries, such as Bangladesh, India and Malaysia, key policy-making positions within the administrative system are held by an elite cadre of generalist administrators. This is resented in varying degrees by the professional staff of technical departments such as agriculture, industry and health. Technical department personnel therefore, look more to their superiors at headquarters for direction in project identification and implementation than to regional and subregional level generalist administrators. While this process facilitates sectoral coordination, it is not conducive to the harmonization of the various departments' activities at the grass roots. Political interventions and favouritism frequently hinder the choice of appropriate officials as regional and subregional coordinators.

Bureaucratic attitudes and behavioural patterns also constrain effective programme coordination and implementation. Most developing countries have inherited colonial administrative systems which for the most part were aimed at the maintenance of law and order, the collection of resources, and the development of infrastructural facilities for extracting resources to meet colonial economic requirements. In most countries, such as India, Malaysia and Sri Lanka, an elite civil service cadre emerged which was expected to serve as a link between the colonial rulers and the vast rural poor majority. Obviously, the bureaucracy assumed a predominant position in power, prestige and living standard within the society. Soon after independence, a rapid expansion took place in the government's developmental activities as well as in the government's economic intervention objectives. Reflecting the people's rising expectations which accompanied independence, regional and subregional level political leaders increasingly asserted their power as representatives of the people. Bureaucratic attitudes and behavioural patterns, however, have not been completely reconciled with the new situation. To varying degrees, the problem still exists. In general, as Rondinelli and Ingle point out, government officials have adverse attitudes and behaviour towards rural people; their orientation is paternalistic, and they "expect and demand deference from farmers and villagers"; they show tremendous reluctance in making decisions for fear of committing mistakes; sometimes they rigidly follow detailed procedures even for routine tasks, while they are ignorant of or deviate from procedures on other occasions; they distrust local leaders and administrators and show a lack of confidence in the latter's capacity to undertake various development planning and implementation tasks.[30]

A country's territorial subdivision patterns considerably affect coordination processes, particularly within federal systems. In India, for example, coordination with different political parties in power at the national and state levels becomes difficult because the country has a federal structure which constitutionally recognizes the states' powers. In Malaysia, due to state government control, several federal government-sponsored land development projects are delayed. Furthermore, the coordination process at the district level is complicated because the agencies involved belong to both government tiers. In both India and Malaysia, the governments' desire to spatially integrate developmental activities must be reconciled with the need for political authority devolution to facilitate the processes of nation building and government legitimacy.

FOCAL POINTS OF INSTITUTIONAL REFORM

For three decades after the Second World War, several attempts have been made in the developing countries of Asia to introduce administrative reform. National governments recognized that their administrative capabilities necessitated strengthening in order to enable them to successfully implement planned programmes and projects and to perform other tasks resulting from their increased intervention in the national economy. These efforts, which were considerably influenced by foreign donors through technical assistance personnel, were focused on improving the administrative support systems such as personnel, budget and accounting, supplies, organization and method and central coordination procedures.[31] To improve the delivery of public services, some management techniques were introduced such as performance budgeting and central procurements. Public administration institutes were established in order to examine strategies for strengthening administrative innovation. Several statutory bodies were created at the national level in order to avoid government agency rigidity. An underlying assumption in the above efforts was that the enhanced administrative capacity of the central level agencies would positively affect the line agencies' task performance in the field. The scope of these reforms ranged from most comprehensive to extremely limited ones.[32] Some of these dealt with the administrative system as a whole while others were programme-based. Similarly, there were variations between countries with regards to the national development orientation of these reforms, their focus on techniques vis-a-vis programmes, and the degree of foreign influence in the articulation of these.[33]

---

[31] Milton J. Esman and John D. Montgomery, "The Administration of Human Development" in Peter T. Knight, ed., *Implementing Programmes of Human Development*, pp. 209-12.

[32] Abelardo G. Samonte, "Patterns and Trends in Administrative Reforms" in Hahn-Been Lee and Abelardo G. Samonte, eds., *Administrative Reforms in Asia* (Manila: Eastern Regional Organization for Public Administration, 1970), pp. 287-302.

[33] Ibid.

In most cases, previous administrative reform efforts have led to several consequences: The trend towards centralization within the administrative system has been reinforced; the impact of administrative innovations at the central level has not trickled down to the field level; the imbalance between the government agencies' capacity and the nongovernmental "constituency" organizations has increased; and the new management techniques have proven to be inappropriate within the local context. It has been argued that in their enthusiasm for quick results, the administrative reformers have not properly appreciated the socio-cultural context within which the reforms were to be implemented, the operational feasibility of new techniques and methods, the bureaucratic attitudes and behavioural patterns and the political implications of reforming the administrative support structures without simultaneously strengthening the people's organizations.

The main development concerns of the 1980s — equity, participation, access to government facilities, local organization, provision of basic needs — have necessitated examination of the institutional support structures necessary for operationalizing these. It is widely recognized that bureaucracy alone is not equipped to meet the new challenges and that, therefore, in addition to administrative reform, nonbureaucratic organizations need to be strengthened to effectively perform the increasingly complex tasks involved in development management. In other words, administrative reforms are a necessary but insufficient condition for ensuring plan implementability that emphasizes accessibility and participation by the people.

The analysis of the coordination processes undertaken in this volume substantiates this argument. There is indeed sufficient evidence in these studies upon which to base the contention that coordination is both an administrative and a political process; that the determinants of effective coordination are contextual as well as procedural ones; and that the delineation of coordination procedures that do not provide increased interaction between coordinating agencies and nongovernmental organizations has frequently led to more centralized controls. The institutional infrastructure for ensuring coordination in development programme implementation would thus, require reorganization of the administrative machinery as well as that of the nonbureaucratic organizations.

The peculiarities of the developing Asian countries' respective administrative and political processes and their socioeconomic structures, and the limitations of comparative data, preclude the possibility of delineating an institutional reform strategy applicable in each country at multilevels. However, as the studies in this volume demonstrate, there are several key issues in facilitating institutional capability in general, and in the performance of coordination functions in particular, which are pertinent to most countries. Thus, it would seem that meaningful future efforts for strengthening institutional support structures must be concerned with identifying strategies and mechanisms for accomplishing the following:

1. Strengthening the roles of the regional, subregional and local coordinators.

2. Enhancing the capacity of people's organizations.
3. Re-examining the relative position of statutory bodies vis-a-vis government departments and agencies.
4. Improving the field staff's performance capacity.
5. Deconcentrating administration.
6. Decentralizing financial resources.
7. Striking a balance between politicization and conflict on the one hand, and political stability on the other.
8. Specifying appropriate division of functions between multilevels of government and administration.
9. Improving the information base within the administrative system in order to enhance the quality of administrative decision-making.
10. Improving local resource management and service delivery.

The available evidence suggests that there are a number of methods and approaches which are likely to yield results in the reorganization of the government's administrative machinery. It has been suggested that an attempt to reform the administrative machinery is more likely to succeed if it has the broad based involvement of agencies in its reorganization proposals, takes into consideration ecological and cultural factors, is timely, utilizes local expertise, takes into consideration the political implications, and has the necessary administrative and political support to ensure implementation.[34] Since institutional reform involves both governmental agencies as well as nongovernmental organizations, delineation of appropriate strategies and approaches in this regard is more complex and, therefore, necessitates considerably more comparative information before any concrete prescriptions may be made. Indeed, one of the challenges of scholars, practitioners and policy-makers in the Third World is to identify the appropriate approaches through which the institutional support structures necessary for operationalizing the new development concerns may be identified.

---

[34] Samonte, "Patterns and Trends in Administrative Reforms."

BIBLIOGRAPHY

1. Institutional Dimensions of Regional Development: General

1.1 Source books, literature reviews, etc.

Blase, Melvin G.
Institution Building: A Source Book (Washington, D.C.: Agency for International Development, U.S. Dept. of State, 1973)
Chang, Diana
Asia and Pacific Planning Bibliography No. 5 (Monticello, Ill.: Council of Planning Librarians, 1974) (Exchange Bibliography #540-541)
Chapel, Yves, ed.
Administrative Management for Development: A Reader (Brussels: International Institute of Administrative Sciences; Paris: UNESCO, 1977)
Jones, Garth N., et. al., eds.
Planning, Development and Change: A Bibliography on Development Administration (Honolulu: East-West Center, 1970)
Rondinelli, Dennis A. and Aspy P. Palia, eds.
Project Planning and Implementation in Developing Countries: A Bibliography on Development Project Management (Honolulu: Technology and Development Institute, East-West Center, 1976)
United Nations. Centre for Social Development and Humanitarian Affairs
Innovative Approaches to Popular Participation in Development: The Basic Needs Approach; A Bibliographical Bulletin (New York, 1977) (ESA/SDHA/Misc. 26)
United Nations. Department of International Economic and Social Affairs. Division of Public Administration and Finance
United Nations Directory of National Agencies and Institutions for the Improvement of Public Administration (New York, 1973) (ST/TAO/M/47/Rev. 1)

1.2 Theories and approaches

Ahmad, Yusuf J.
"Administration of Integrated Rural Development Programmes: A Note on Methodology," *International Labour Review,* Vol. III, No. 2, Feb. 1975, pp. 119-42
Blaise, Hans C.
"An Analysis of Selected Strategies of Institution Building for Public Service" in Inayatullah ed., *Management Training for Development: The Asian Experience* (Kuala Lumpur: Asian and Pacific Development Administration Centre, 1975), pp. 285-300
Blase, Melvin, ed.
Institutions in Agricultural Development (Ames: Iowa State University Press, 1971)

Braibanti, Ralph, ed.
Asian Bureaucratic Systems Emergent from the British Imperial Tradition (Durham, N.C.: Published for the Duke University Commonwealth-Studies Center by Duke Univ. Press, 1966)

Braibanti, Ralph, ed.
Political and Administrative Development (Durham, N.C.: Duke University Press, 1969)

Eaton, Joseph W., ed.
Institution Building and Development: From Concepts to Application (Beverly Hills, Cal.: Sage Pub. with the cooperation of the Inter-University Research Program in Institution Building, 1972)

Esman, Milton J. and Hans C. Blaise
"Institution Building Research: The Guiding Concepts" (mimeo), University of Pittsburg, Graduate School of Public and International Affairs, n.d.

Friedmann, John
A Spatial Framework for Rural Development: Problems of Organization and Development: A Report to the U.S. Agency for International Development (Los Angeles: School of Architecture and Urban Planning, University of California, 1974)

Gable, Richard W. and J. Fred Springer
"Administrative Implications of Development Policy: A Comparative Analysis of Agricultural Programs in Asia," *Economic Development and Cultural Change*, Vol. 27, No. 4, July 1979, pp. 687-704

Gross, Bertram
The Administration of Economic Development Planning: Principles and Fallacies (St. Louis, Mo.: Washington University, 1967)

Gruchman, Bohdan
"State of Art of the Methods of Planning for Regional Development: An International Survey Report" (Nagoya: United Nations Centre for Regional Development, 1978) [Paper presented at the Workshop on Improving the Methods of Planning for Comprehensive Regional Development, 16 May-12 June 1978]

Gunderson, Gil
"Epistemology in Public Administration," *Philippine Journal of Public Administration*, Vol. 19, No. 3, July 1975, pp. 145-54

Heaphey, James and Philip Kronenberg
Toward Theory Building in Comparative Public Administration: A Functional Approach, Occasional Paper (Washington D.C.: Comparative Administrative Group, American Society for Public Administration, 1966)

Katz, Saul M.
A System Approach to Development Administration: A Framework for Analysing Capability of Action for National Development (Chicago: Comparative Administration Group of the American Society for Public Administration, 1965)

Kriesberg, Martin, ed.
Public Administration in Developing Countries (Washington, D.C.: Brookings Institution, 1963)

Lee, Hahn-Been and Abelardo Samonte, eds.
Administrative Reform in Asia (Manila: Eastern Regional Organization for Public Administration, 1971)

Mauzy, Diane K.
"Two Rural Development Strategies: Organization, Administrative Performance and Political Priorities in India and Malaysia," *Philippine Journal of Public Administration*, Vol. 19, Nos. 1 & 2, Jan.-Apr. 1975, pp. 84-112

Montgomery, John D.
Technology and Civic Life: Making and Implementing Development Decisions (Cambridge, Mass.: MIT Press, 1974)

Montgomery, John D., and William J. Siffin, eds.
Approaches to Development: Politics, Administration and Change (New York:

McGraw-Hill, 1966)
Nieuwenhuijze, C.A.O.
Public Administration, Comparative Administration, Development Administration: Concepts and Theory in Their Struggle for Relevance (The Hague: Institute of Social Studies, 1973) (Occasional Paper No. 24)
Philips, Hiram S.
Guide for Development: Institution-Building and Reform (New York: Praeger, 1969)
Philips, Hiram S.
Handbook for Development: Changing Environments and Institutions (Washington, D.C.: Praeger, 1968)
Riggs, Fred W.
Administration in Developing Countries: The Theory of Prismatic Society (Boston: Houghton Mifflin, 1964)
Riggs, Fred W.
Frontiers of Development Administration (Durham, N.C.: Duke University Press, 1971)
Rodman, Peter W.
Development Administration: Obstacles, Theories and Implications for Planning (Paris: International Institute of Educational Planning, UNESCO, 1968)
Rondinelli, Dennis A.
"National Investment Planning and Equity Policy in Developing Countries: The Challenge of Decentralized Administration," *Policy Sciences,* Vol. 10, No. 1, Aug. 1978, pp. 45-74
Rondinelli, Dennis A. and Kenneth Ruddle
Urbanization and Rural Development: A Spatial Policy for Equitable Growth (New York: Praeger, 1978)
Rothwell, Kenneth J., ed.
Administrative Issues in Developing Economies (Lexington, Mass.: Lexington Books, 1972)
Shaw, Carroll K. and F.W. Riggs
Research on Development Administration (New York: Asia Society, Southeast Asia Development Advisory Group, 1967) (SEADAG papers on problems of development in Southeast Asia, No. 15)
Southeast Asia Development Advisory Group
Development Administration Panel Seminar on Rural Local Government and Development Administration in Southeast Asia, Cornell University, Ithaca, New York, April 4-6, 1974 (New York: Asia Society, SEADAG, 1974) (SEADAG report, No. 8)
Swerdlow, Irving, ed.
Development Administration: Concepts and Problems (Syracuse: Syracuse Univ. Press, 1963)
Swerdlow, Irving
The Public Administration of Economic Development (New York: Praeger, 1975)
United Nations Centre for Regional Development
Role of Governments in the Regional Development Process (Nagoya, 1977) (Sales no. E.77.II.F.CRD 32)
United Nations. Department of International Economic and Social Affairs. Division of Public Administration
Decentralization for National and Local Development (New York, 1962) (ST/TAO/ M/19) (Sales no. E.62.II.H.2)
United Nations. Department of International Economic and Social Affairs
Development Administration: Current Approaches and Trends in Public Administration for National Development (New York, 1975) (ST/ESA/SER.E.3) (Sales no. E.76.UU.H.1)
United Nations. Department of International Economic and Social Affairs
Interregional Seminar on Major Administrative Reforms in Developing Countries (New York, 1973) 3 vol. (ST/TAO/M/62)

258

United Nations. Department of International Economic and Social Affairs
Interregional Seminar on the Use of Modern Management Techniques in the Public Administration of Developing Countries (New York, 1970) 3 vol. (ST/TAO/M/52)
United Nations. Department of International Economic and Social Affairs
Local Government Reform: Analysis of Experience in Selected Countries (New York, 1975) (ST/ESA/SER.E/2) (Sales no. E.75.II.H.1)
United Nations. Department of International Economic and Social Affairs
Proceedings of the Interregional Seminar on Organization and Administration of Development Planning Agencies (Kiev, USSR, 1972) (New York, 1974) (ST/TAO/M/64) Vol. 1: Report and general technical papers. (Sales no. E.74.II.H.2)
United Nations. Department of International Economic and Social Affairs
Public Administration in the Second United Nations Development Decade: Report of the Second Meeting of Experts, 16-26 January 1971 (New York, 1971) (ST/TAO/M/57) (Sales no. E.71.II.H.3)
United Nations. Department of International Economic and Social Affairs
United Nations Programme in Public Administration: Report of the Meeting of the Experts (New York, 1967) (E/4296) (ST/TAO/M/38)
United Nations. Department of International Economic and Social Affairs
Strengthening Public Administration and Finance for Development in the 1980s: Issues and Approaches (New York, 1978) (ST/ESA/SER.E/13) (Sales no. E.78.II.H.6)
United Nations. Economic Commission for Africa. Public Administration Section
Administration for Development (New York, 1971) (E/CN.14/UAP/184) (Sales no. E.71.II.K.13)
United Nations. Economic Commission for Asia and the Pacific
"Administrative Machinery for Planning," *Economic Bulletin for Asia and the Far East,* Vol. 12, No. 3, Dec. 1961, pp. 26-51
United Nations. Economic Commission for Latin America
Administrative Aspects of Planning: Papers of a Seminar on Administrative Aspects of Plan Implementation (Santiago, 1968) (E/CN.12/811) (Sales no. E.69.II.G.2)
Weidner, Edward W., ed.
Development Administration in Asia (Durham, N.C.: Duke University Press, 1970)

1.3 Development indicators

Baster, N., ed.
Measuring Development (London: Frank Cass, 1972)
Cant, R.G.
"Territorial Indicators and National Planning: A Report on Country Studies in Thailand and the Philippines," *Economic Bulletin for Asia and the Pacific,* Vol. 27, No. 2, Dec. 1976, pp. 26-53
Drewnowski, Jan
On Measuring and Planning the Quality of Life (The Hague: Mouton, 1974)
Hicks, Norman and Paul Streeten
"Indicators of Development: The Search for a Basic Needs Yardstick," *World Development,* Vol. 7, 1979, pp. 567-80
Mangahas, Mahar, ed.
Measuring Philippine Development: Report of the Social Indicators Project (Makati: Development Academy of the Philippines, 1976)
McGranahan, D.V., et. al.
Contents and Measurement of Socioeconomic Development: A Staff Study (New York: Praeger, 1972) (Praeger special studies in international economics and development)
Sarup, Anand and K.V. Sundaram
"Country Report on India" (Nagoya: United Nations Centre for Regional Development, 1978) [Paper presented at the Workshop on Improving the Methods of Planning for Comprehensive Regional Development, 16 May-12 June 1978.]

Schwefel, Detlef
  Who Benefits from Production and Employment? Six Criteria to Measure the Impact of Development Projects on Poverty and Satisfaction of Basic Needs (Berlin: German Development Institute, 1975) (Occasional Paper No. 29)
Scott, Wolf
  Measurement of Real Progress at the Local Level: An Overview Report on a Joint Project by Research Institutes and Scholars in Seven Countries (Geneva: United Nations Research Institute for Social Development, 1977)
Strumpel, Burkhard, ed.
  "Subjective Elements of Well-Being" (Paris: OECD, 1974) [Paper presented at a Seminar of the Organization for Economic Co-operation and Development, Paris, May 15-17, 1972.]
Subido, C.T.
  "Use of Social Indicators in Development Planning and Appraisal in the Philippines," *Economic Bulletin for Asia and the Pacific,* Vol. 27, No. 1, June 1976, pp. 28-40
United Nations. Commission for Social Indicators
  Social Indicators: Current National and International Activities in the Field of Social Indicators and Social Reporting, Report of the Secretary-General (New York, 1975) (E/CN.5/518)
United Nations. Statistical Commission
  Draft Guidelines on Social Indicators (New York, 1976) (E/CN.3/488)
United Nations University
  Report on the State of the Arts: Indicators of Human and Social Development (Tokyo: UNU, 1977) 8 vol. (HSD/RP/1)

1.4 Administrative performance

Basu, P.K., ed.
  Towards a New Managerial Order in Asia (Kuala Lumpur: Asian and Pacific Development Administration Centre, 1977)
Basu, P.K. and Alec Nove, eds.
  Performance Criteria for Asian Public Enterprises: Studies on Public Enterprise Policy on Investment, Pricing and Surplus Generation (Kuala Lumpur: Asian and Pacific Development Administration Centre, n.d.)
Gross, Bertram
  "Some Factors Involved in Appraising Administrative Performance in Development Planning," in United Nations, Economic Commission for Latin America, *Administrative Aspects of Planning* (New York, 1969), pp. 226-37
Inayatullah, ed.
  Management Training for Development: The Asian Experience (Kuala Lumpur: Asian and Pacific Development Administration Centre, 1975)
Mundel, Marvin E.
  Measuring and Enhancing the Productivity of Service and Government Organizations (Tokyo: Asian Productivity Organization, 1975)
United Nations. Department of International Economic and Social Affairs. Public Administration Division
  Appraising Administrative Capability for Development: A Methodological Monograph Prepared by the International Group for Studies in National Planning (INTERPLAN) (New York, 1969) (ST/TAO/M/46) (Sales no. E.69.II.H.2)
United Nations. Department of International Economic and Social Affairs
  Interregional Seminar on Administration of Management Improvement Services (New York, 1971) 2 vol. (ST/TAO/M/56)
Whang, In-Joung
  Administrative Feasibility Analysis for Development Projects: Concept and Approach (Kuala Lumpur: Asian and Pacific Development Administration Centre, 1978) (Occasional Paper No. 4)

260

2. Selected Aspects

2.1 Coordination

Anthony, Robert N.
Planning and Control Systems: A Framework of Analysis (Cambridge, Mass.: Harvard University Press, 1965, 1979 printing)

Barrett, John H.
"Power, Influence and Control in Organizations" in Stanley E. Seasore and Robert J. McNeill, eds., *Management of the Urban Crisis* (New York: Free Press, 1971)

Carada, Wilfredo
"Techniques of Supervision for Rural Development Supervisor — Coordinators" in Amara Raksasataya and L.J. Fredericks, eds., *Rural Development Training to Meet New Challenges,* Vol. 2 (Kuala Lumpur: Asian and Pacific Development Administration Centre, 1978), pp. 290-332

Chamong, Vudhichai
Coordination in the Implementation of Family Planning Programs (Kuala Lumpur: Asian and Pacific Development Administration Centre, 1978)

Dahl, Robert A. and Charles E. Lindblom
Politics, Economics and Welfare: Planning and Politico-economic Systems Resolved into Basic Social Processes (Chicago: Univ. of Chicago Press, 1976)

Hussain, Mohammad
"Instruments for Budget-Plan Coordination in Pakistan," *Pakistan Administration,* Vol. 16, No. 1, Jan. 1979

Iglesias, Gabriel U., ed.
Implementation: The Problem of Achieving Results: A Casebook on Asian Experiences (Manila: Eastern Regional Organization for Public Administration, 1976)

McGinnis, L.F. and H.L.W. Nuttle
"The Project Coordinator's Problem," *Omega: The International Journal of Management Science,* Vol. 6, No. 4, 1978, pp. 325-30

Muttalib, M.A.
"The Theory of Coordination Re-discovered and Re-formulated," *The Indian Journal of Public Administration,* Vol. 24, No. 2, April-June 1978, pp. 374-84

Nagamine, Haruo
"Methods of Planning for Comprehensive Regional Development: A Paradigm," *Asian Development Dialogue,* Nos. 5 and 6, 1977, pp. 7-27

Payad, Aurora
"Communication for Effective Supervision and Coordination" in Amara Raksasataya and L.J. Fredericks, eds., *Rural Development Training to Meet New Challenges,* Vol. 2, (Kuala Lumpur: Asian and Pacific Development Administration Centre, 1978), pp. 333-62

Sadique, Abu Sharaf H.K., ed.
Public Enterprises in Asia: Studies on Coordination and Control (Kuala Lumpur: Asian and Pacific Development Administration Centre, 1976)

Whang, In-Joung
A Framework of Coordination in the Implementation of Family Planning programmes (Kuala Lumpur: Asian and Pacific Development Administration Centre, 1976)

2.2 Annual planning, programming

Haq, Mahbub ul
"Annual Planning in Pakistan," *Journal of Development Planning,* No. 2, 1979, pp. 81-114

Kim, Kwang Woong

Management Planning for Implementation of Family Planning Programmes (Kuala Lumpur: Asian and Pacific Development Administration Centre, 1978)

Middleton, John
  Managing Family Planning Communication Activities (Kuala Lumpur: Asian and Pacific Development Administration Centre, 1978)

Unakul, Snoh
  "Annual Planning in Thailand," *Economic Bulletin for Asia and the Pacific,* Vol. 20, No. 1, June 1969, pp. 68-80

United Nations. Department of International Economic and Social Affairs
  Administration of Development Programmes and Projects: Some Major Issues (New York, 1971) (Sales no. E.71.II.H.4)

Wanasinghe, Shelton
  Administrative Support Planning for Development Projects (Kuala Lumpur: Asian and Pacific Development Administration Centre, 1978)

2.3 Budgeting, financing

Caiden, Naomi and Aaron Wildavsky
  Planning and Budgeting in Poor Countries (New York: Wiley, 1974)

Colm, G.
  Integration of National Planning and Budgeting (Washington, D.C.: Centre for Development Planning, National Planning Association, 1968) (Planning methods series, No. 5)

Hovey, Harold
  The Planning-Programming-Budgeting System: An Appraisal (New York: Praeger, 1968)

Prawiraatmadja, Abdul K., et. al., eds.
  Integrated Approach to Budgeting (Kuala Lumpur: Asian and Pacific Development Administration Centre, 1967) Vol. 1: Workshop findings and technical papers, Vol. 2: Country reviews

United Nations. Department of International Economic and Social Affairs
  A Manual for Programme and Performance Budgeting (New York, 1965)

United Nations. Economic and Social Commission for Asia and the Pacific
  Regional Seminar on Local Government Finance: Report of Seminar and Technical Papers, Kuala Lumpur and Penang, 5-17 August 1974 (Bangkok: United Nations Economic Commission for Asia and the Pacific, 1974)

2.4 Monitoring and evaluation, implementation management

Ahmed, Meshah Uddin
  "Project Monitoring in Bangladesh," *Economic Bulletin for Asia and the Pacific,* Vol. 27, No. 2, Dec. 1976, pp. 54-60

Bachrach, P.
  Evaluating Development Programmes: A Synthesis of Recent Experience (Paris: Development Centre, Organization for Economic Cooperation and Development, 1977)

Barkin, David
  "A Case Study of the Beneficiaries of Regional Development," *International Social Development Review,* No. 4, 1972 (ST/SOP/SER.X/4) pp. 84-94

Cacho, C.P.
  "The Road to Plan Implementation," *Finance and Development,* Vol. 12, No. 4, Dec. 1975, pp. 42-45

Consultative Meeting on Monitoring and Evaluation of Social Development Programmes, Manila, 1978

262

"Monitoring and Evaluation of Social Development Programmes: Summary Report of a Consultative Meeting, Manila, 15-23 Feb. 1978" (Bangkok: United Nations Asian and Pacific Development Institute: United Nations Centre for Regional Development: United Nations Children's Fund, 1979)

Dolbeare, Kenneth M., ed.
Public Policy Evaluation (Beverly Hills, Cal.: Sage Pub., 1975)

Esman, Milton
"Monitoring the Progress of Projects: The Redbook and Operations Room" in Dennis Rondinelli, ed., *Planning Development Projects* (Stroudsburg, Pa.: Dowden, Hutchinson and Ross, 1977)

Friedmann, John
"The Implementation of Regional Development Policies: Lessons of Experience," *International Social Development Review,* No. 4, 1972 (ST/SOA/SER.X/4) pp. 95-105

Gable, Richard W. and Fred Springer
Administering Agricultural Development in Asia: A Comparative Analysis of Four National Programs (Boulder, Col.: Westview Press, 1976)

Goodman, Louis J. and Ralph Ngatata Love, eds.
Management of Development Projects: An International Case Study Approach (New York: Pergamon Press, 1979)

Haque, Wahidul, et. al.
An Approach to Micro-level Development: Designing and Evaluation of Rural Development Projects (Bangkok: United Nations Asian and Pacific Development Institute, 1977)

Hayes, Samuel P.
Evaluating Development Projects (Paris: United Nations Educational, Scientific, and Cultural Organization, 1959)

Heseltine, Nigel
"Administrative Structures and the Implementation of Development Plans," *Journal of Administration Overseas,* April 1967

Iglesias, Gabriel U., ed.
Implementation: The Problem of Achieving Results: A Casebook on Asian Experiences (Manila: Eastern Regional Organization for Public Administration, 1976)

International Bank for Reconstruction and Development
Technical Workshop on Monitoring and Evaluation of Rural Development Projects and Programs (Washington, D.C., 1977)

Khan, Akhtar Hameed
Four Rural Development Programmes: An Evaluation (Peshawar: Pakistan Academy for Rural Development, 1974)

Kim, Shin Bok
Personnel Administration for Family Planning Program Managers (Kuala Lumpur: Asian and Pacific Development Administration Centre, 1978)

Mangahas, Mahar and Chita T. Subido
"Development Planning, Appraisal and Performance Evaluation with Special Reference to the Philippines," *Economic Bulletin for Asia and the Pacific,* Vol. 27, No. 1, June 1976, pp. 13-27

McFadden, D.
"The Evaluation of Development Programmes," *Review of Economic Studies,* 97, Jan. 1967

Rondinelli, Dennis A. and Kenneth Ruddle
"Local Organization for Integrated Rural Development: Implementing Equity Policy in Developing Countries," *International Review of Administrative Sciences,* Vol. 43, 1977, pp. 20-30

Schneider, Hartmut
Linkages Between Social and Economic Aspects in Rural Development and Their Implications for Project Design and Implementation (Paris: Development Centre, Organization for Economic Cooperation and Development, 1977)

Suchman, Edward A.
    Evaluative Research: Principles and Practice in Public Service and Social Action Programs (New York: Russel Sage Foundation, 1967)
Taake, Hans-Helmut
    "The Implementation of Development Plans: Organization and Policies," *Developing Economies,* Vol. 13, No. 1, 1975, pp. 22-37
United Nations. Correspondence Course in Social Planning
    "Plan Implementation and Progress Reporting and Evaluation" Lecture 8 (New York, 1972) (ESA/SD/CCCP.III/16)
United Nations. Department of International Economic and Social Affairs
    Administration of Development Programmes and Projects (New York: United Nations, 1971) (ST/TAO/M/55)
United Nations. Department of International Economic and Social Affairs
    Systematic Monitoring and Evaluation of Integrated Development Programmes: A Source-Book (New York, 1978) (ST/ESA/78) (Sales no. E.78.IV.11)
United Nations. Economic and Social Commission for Asia and the Pacific
    "Evaluation in Planning and Policy-Making," *Economic Bulletin for Asia and the Pacific,* Vol. 27, No. 1, June 1976, pp. 1-12
United Nations. Economic Commission for Asia and the Pacific
    "Progress Reporting and Evaluation," *Economic Bulletin for Asia and the Pacific,* Vol. 23, No. 2, Sep. 1972, pp. 10-18
United Nations. Industrial Development Organization
    Guidelines for Project Evaluation (New York: United Nations, 1972)
United States. Agency for International Development. Office of Development Program Review and Evaluation
    Project Evaluation Guidelines (Washington, D.C., 1974)
Weiss, Carol H.
    Evaluating Action Programmes: Readings in Social Action and Evaluation (Boston, Mass.: Allyn and Bacon, 1972)
Weiss, Carol H.
    Evaluation Research: Methods for Assessing Program Effectiveness (Englewood Cliffs, N.J.: Prentice-Hall, 1972)
Whang, In-Joung
    Management of Family Planning Programmes in Asia: Concepts, Issues, and Approaches (Kuala Lumpur: Asian and Pacific Development Administration Centre, 1976)

2.5 *Popular participation and local organizations*

Food and Agriculture Organization
    Participation of the Poor in Rural Organizations (Rome, 1979)·
Inayatullah, et. al., eds.
    Cooperatives and Development in Asia: A Study of Cooperatives in Fourteen Rural Communities of Iran, Pakistan and Ceylon (Geneva: United Nations Research Institute for Social Development, 1972)
Inayatullah, ed.
    Rural Organizations and Rural Development: Some Asian Experiences (Kuala Lumpur: Asian and Pacific Development Administration Centre, 1978)
Montgomery, John D. and Milton J. Esman
    "Popular Participation in Development Administration," *Journal of Comparative Administration,* Vol. 3, 1971-72
United Nations. Department of International Economic and Social Affairs
    Local Government Reform: Analysis of Experience in Selected Countries (New York, 1975) (Sales no. E.75.II.H.1)
United Nations. Department of International Economic and Social Affairs
    Popular Participation for Decision Making for Development (New York, 1975)

United Nations. Department of International Economic and Social Affairs
Popular Participation in Development: Emerging Trends in Community Development
(New York, 1971) (Sales no. E.71.IV.2)
United Nations Research Institute for Social Development
Rural Cooperatives as Agent of Change: A Research Report and a Debate (Geneva, 1975)
United Nations. Social Development Division
Local Participation in Development Planning: A Preliminary Study of the Relationship of Community Development to National Planning (New York, 1967)
Uphoff, Norman and Milton J. Esman
Local Organization for Rural Development: Analysis of Asian Experience (Ithaca, N.Y.: Rural Development Committee, Center for International Studies, Cornell Univ., 1974) (Special series on rural local government; RLG no. 19)
Wehmhoerner, Arnold, ed.
Organization of Peasants in Asia (Bangkok: Friedrich-Ebert-Stiftung, 1974)

3. Institutional Dimensions of Regional Development: Selected Countries

3.1 Bangladesh

Abdullah, M.M.
Public Administration Today (Dacca: Lion Publications, 1979)
Abdullah, M.M.
Rural Development in Bangladesh (Comilla: Bangladesh Academy for Rural Development, 1978)
Ahmed, Badruddin
Manual on Comilla Co-operatives (Comilla: Bangladesh Academy for Rural Development, 1972)
Ahmed, Ziauddin
The District Administration in Bangladesh (Dacca: National Institute of Public Administration, 1979)
Alamgir, Mohiuddin
Famine 1974: Political Economy of Mass Starvation in Bangladesh; A Statistical Annex (Dacca: Bangladesh Institute of Development Studies, 1977)
Ali, Ahmed
Administration of Local Self-Government for Rural Areas in Bangladesh (Dacca: Local Government Institute, 1979)
Ali, Ahmed
Effectiveness of "Own Village Development Programme" in Rural Development of Bangladesh (Dacca: National Institute of Public Administration, 1979)
Ali, Qazi A.
District Administration in Bangladesh (Dacca: National Institute of Public Administration, 1978)
Aminuzzaman, S.M.
Rural Elite and Rural Development (Dacca: Univ. Grants Commission, 1980)
Anisuzzaman, M.
Bangladesh Public Administration and Society (Dacca: Bangladesh Books International, 1979)
Bangladesh Academy for Rural Development
Rural Leadership and Its Emerging Patterns in Bangladesh (Comilla: BARD, 1972)
Blair, Harry W.
The Elusiveness of Equity: Institutional Approaches to Rural Development in Bangladesh (Ithaca, N.Y.: Rural Development Committee, Center for International Studies, Cornell Univ., 1974) (Special series on rural local government; RLG no. 1)
Choldin, Harvey M.

"An Organizational Analysis of Rural Development Projects at Comilla, East Pakistan," *Economic Development and Cultural Change,* Vol. 20, No. 4, July 1972, pp. 671-90

Chowdhury, Anwarullah A.
A Bangladesh Village: A Study of Social Stratification (Dacca: Centre for Social Studies, 1978)

Civil Servants' Training Academy
Thana Administration and Rural Development (Dacca: The Civil Servants' Training Academy, 1976)

Haq, M. Nurul
Village Development in Bangladesh: A Study of Monogram Village (Comilla: Bangladesh Academy for Rural Development, 1973)

Huq, M. Ameerul
Exploitation and Rural Poor: A Working Paper on the Rural Power Structure in Bangladesh (Comilla: Bangladesh Academy for Rural Development, 1978)

Islam, Shamsul
Public Corporations in Bangladesh (Dacca: Local Government Institute, 1975)

Khan, Akhtar Hameed
Tour of Twenty Thanas: Impressions of Drainage-roads, Irrigation and Co-operative Programmes (Comilla: Bangladesh Academy for Rural Development, 1971)

Khan, Ali Akhter
Rural Credit Program of Agricultural Co-operative Federation (Comilla: Bangladesh Academy for Rural Development, 1971)

Khan, Fazlur Rashid
"District Town Elites in Bangladesh," *Asian Survey,* Vol. 19, No. 5, May 1979, pp. 468-84

Nandy, P.K.
Problems of District Administration (Dacca: National Institute of Public Administration, 1980)

Sultan, K.M. Tipu
Government and Citizens in Politics and Development (Comilla: Bangladesh Academy for Rural Development, 1978)

Sultan, K.M. Tipu
Problems of Rural Administration in Bangladesh (Comilla: Bangladesh Academy for Rural Development, 1974)

Swadesh, Bose
The Comilla Co-operative Approach and the Prospects for Broad-base Green Revolution in Bangladesh (New York: Oxford University Press, 1974)

Swedish International Development Authority
Contradictions and Distortions in a Rural Economy: The Case of Bangladesh (Stockholm: Policy Development and Evaluation Division, 1979)

3.2 India

Alexander, William
"Government in the Villages of Modern India," *Journal of Administration Overseas,* Vol. 7, No. 1, 1968, pp. 303-10

Barnabas, A.P. and Donald C. Pelz
Administering Agricultural Development: Coordination, Initiative and Communication in Three North Indian States (New Delhi: Indian Institute of Public Administration, 1969)

Bhalerao, C.N.
"Changing Pattern of Development Administration in the District" in C.N. Bhalerao, ed., *Administration Politics and Development in India* (Bombay: Lalvani, 1972) pp. 336-76

Bhalerao, C.N.
"Some Social, Political and Administrative Consequences of Panchayati Raj," *Asian Survey,* Vol. 4, 1964, pp. 804-11

Bhalla, G.S. and Y.K. Alagh
Performance of Indian Agriculture: A District-Wise Study (New Delhi: Sterling, 1979)

Bhambhri, C.P.
"Contextual Framework of Public Administration in Indian States," *Indian Journal of Public Administration,* Vol. 22, No. 3, July-Sept. 1976, pp. 330-48

Bhargava, B.S.
Grass Roots Leadership in Panchayati Raj Institutions (Delhi: Ashish Publishing House, 1979)

Bhargava, B.S.
Politico-administrative Dynamics in Panchayati Raj System (New Delhi: Ashish Publishing House, 1978)

Bhatnagar, S.
Rural Local Government in India (New Delhi: Light & Life, 1978)

Bitcheeck, John T.
"Centrally Planned Rural Development in India: Some Problems," *The Economic Weekly,* March 11, 1961, pp. 435-41

Chatterji, M.
"A Scheme of Decentralized Decision-Making in India," *Indian Journal of Public Administration,* Vol. 16, No. 4, Oct.-Dec. 1970, pp. 521-40

Chaturvedi, H.R.
Bureaucracy and the Local Community: Dynamics of Rural Development (Bombay: Allied Publishers, 1977)

Datta, Abhijit
"Rural Administration in India: A Research Survey during 1950-70," *Journal of Administration Overseas,* Vol. 17, No. 1, Jan. 1978, pp. 35-42

Davies, Morton R.
"The Machinery of Planning in Uttar Pradesh," *Development Policy and Administration Review,* Vol. 4, No. 1, Jan.-June 1978, pp. 20-42

Dayal, Ishwar, et. al.
Bench-mark Studies of Field Administration in India (New Delhi: Indian Institute of Public Administration, n.d.)

Dayal, Ishwar, et. al.
District Administration: A Survey for Reorganization (Delhi: Macmillan Co. of India, 1976)

Dubey, S.N.
"Environment, Technology and Decision Making in Panchayati Raj Institutions," *Economic and Political Weekly,* Vol. 10, No. 3, Jan. 18, 1975, pp. 75-82

Dubey, S.N. and R. Murdia
Structure and Process of Decision-making in Panchayati Raj Institutions (Bombay: Somaiya Pub., 1976)

Dubhashi, P.R.
Economics, Planning and Public Administration (Bombay: Somaiya Pub., 1976)

Dutta, V.R.
"Emerging Power Patterns at the Zila Parishad Level: A Case Study of Varanasi Zila Parishad," *Indian Journal of Political Science,* Vol. 31, No. 3, Jul.-Sep. 1970, pp. 291-300

Fliegel, Frederick C.
"Community Organization and Acceptance of Change in Rural India," *Rural Sociology,* Vol. 34, No. 2, June 1969, pp. 167-81

Gaikwad, V.R.
Panchayati Raj and Bureaucracy: A Study of the Relationship Patterns (Hyderabad: National Institute of Community Development, 1969)

Grover, V.P., et. al.

Panchayati Raj Administration (Agra: Lakshmi Narain Agarwal, 1973)

Haldipur, R.N.
Local Government, Rural Development and Micro-level Planning (New Delhi: Training Division, Department of Personnel and Administrative Reforms, 1974)

Haldipur, R.N. and V.R.K. Pramahansa, eds.
Local Government Institutions in Rural India: Some Aspects (Hyderabad: National Institute of Community Development, 1970)

Haragopal, G.
Administrative Leadership and Rural Development in India (New Delhi: Light & Life, 1980)

Hooja, Rakesh
"The District as a Planning Unit: Style and Locus," *Indian Journal of Public Administration,* Vol. 19, No. 3, Jul.-Sept. 1973, pp. 393-406

India. Department of Personnel and Administrative Reforms
Journal of the Lal Bahadur Shastri National Academy of Administration: Special Issue on District Planning, Vol. 20, No. 1, Spring 1975

India. Department of Rural Development
Planning and Administration of Special Public Works Schemes in India: Country Report (Inter-Regional I.L.O. Project No. INT/74/022) (July 1976)

Indian Institute of Public Administration
New Challenges in Administration (New Delhi: IIPA, 1972)

Jain, C.M.
"Rural Development: Some Aspects of Institutional and Administrative Change," *Administrative Change,* Vol. 4, No. 2, Jan.-June 1977, pp. 236-42

Johl, S.S.
The Dynamics of Institutional Change and Rural Development in Punjab, India (Ithaca, N.Y.: Rural Development Committee, Center for International Studies, Cornell Univ., 1974) (Special series on rural local government; RLG no. 5)

Kabra, Kamal Nayan
Planning Process in a District (New Delhi: Indian Institute of Public Administration, 1977)

Khera, Sucha Singh
District Administration in India (London: Asia Publishing House, 1964)

Maddick, Henry
Panchayati Raj: A Study of Rural Local Government in India (London: Longmans, 1970)

Masaldan, P.N.
"The Planner's Attitude to Administrative Reforms in India," *Indian Journal of Politics,* Vol. 5, No. 1, Apr.-June 1971, pp. 49-56

Mathur, Kuldeep
"Administrative Institutions, Political Capacity and India's Strategy for Rural Development" in Inayatullah, ed., *Approaches to Rural Development: Some Asian Experiences* (Kuala Lumpur: Asian and Pacific Development Administration Centre, 1979) pp. 171-97

Mathur, Kuldeep
Bureaucratic Response to Development (Delhi: National Publishing House, 1972)

Mathur, Kuldeep
"Training and Administrative Reform in India: The Real Challenge," *Indian Administrative and Management Review,* Vol. 4, No. 1, Jan.-Mar. 1972, pp. 19-23

Menge, Paul Erich
Management for Development: Executive Budget-making in Indian Government (Ann Arbor: Michigan Univ. Microfilms, 1971)

Mundle, Sudipto
District Planning in India (New Delhi: Indian Institute of Public Administration, 1977)

Muttalib, A.
Development Administration in Rural Government for Agricultural Production

(Hyderabad: Osmania University, 1973)

Narain, Iqbal
"Democratic Decentralization and Rural Leadership in India: The Rajasthan Experiment," *Asian Survey,* Vol. 4, No. 8, Aug. 1964, pp. 1015-22

Narayan Prasak, P.S.
"Work of the Planning Commission," *Indian Express,* 24 Aug. 1977, p. 4; 25 Aug. 1977, p. 4; 26 Aug. 1977, p. 4

Natraj, V.K.
Decentralization of Planning in India (Mysore: Institute of Development Studies, University of Mysore, 1974)

Nayar, P.K.B.
Leadership, Bureaucracy and Planning in India: A Sociological Study (New Delhi: Associated Pub. House, 1969)

Pai Panandiker, V.A., ed.
Development Administration in India (Delhi: Macmillan, 1974)

Park, Richard L. and Irene Tinker, eds.
Leadership and Political Institutions in India (Princeton, N.J.: Princeton University Press, 1959)

Potter, David C.
Government in Rural India: An Introduction to Contemporary District Administration (London: Bell and Sons, 1964)

Prasad, Awadhesh
Block Development Officer: A Portrait of Bureaucracy in India (Patna: Associated Book Agency, 1976)

Raghavulu, C.V.
"Administrative Reform: A Study of an Intensive Agricultural Programme in India," *Journal of Administration Overseas,* Vol. 17, No. 3, July 1978, pp. 191-200

Rahman, A.T.R.
"Rural Institutions in India and Pakistan," *Asian Survey,* Vol. 8, No. 9, Sep. 1968, pp. 792-805

Rai, H.
"Politico-Administrative Bases of Indian Field Administration: The Patterns of the District Officer System under the British," *Indian Journal of Public Administration,* Vol. 16, No. 4, Oct.-Dec. 1970, pp. 457-86

Rai, Haridwar and Awadhesh Prasad
"Panchayati Raj, Bureaucracy and Development: A Study in the Impact of Democratisation of Block Administration," *Indian Journal of Political Science,* Vol. 34, No. 3, Jul.-Sep. 1973, pp. 281-98

Ramayyar, M.S.
Indian Audit and Accounts Department: Its Evolution, Organisation and Functions (New Delhi: Indian Institute of Public Administration, 1967)

Rao, N.R.
Union-State Financial Relations in India (Dharwal: Karnataka Univ., 1972)

Ray, Amal
Organizational Aspects of Rural Development: Taluk-level Administration in an Indian State (Calcutta: World Press, 1976)

Reddy, Y. Venugopal
Multilevel Planning in India (Delhi: Vikas, 1979)

Roy, Ramashray
Bureaucracy and Development: The Case of Indian Agriculture (New Delhi: Manas Publications, 1975)

Sadasivan, S.N.
"District Level Co-ordination in India (the Madras Experience)," *Indian Journal of Public Administration,* Vol. 18, No. 1, Jan.-Mar. 1972, pp. 78-96

Saxena, A.P.
"Improving State Administration: Search for Directions," *Indian Journal of Public*

Administration, Vol. 22, No. 3, Jul.-Sep. 1976, pp. 392-402
Seshadri, K.
"Administrative Institutions and Agricultural Development" in Waheeduddin Khan,
ed., *Papers and Proceedings of Workshop-cum-Seminar on Rural Institutions and
Agricultural Development* (Hyderabad: National Institute of Community Develop-
ment, 1972)
Sharan, P.
Public Administration in India (Meerut: Meenakshi Prakashan, 1978)
Sharma, Arvind K.
"The Planning Commission in India: A Case for Reorganization," *Journal of Adminis-
tration Overseas,* Vol. 9, No. 1, Jan. 1979, pp. 4-12
Shiviah, M., et al.
Block-level Administration: An Analysis of Salient Dimensions (Hyderabad: National
Institute of Rural Development, 1979)
Shukla, J.D.
State and District Administration in India (New Delhi: Published under the auspices
of Indian Institute of Public Administration by National Publishing House, 1976)
Singh, M.P., N.K. Jaiswal and B.N. Singh
"Relative Importance of the Factors Influencing Co-ordination among Personnel
Working in the Intensive Agriculture District Programme," *Behavioural Science and
Community Development,* Vol. 3, No. 1, Mar. 1969, pp. 1-12
Singh, Sahab
Process of Plan Formulation at District Level (New Delhi: Indian Institute of Public
Administration, 1979)
Thavaraj, M.J.K. and K.L. Handa
Financial Control and Delegation (New Delhi: Indian Institute of Public Administra-
tion, 1973)
Tinker, Hugh
"Authority and Community in Village India," *Pacific Affairs,* Vol. 32, No. 4, Dec. 1959,
pp. 354-75

3.3 Malaysia

Affandi, Raja Mohammed
Public Enterprises in Malaysia: Roles, Structure and Problems (Kuala Lumpur:
Malaysian Centre for Development Studies, 1979) (Occasional paper no. 6)
Ahad, R.M.
"FELDA Activities and Development Trends" [Paper prepared for presentation at the
FELDA Officers' Conference, 1974]
Ahmad, Abdullah Sanusi
"Administrative Reform for Development in Malaysia: Focus on Grassroot Organi-
zation" [Paper presented at Expert Group Meeting on Administration Reform for
Decentralized Development organized by APDAC, New Delhi, Sep. 17-21, 1979]
Hamid, Ahmad Sarji bin Abdul
"Farmers' Organization: An Integrated Approach to Rural Economic Development,"
(mimeo) (Kuala Lumpur: Farmers' Organization Authority, 1973)
Beaglehole, J.H.
The District: A Study in Decentralization in West Malaysia (London: Published for
the Univ. of Hull by the Oxford Univ. Press, 1976)
Beaglehole, J.H.
"Local Government in West Malaysia: The Royal Commission Report," *Journal of
Administration Overseas,* Vol. 13, No. 2, Apr. 1974, pp. 348-57
Chee, Stephen
Rural Development and Development Administration in Malaysia (New York: Asia
Society, Southeast Asia Development Advisory Group, 1974)

Chee, Stephen
    Rural Local Governance and Rural Development in Malaysia (Ithaca, N.Y.: Rural Development Committee, Center for International Studies, Cornell University, 1974)
Cheema, G. Shabbir
    "The Administration of Public Enterprises in Malaysia," *Journal of Administration Overseas*, Vol. 18, 1979, pp. 95-106
Cheema, G. Shabbir
    "Administrative Responses to Urbanization in West Malaysia," *Journal of Administration Overseas*, Vol. 16, No. 4, 1977, pp. 240-47
Cheema, G. Shabbir
    "Changing Patterns of Administration in the Field: The Malaysian Case," *International Review of Administrative Sciences*, Vol. 45, 1979, pp. 64-8
Cheema, G. Shabbir
    "Rural Organizations and Participation in Malaysia" (Penang: School of Comparative Social Sciences, Universiti Sains Malaysia, 1978) [Prepared for the World Conference on Agrarian Reform and Rural Development, Food and Agriculture Organization of the United Nations, Rome, Italy]
Cheema, G. Shabbir and S. Ahmad Hussein
    "Local Government Reform in Malaysia," *Asian Survey*, Vol. 19, June 1978, pp. 577-91
Esman, Milton J.
    Administration and Development in Malaysia: Institution Building and Reform in a Plural Society (Ithaca, N.Y.: Cornell University Press, 1972)
Ghani, Mohamed Noor
    "Evaluation Techniques in Malaysia" [Paper presented at UNESCO Regional Seminar on the Application of Evaluation Techniques in Social Action Projects in Asia, Kuala Lumpur, No. 26-30, 1979]
Milne, R.S.
    "Bureaucracy and Bureaucratic Reform in Malaysia," *Philippine Journal of Public Administration*, Vol. 10, 1966
Ness, Gayl D.
    Bureaucracy and Rural Development in Malaysia: A Study of Complex Organizations in Stimulating Economic Development in New States (Berkeley: Univ. of California Press, 1967)
Norris, Malcolm
    "Local Government in West Malaysia: The Royal Commission Report and After," *Studies in Comparative Local Government*, Vol. 8, No. 1, Summer 1974, pp. 5-21
Puthucheary, Mavis
    The Politics of Administration: The Malaysian Experience (Kuala Lumpur: Oxford Univ. Press, 1978)
Rani, Kamaruddin
    National and Regional Development Planning System in Malaysia: The Formulation and Implementation Process (Nagoya: UNCRD, 1979) [Paper presented at the Colloquium on Methods of Planning for Comprehensive Regional Development, Nagoya, 25 Oct.-1 Nov. 1976]
Rogers, Marvin L.
    "Patterns of Leadership in a Rural Malay Community," *Asian Survey*, Vol. 15, No. 5, May 1979, pp. 407-21
Rudner, Martin
    Nationalism, Planning and Economic Modernization in Malaysia: The Politics of Beginning Development (Beverly Hills, Cal.: Sage, 1975)
Sivalingam, G.
    "The Relationship between Leadership Style and Productivity in Two Agricultural Re-Development Schemes in West Malaysia," *Philippine Journal of Public Administration*, Vol. 19, No. 3, July 1975, pp. 209-224
Tilman, Robert O.
    Bureaucratic Transition in Malaya (Durham, N.C.: Duke University Press, 1964)

Wahab, Subkey B. Abdul
Development Planning and Administration in Malaysia (Honolulu: East-West Technology and Development Institute, 1977) (Country-specific materials no. 1)

3.4 Sri Lanka

Blackton, John S.
Local Government and Rural Development in Sri Lanka (Ithaca, N.Y.: Rural Development Committee, Center for International Studies, Cornell University, 1974)
Fernando, Neil
Regional Administration in Sri Lanka (Colombo: Academy of Administrative Studies, 1973)
Fernando, Neil, et. al.
"Kurunegala Rural Development Project: Administrative and Organization Infrastructure Component" (Colombo: Ministry of Public Administration and Home Affairs, 1978) (Management consultancy report)
Kanesaligam, V.A.
A Hundred Years of Local Government in Ceylon (1865-1965) (Colombo: Modern Plastic Works, 1971)
Kulatilake, T.M.
"Development at the Local Level," *Journal of Development Administration,* Vol. 2, No. 1, Nov. 1971, pp. 26-9
Leitan, G.R.T.
"The Role of the Government Agent in Sri Lanka," *Journal of Administration Overseas,* Jan. 1976, pp. 15-25
Marga Institute
Local Level Planning within the Framework of Overall National Planning: Sri Lanka (Colombo: the Institute, 1976)
Marga Institute
Welfare and Growth: A Case Study of Sri Lanka (Colombo: the Institute, 1974) [Prepared for UNRISD project "The Unified Approach to Development Planning and Analysis"]
Mendis, M.W.J.G.
Local Government in Sri Lanka (Colombo: Apothecaries, 1976)
Sri Lanka. Committee of Inquiry on Local Government
Report of the Committee of Inquiry on Local Government (Colombo: Printed at the Dept. of Government Print, 1972) (Sessional paper no. 7)
Wanigasekera, Earle
"Popular Participation and Local Level Planning in Sri Lanka," *Marga Quarterly Journal,* Vol. 4, No. 4, 1977, pp. 37-77
Wanninayake, P.B.
"The Organisation for the Formulation and Implementation of the District Agricultural Programme in Sri Lanka," *Journal of Development Administration,* Vol. 6, No. 2, Nov. 1976, pp. 15-21
Weerakoon, Bradman
"Role of Administrators in a Changing Agrarian Situation: The Sri Lanka Experience," *Journal of Administration Overseas,* Vol. 16, No. 3, July 1977, pp. 148-61
Wijeweera, B.S.
"Some Reflections on Current Administrative Reforms on the District Administration," *Journal of Development Administration,* Vol. 5, No. 1, May 1974, pp. 13-46

3.5 Thailand

Buranasiri, P. and Snoh Unakul

"Obstacles to Effective Planning Encountered in the Thai Planning Experience," *The Philippine Economic Journal,* Vol. 4, No. 2, 1965, pp. 327-40

Dhiravegin, Likhit

The Bureaucratic Elite of Thailand: A Study of Their Sociological Attributes, Educational Backgrounds and Career Advancement Pattern (Bangkok: Thai Khadi Research Institute, Thammasat Univ., 1978)

Dhiravegin, Likhit

"The Local Government System in Thailand" [Paper prepared for the Seminar on Financing Local Development organized by APDAC, Kuala Lumpur, 10-27 May 1976]

Krannich, Ronald L.

"The Politics of Intergovernmental Relations in Thailand," *Asian Survey,* Vol. 19, No. 5, May 1979, pp. 506-522

Nakajud, Arb

A Study of Provincial and Local Government in the Province of Udornthani, Thailand with Special Reference to Agriculture (Bangkok: Dept. of Agricultural Economics, Kasetsart University, 1973) (Research report no. 5)

Nilpanich, Chit

"Decentralization and Local Government: A Focus on the Thai Municipality" [Paper presented at the Seminar on Development and Finance of Local Government in Thailand, organized by UNADI, NESDB and SEADAG, Chiengmai, 2-3 Feb. 1976]

Riggs, Fred W.

Thailand: The Modernization of a Bureaucratic Polity (Honolulu: East-West Center Press, 1966)

Saihoo, Pathya

A Report on Leadership in the Southern Provinces (Bangkok: Community Development Division and Faculty of Political Sciences, Chulalongkorn Univ., 1966)

Siffin, William

The Thai Bureaucracy (Honolulu: East-West Center Press, 1966)

Trombley, W.G., et al.

Thai Government and Its Setting: A Selective, Annotated Bibliography (Bangkok: National Institute of Development Administration, 1967)

CONTRIBUTORS

ALI, Shaikh Maqsood, Director-General, National Institute of Public Administration, Dacca, Bangladesh

CHATURVEDI, T.N., Director, Indian Institute of Public Administration, New Delhi, India

CHEEMA, G. Shabbir, Development Administration Planner, United Nations Centre for Regional Development, Nagoya, Japan

ESMAN, Milton J., Professor, Center for International Studies, Cornell University, Ithaca, N.Y., U.S.A.

FABELLA, Armand V., Chairman, Presidential Commission on Reorganization, Manila, Philippines

FERNANDO, P.N.M., Additional Secretary, Ministry of Education, Colombo, Sri Lanka

IGLESIAS, Gabriel U., Expert, Asian and Pacific Development Centre, Kuala Lumpur, Malaysia

INGLE, Marcus D., Senior Consultant of the staff of Practical Concepts Incorporated (PCI), Washington, D.C., U.S.A.

MAT, Johari, Deputy Director and Head, Centre for Local, Urban and Regional Administration, National Institute of Public Administration (INTAN), Petaling Jaya, Malaysia

NORANITIPADUNGKARN, Chakrit, Professor, Research Centre, National Institute of Development Administration, Bangkok, Thailand

PERERA, K.P.G.M., Director, Regional Development, Ministry of Plan Implementation, Colombo, Sri Lanka

RONDINELLI, Dennis A., Professor and Director, The Maxwell School, Syracuse University, Syracuse, N.Y., U.S.A.

SAXENA, A.P., Director, Management Services, Ministry of Finance, New Delhi, India

INDEX

The Regional Development Series